STUDY GUIDE PLUS

FOR

BARON

ESSENTIALS OF
PSYCHOLOGY

Catherine Seta
Wake Forest University

John Seta
University of North Carolina at Greensboro

Paul Paulus
University of Texas at Arlington

Allyn and Bacon
Boston · London · Toronto · Sydney · Tokyo · Singapore

ISBN 0-205-18541-X

Printed in the United States of America

10 9 8 7 6 5 4 3 2 1   00 99 98 97 96 95

PREFACE
STUDY GUIDE OVERVIEW: ITS PURPOSE AND AIMS

It might be helpful for you to know what our goals were as we wrote this guide. First and foremost, our goal is to help you study the material that is in your text. The purpose of this guide is to supplement, not substitute for, your book. It is designed to help you review the material and includes exercises that will check for your comprehension and ability to think critically about the material in your text. Using this study guide along with careful study of your text should help you do well in the course. In addition, we have tried to provide exercises that will help you apply psychology to your everyday lives. Psychology is a useful science and your experiences in your psychology course should help you understand the world of people that we live in.

As we wrote this guide, we tried to approach it from the student's perspective. We sought the advice of a number of students in our classes concerning what kinds of exercises would be both enjoyable and beneficial for learning about psychology. In addition, we sought out what the experts have to say about effective learning strategies and incorporated many of these suggestions.

After a considerable amount of research, we developed three primary strategies. First, we decided that we would include a very active approach to learning. That is, we want to get you involved in this material! As you will see, there are many opportunities for you to analyze information and to apply psychology to your life. Second, we wanted to help you organize the material in the text. We have provided outlines with relevant learning objectives and survey/question sections that emphasize the major concepts contained in each chapter. Use these as tools for seeing how the components of the chapter fit together. Third, we wanted to give you multiple opportunities to test your knowledge of the material. Practice tests are presented for each chapter and supplemental tests are included at the end of the study guide.

We will now turn to a more detailed discussion of how to use the study guide, and then consider some tips on how to improve your studying. We wish you well in your course and hope that you enjoy psychology as much as we love the field!

Outline: Develop a Study Plan

As the name of this section implies, the purpose of this section is to help you develop a study plan. It is important to have a plan of study because it helps you organize your time and make the most of your study periods. We have included learning objectives for each major topic area in this section. Using this outline will help you grasp the organizational structure of the chapter content - seeing "the big picture," followed by filling in the details, is an effective learning strategy.   Space has been provided to write any notes or questions that come to mind as you begin your study of each topic. After you have developed your study plan and have a feel for "the big picture," go onto the second section which begins to add some detail.

Survey and Question

Using the chapter outline as a guide, this section presents the major topics and ideas of each chapter. It is very important for you to realize that this section is not a substitute for reading the text. You should read the appropriate chapter prior to completing this section. After you have read the chapter, you can use this section as a tool for seeing how the components of the chapter fit together. In this section, we also give you an opportunity to check on your comprehension of the material. Questions that relate to the major learning objectives are presented. If you can answer these questions, you have come a long way toward mastering the material.

Here's another suggestion for using this section. Review this material again several times before the exam. Along with additional reading of the chapter and studying your class notes, this section can be used as a final review for an exam.

Making Psychology Part Of Your Life: Key Terms and Concepts

Knowing the important concepts and key terms contained in each chapter is a very important part of mastering the material. In this section, we have presented some of the key terms and concepts. Check on your understanding of this material by defining those that are listed in this section. Research has also shown that providing examples of concepts is a good way to increase your memory for them. Therefore, we have provided space for you to write an example of each. Try to be as specific as possible. Research has also shown that relating material to your own personal experiences is an extremely effective learning strategy. So, whenever possible try to use your own personal experiences when thinking of an example. As you will see, the author of your book (Robert Baron) has provided many examples of important concepts from his personal experiences. Try to follow his lead and relate this material to your life.

Challenge: Develop Your Critical Thinking Skills

Robert Baron points out in your textbook that one "hidden bonus" of taking introductory psychology is that it will help you develop your critical thinking skills. We definitely agree with him! These skills are a must in today's world. In this section, we have given you exercises that will help you develop the ability to think critically. We also discuss the particular skill that the exercise is designed to develop, along with a brief discussion of why this skill is important.

The best way to use these exercises is to complete them when you feel you have a good grasp of the material in the chapter. Completing the exercise will reinforce your understanding and will also give you feedback about whether you indeed have a true understanding of the material. We consulted a number of students while developing these exercises (and those presented in the next section); they reported that they found them quite enjoyable. So, we hope that you share their impressions and will enjoy "stretching your mind."

Challenge: Making Psychology Part of Your Life

This section is designed to encourage you to use what you've learned. The exercises vary in format - sometimes we give you a situation and ask you about how you'd deal with it. Sometimes we ask you to play the role of psychologist and provide your expert opinion. In all cases, the goal is to get you to apply psychology to your life. Of course, this will help you learn the material and do better on your exams. But more importantly, it will give you an appreciation for how your knowledge of psychology can enrich your day to day life.

Challenge: Review Your Comprehensive Knowledge

In this section, we present you with 20 sample multiple choice questions. This is an opportunity to check on your mastery of the material after you have finished your studying but while you still have some time left for review. There are skills involved in taking multiple choice tests. Practicing these skills will help you develop these skills. To help you grasp the logic of multiple choice testing, we have provided explanations for why a given item is the best response to the question. We have also given you the page number in your text that corresponds with the subject of each question. If you miss a question, go back an review that material. There is also a supplementary practice quiz for each chapter at the end of the study guide.

The items on this quiz are similar to the ones that may be used by your instructor on actual class tests. It should give you an idea of how well you'll do on your exam. We have also provided you with additional multiple choice questions at the end of the study guide. You should use these as an additional check on your mastery. A strong word of caution is due at this time. Do not rely only on these questions to assess your readiness for the exam. They are only a sample of the kinds of questions you might expect. Be sure you have mastered the learning objectives, the survey material, your class notes, and the key concepts and terms.

Some Study Tips

In the psychology course for which you have enrolled, inevitably some students will do quite well and others not so well. This fact often leads us to assume that these students differ in their intelligence or their intellectual ability. While this may be the case to some extent, a large portion of these differences in performance is probably due to differences in the way in which students approach their studies. Some are not motivated to work hard and so spend little time in actual study. Others may spend a lot of time studying but may have poor study habits. Let's briefly discuss how each of these two problems can be overcome.

Motivation to Learn

Unless you are motivated to learn or do well in a course, you are not likely to perform well in it even if you have all the best study habits. There are, of course, many obvious reasons to be motivated to do well in a course. Personal satisfaction of doing well, approval from your instructors, and the benefits derived from good grades (e.g., getting good jobs or gaining entrance to graduate or professional schools) are often sufficient to motivate many students. If these factors are not important to you (and even if they are), you should try to learn to derive satisfaction from learning itself. The discovery of new ideas and facts and the mastery of new concepts is often an inherent source of pleasure. You can probably increase the satisfaction derived from the learning by relating these facts, ideas, and concepts to your everyday life. Another technique that may help your motivation is breaking up the material in a chapter into smaller sections. After you have read and/or reviewed a major section of your chapter, provide yourself with a reward such as a drink, a snack, a walk outside, or a brief visit with friends. Then return to your studies and cover an additional section. Be sure not to reward yourself until you have finished an entire section. This procedure should not only help motivate your studying, but also will help build good study habits.

Study Habits

Let's assume you are highly motivated to do well in a course. You should now be strongly interested in the most efficient way to study. One of the important factors is **where** you study. It's important to study in a quiet area that is free from outside distractions and interruptions. A quiet corner of the library may do. Your own room may also be fine, if you can control your roommates and/or friends. Set up definite study periods and make others respect these. Make sure your desk is not cluttered with distracting material. You can even listen to light music but avoid programs which involve talking. Do not study by the TV. It is best to study in the same place each time so that it will become a habit when you are there (don't do anything else there except study!). Also be sure you have good lighting. It is best to have your light off to the side so as to minimize glare.

The next issue is **how** to study. One concern is how long you should study at one time. All of us have a span of concentration. Some of us can study for hours without a break. Others feel the need for a break after 10 minutes of study. In general, it is best not to study too long at one time since fatigue will set in and you won't be accomplishing very much anyway. So be sure to take breaks at appropriate times. You may need one every hour or every half-hour, or even after every 15 minutes. In fact, you can use these to reward yourself for studying certain amounts of material. Again, be sure to decide how much material you plan to cover before taking a break. Then, make sure you finish this material before you do take the break.

Another tactic that may help your studying is that of working on different subjects during each study session. This will prevent you from getting bored with one kind of study. You might want to do the least preferred subjects or tasks first, so that doing the more enjoyable ones will serve as a reward for completing the less preferred ones. Another important factor is your technique of study. One frequently suggested method of study involves a number of related steps: Survey, Question, Read, Recite, and Review (Robinson, 1970; Shepherd, 1987).

Survey. When you first begin with a chapter, glance through the entire chapter briefly to note the major topics covered. Use the headings contained in the chapters since they indicate the major points of the chapter. Also read the summary at the end of the chapter. Now you will know what you will have to learn in the chapter and how to organize the material as you read it. You may want to study one section before going on to the next, especially if a section contains a lot of information. The Learning Objectives can also help you survey the chapter.

Question. As you now read through the chapter, turn the headings into questions. This will give you an active and receptive set as you read through each section. An active learning set is very helpful in learning the test material. Also be sure to look at the Learning Objectives and Essay Questions sections of the manual for additional questions.

Read. Next you should read the material in the text to answer the questions you now have. Do not read as if you were reading a novel, but read as if preparing for a test (which, of course, you are!). Read in order to remember the material at a later time. Make sure to read everything as you go along. Don't omit the graphs, tables, and boxes since they are important additions to your chapter. Organize your reading by underlying and taking notes.

Recite. As you finish each section, you should see if you now can answer the questions you asked yourself at the beginning. You can do this verbally or by briefly jotting down the major points of the section. Then go back and see if you were correct. As you go through the chapter, you may want to go back and recite the major points of each section. Recitation is also designed to make you an active and involved learner. It is one of the most important of the study techniques and should take up a good part of your study time (e.g., one-third). Continue to question, read, and recite until you finish the chapter.

Review. After you have finished the chapter, you should review all of the material immediately. You can use your notes of the main topics or the main headings for this. Try to briefly summarize the major points of each of these sections. This should take only 10 minutes or so. This review is very important. If material is not reviewed immediately, much of it is soon forgotten. This review should be repeated at spaced intervals (e.g., every few days) and just prior to the examination. The Guided Review, of course, can be used for this type of review. Your reviews should consist of both recitation and re-reading of the material, depending on your level of mastery.

We have only been able to make a few suggestions on how to improve your studying. If you have serious difficulties with your studying or reading, you should try to take a study skills and reading course. Many colleges and universities offer such courses, and they may be well worth the required investment of time. You should also periodically come back to this section to remind yourself about good study techniques. However, if you follow the above study suggestions carefully, you won't need to be reminded, and you should find yourself doing better than ever in your course work. Good luck and enjoy your study of psychology.

Catherine E. Seta
Wake Forest University

John J. Seta
University of North Carolina at Greensboro

Paul B. Paulus
University of Texas at Arlington

REFERENCES

Robinson, F. P. (1970). Effective study. New York: Harper & Row Publisher.

Shepherd, J. F. (1987). College study skills (3rd ed.). Boston: Houghton Mifflin Company.

Acknowledgements

We are grateful to a number of persons for their help with this study guide. Several students have contributed suggestions about this guide and have helped with its completion -- Katherine Vickers, Lori Dawkins, Casey Goodman, and Amanda Muelchi. We very much appreciate their help! In addition, we would like to thank Rod Bedoya for helping with the glossary sections. We would like to thank Teresa Hill for preparing the text copy. We could not have done this without her. Finally, we are grateful to Beth Brooks, Laura Ellingson, and Susan Gleason for their suggestions and proofing.

TABLE OF CONTENTS

Page

CHAPTER 1
PSYCHOLOGY: ITS NATURE, SCOPE, AND METHODS

OUTLINE: Develop a Study Plan

Use this outline to help you grasp the organizational structure of the chapter contents. The learning objectives (LOs) for each section are included. Use them as tools for developing your study plan. Space has been provided for you to write any notes or questions that come to mind as you begin your exploration into this material.

Heading:	Learning Objective:	Your Notes:
I. Psychology: What It Is and How It Developed		
A. Philosophy and Science: The Dual Roots of Modern Psychology	**L.O. 1.1:** Describe the roots of psychology.	
B. Psychology: Some Early Views	**L.O. 1.2:** Compare and contrast structuralism, functionalism, and behaviorism.	
C. Psychology During the Twentieth Century: How It Developed and Grew	**L.O. 1.3:** Describe the growth and development of psychology within the twentieth century.	
D. Modern Psychology: Some Key Perspectives	**L.O. 1.4:** Compare and contrast the key perspectives within modern psychology.	
E. Psychology in a Diverse World: The Multicultural Perspective	**L.O. 1.5:** Discuss the implications of growing cultural diversity for psychology.	
F. Psychology: Some Basic Questions	**L.O. 1.6:** Answer the questions: "Is psychology really scientific?" and "Is psychology merely common sense?"	
II. Psychology: Who and What		
A. Who: The Background and Training of Psychologists	**L.O. 1.7:** Describe the background and training of psychologists. Describe the specialties that exist within psychology.	
B. What: Specialties Within Psychology		

Heading:	Learning Objective:	Your Notes:
III. Adding To What We Know: The Process of Psychological Research **A.** Naturalistic Observation: Scientists as Explorers	**L.O. 1.8:** Describe the naturalistic observation, case study, and survey methods of psychological research and discuss their positive and negative features.	
B. Case Studies: Generalizing from the Unique **C.** Surveys: The Science of Self-Report **D.** The Correlational Method: Knowledge through Systematic Observation **E.** Experimentation: Knowledge through Systematic Intervention		
F. Interpreting Research Results: Statistics as a Tool	**L.O. 1.9:** Describe the role of statistics and theory in psychological research.	
G. The Role of Theory in Psychological Research		
IV. Ethical Issues in Psychological Research	**L.O. 1.10:** Discuss the major ethical issues that psychologists face in their research with humans and animals.	
A. Deception: Is It Ever Appropriate for Psychologists to Lie to Research Participants? **B.** Research with Animals: Is It Acceptable?		
C. Ethical Issues in the Practice of Psychology	**L.O. 1.11:** Discuss the major ethical issues that psychologists face in the practice of psychology.	

Heading:	Learning Objective:	Your Notes:
V. Using This Book: A Note on Its Features		
VI. Using the Knowledge in This Book: Some Tips on How to Study	**L.O. 1.12:** Be able to describe how you can improve your study habits.	
VII. Making Psychology Part of Your Life		
A. Practice in Critical Thinking: The Hidden Bonus in Introductory Psychology	**L.O. 1.13:** Know how you can improve your critical thinking.	

SURVEY AND QUESTION

This section presents the major topics and ideas from the chapter. Use it as a tool for seeing how the components of the chapter fit together. At the end of each major topic, we have asked you a question that relates to the major learning objectives. If you can answer these questions, you have taken a major step toward mastering this material.

I. Psychology: What It Is and How It Developed

A. Philosophy and Science: The Dual Roots of Modern Psychology

Your text defines psychology as the science of behavior and cognitive processes. Psychology was heavily influenced by philosophy and science. The text discusses several philosophical views that were important for the emergence of psychology. These are: Empiricism -- the view that knowledge can be acquired through observation; Rationalism -- the view that knowledge can be acquired by logic and reasoning; and Interactionism -- the view that mind and body interact (the mind can influence the body and the body can influence the mind).

B. Psychology: Some Early Views

Psychologists have defined their field in different ways during its brief history. Structuralists believed that psychology should focus on analyzing conscious experience into its basic components. Wundt was a structuralist and was the founder of the first psychological laboratory. Functionalists believed that psychologists should study the way conscious experience helps us adapt to and survive in the world. One of the influential functionalists was William James. He wrote an early influential text, Principles of Psychology. The founder of the behaviorist approach was John Watson. He felt that psychology should focus on only observable activities that could be studied in a scientific manner. Because of his influence, for many years psychology was defined as the science of behavior.

C. Psychology during the Twentieth Century: How It Developed and Grew

In the 1930s and 1940s behaviorists focused on the study of learning. The study of human development, motivation, and the brain were major concerns in the 1950s. Environmental psychology and the study of psychology and law emerged in the 1960s. In the 1970s and 1980s the areas of adult development, gender differences, and health psychology became popular.

D. Modern Psychology: Some Key Perspectives

Modern psychology studies behavior and cognitive processes from several different perspective. The study of observable events is the behavioral perspective. Another perspective studies cognitive processes such as thinking, expecting, remembering, and deciding. The role of unconscious forces is the focus of the psychodynamic perspective. The humanistic perspective suggests that people have free will and concentrates on personal growth. The biopsychological or neuroscience perspective focuses on biological factors. The evolutionary perspective studies the adaptive pressures arising over the course of evolution and the mechanisms that evolved in response to these pressures. The socio-cultural perspective emphasizes the influence of social and cultural systems.

E. Psychology in a Diverse World: The Multicultural Perspective

Many countries are experiencing growing cultural and ethnic diversity. The field of psychology has also become more diverse in that there are more women and more psychologists that are not of European descent. However, although cultural diversity is becoming a focus of interest, there is still some indication of sex bias in the field. There is also a decline in the proportion of articles in the psychology literature that deal with African-Americans.

F. Psychology: Some Basic Questions

A scientific field of study is distinguished by its use of certain methods and its adherence to key values or standards. The scientific method involves systematic observation and direct experimentation. The main standards of science are objectivity, accuracy, and skepticism. Because psychology uses the scientific method and adheres to these standards, it can be considered to be a science.

Some people think that psychology is merely "common sense." However, the problem with common sense is that it often suggests contradictory answers; sometimes we assume we knew it "all-along." Studies have shown that actual predictions of research results are often wrong. Thus, it is clear that psychology is not just "common sense."

There are many subfields in psychology, including cognitive psychology, developmental psychology, educational psychology, industrial/organizational psychology, psychobiology, social psychology, and experimental psychology.

Questions:

1-1.   What ideas influenced the emergence of psychology? _____

_____

_____

_____

1-2.   What are structuralism, functionalism, and behaviorism? _____

_____

_____

_____

1-3.   Give a brief overview of how psychology developed in the twentieth century. _____

_____

_____

_____

1-4.   What are the key perspectives within modern psychology? _____

_____

_____

_____

1-5.   Discuss the implications of growing cultural diversity for the future of psychology. _____

_____

_____

_____

1-6.   Discuss why psychology is scientific and not merely "common sense." _____

_____

_____

_____

II.   Psychology: Who and What

A. Who: The Background and Training of Psychologists

Although many persons think that psychiatrists and psychologists are the same professions, they are quite different in training. Psychiatrists are physicians who specialize in the treatment of mental disorders after completing their medical studies. Psychologists receive their training in graduate schools specializing in psychology. This usually involves five years of advanced study.

B. What: Specialties Within Psychology

Although nearly half of all psychologists are involved in clinical or counseling activities, there are many other specialties within psychology. These are a few of the subfields:

(1) clinical psychology: studies the diagnosis, causes and treatment of mental disorders
(2) counseling: assists individuals in dealing with personal problems that do not involve psychological disorders
(3) developmental: studies how people change physically, cognitively, and socially over the life span
(4) educational psychology: studies the educational process
(5) cognitive psychology: investigates all aspects of cognition
(6) industrial/organizational psychology: studies behavior in work settings
(7) psychobiology: studies the biological bases of behavior
(8) social psychology: studies social behavior and thought
(9) experimental: studies learning, perception, and motivation

As you can see, psychologists study a number of different things. The shared goals, values, and methods used by psychologists unifies the field.

Questions:

1-7.   Describe the background and training of psychologists. _____

_____

_____

_____

1-8.   Describe the specialties that exist within psychology. _____

_____

_____

_____

III. Adding to What We Know: The Process of Psychological Research

A-C. Naturalistic Observation, Case Studies, and the Survey Methods

Psychologists use many different methods. Observing humans or animals in their natural settings is called naturalistic observation. An advantage is that subjects are likely to act in a natural manner. However, the data is sometimes relatively informal in nature. The detailed study of a few individuals is the case method of research. One problem with case method may be a lack of objectivity. One advantage is that when the behavior involved is very unusual, this method can uncover valuable insights.

The method that involves large numbers of individual completing questionnaires is called the survey approach. Problems with the survey approach are that people may not answer truthfully or accurately, and the persons surveyed may not be representative of the larger population to which the findings are to be generalized.

D. The Correlational Method: Knowledge through Systematic Observation

An important goal for psychology is prediction -- the ability to forecast future events from present ones. One such technique involves examining the association of changes in one variable with those of another one. This is called the correlational method. Statistical procedures are used to determine the size of the correlation (or relationship between variables). Correlations can range from -1.00 to +1.00. The greater their departure from 0, the stronger the assumed relationship between the variables.

Advantages of the correlational method are that: (1) it is efficient, (2) it can be used in naturalistic settings, (3) it allows us to examine many variables at once, and (4) it is often the only method feasible from a practical or ethical standpoint. One drawback of the correlational method is that it is not conclusive as to cause-and-effect relationships. If two variables are correlated, it does not mean one causes the other.

E. Experimentation: Knowledge through Systematic Intervention

Experimentation is the method that is preferred by psychologists because of its ability to help uncover why a relationship exists. Answering the question "why" serves the goal of explanation in science. Experimentation can provide fairly clear evidence about causality.

The experimental method involves systematically altering some factor believed to affect behavior and measuring the effects of such variations. The factor systematically varied is called the independent variable. The behavior or cognitive process studied is the dependent variable.

There are two requirements for the success of experiments. First, all participants in an experiment must have an equal chance of being exposed to any level of the independent variable. This is accomplished by random assignment of subjects to experimental conditions. Secondly, all factors that might affect subjects aside from the independent variable must be held constant. If this is not done, the independent variable is confounded with the other variables.

When researchers unintentionally influence the behavior of subjects, experimenter effects can result. When the hypothesis behind the study is communicated through the experimental procedures, we have demand characteristics. A procedure which minimizes these problems involves having research assistants who are unfamiliar with the hypothesis and the condition to which the subject is assigned conduct the study. This is known as the double-blind procedure.

F. Interpreting Research Results: Statistics as a Tool

Inferential statistics are used to determine whether a particular finding may have occurred due to chance. Only when the likelihood of a chance finding is low are the results described as significant.

A meta-analysis combines the results of many different studies to estimate both the direction and size of the effects of independent variables.

G. The Role of Theory in Psychological Research

Ideas for studies can come from informal observation or findings of other studies. However, the most important source is theories. These are attempts to understand why events occur. That is, they seek to explain. Theories consist of basic concepts and statements about the relationships between concepts. Predictions or hypotheses derived from the theory can be tested. From a scientific perspective, theories are useful only to the extent that they lead to testable predictions.

Questions:

1-9.   What are the naturalistic observation, case study, and survey methods of psychological research? Identify their positive and negative features. _____

_____

_____

_____

1-10.   What is the correlational method and what are its advantages and disadvantages? _____

_____

_____

_____

1-11. What are the basic characteristics of the experimental method? Why is it frequently the method of choice in psychology? _____

_____

_____

_____

1-12. What are two requirements that must be met in order for an experiment to be valid? _____

_____

_____

_____

1-13. Define experimenter effects, demand characteristics, and the double-blind procedure. _____

_____

_____

_____

1-14. What is the role of statistics in psychological research? _____

_____

_____

_____

1-15. What is the role of theory in psychological research? _____

_____

_____

_____

IV. Ethical Issues in Psychological Research

A. Deception: Is It Ever Appropriate for Psychologists to Lie to Research Participants?

Sometimes it is necessary to conceal certain aspects of an experiment. This is called deception. To counteract the negative effects of deception (such as discomfort, stress, and negative shifts in self-esteem) subjects are usually given as much information as possible prior to the experiment. This is known as informed consent. Full information after the experiment is called debriefing. Those who have participated in deception experiments generally view it as acceptable. Effective debriefing seems to eliminate many potentially negative effects of deception.

B. Research With Animals: Is It Acceptable?

Animal research makes it possible to do important research which, for health and safety reasons, cannot be done with humans. Because of their brief lifespans, animals are also useful for studying development. Animal studies by psychologists have resulted in a variety of practical benefits. The ethical issues that confront animal research are complex and whether the "benefits outweigh the costs" is a value judgment.

C. Ethical Issues in the Practice of Psychology

Many of the ethical issues that are involved in practicing psychology center around confidentiality issues. Confidentiality problems arise when professional ethics require the psychologist to withhold information when they feel the information should be revealed.   In addition, ethical issues involve situations in which the psychologist is in a conflicted relationship with a client or is sexually attracted to the client. Practicing psychology requires adherence to the highest of professional standards.

Questions:

1-16.   What are the major ethical issues surrounding research with humans? _____

_____

_____

_____

_____

1-17.   What are the major ethical issues that psychologists face in their research with animals? _____

_____

_____

_____

1-18.   What are the ethical issues that psychologists face in the practice of psychology? _____

_____

_____

_____

V. Using This Book: A Note on its Features

This book contains a number of features that makes it easier to read. Make notes of key terms printed in bold text. Also, note the key points in the margins. There are also a number of special sections that you'll find interesting and entertaining. BE SURE AND READ THESE SECTIONS.

VI. Using the Knowledge in This Book: Some Tips on How to Study

Your text provides six guidelines for effective studying: 1) Begin with an overview; 2) Eliminate or minimize distractions; 3) Recognize the limitations of your span of concentration; 4) Set specific, challenging, but attainable goals; 5) Reward yourself for progress; and 6) Engage in active, not passive, studying.

Question:

1-19. How will you incorporate the six guidelines for effective studying in your study routine? _____

_____

_____

_____

VII. Making Psychology Part of Your Life

A. Practice in Critical Thinking: The Hidden Bonus in Introductory Psychology

Your course in introductory psychology offers you the opportunity to develop your critical thinking skills. Critical thinking is inherent in the scientific approach to psychology. In addition, you will learn much about topics such as problem-solving and decision-making that will give you insight into critical thinking. In this study guide, we give you an opportunity to develop and practice your critical thinking skills in the "Challenge" sections that accompany each chapter.

Question:

1-20. What are the components of critical thinking and how can you improve your skills? _____

_____

_____

_____

YOUR NOTES:

MAKING PSYCHOLOGY PART OF YOUR LIFE: Key Terms and Concepts

Knowing the important concepts and key terms contained in this chapter is a very important part of mastering the material. We have presented a sample of these concepts below. Define each concept and check your definition with that presented in the chapter. It will also be beneficial for you to think of an example of each concept. Whenever possible, use your own personal experience to provide an example of each term below.

1-1.   **Behaviorism:** _____

      Example: _____

1-2.   **Case Method:** _____

      Example: _____

1-3.   **Cognitive Processes:** _____

      Example: _____

1-4.   **Correlational Method of Research:** _____

      Example: _____

1-5.   **Critical Thinking:** _____

      Example: _____

1-6.   **Debriefing:** _____

      Example: _____

1-7.   **Deception:** _____

      Example: _____

1-8.   **Demand Characteristics:** _____

      Example: _____

1-9.   **Dependent Variables:** _____

      Example: _____

1-10. **Double Blind Procedure:** _____

Example: _____

1-11. **Evolutionary Psychology:** _____

Example: _____

1-12. **Experimenter Effects:** _____

Example: _____

1-13. **Experimentation:** _____

Example: _____

1-14. **Functionalism:** _____

Example: _____

1-15. **Humanistic Perspective:** _____

Example: _____

1-16. **Hypothesis:** _____

Example: _____

1-17. **Independent Variable:** _____

Example: _____

1-18. **Inferential Statistics:** _____

_____

1-19. **Informed Consent:** _____

_____

1-20. **Meta-Analysis:** _____

_____

1-21. **Multicultural Perspective**: _____

       Example: _____

1-22. **Naturalistic Observation**: _____

       Example: _____

1-23. **Psychodynamic Perspective**: _____

       Example: _____

1-24. **Psychology**: _____

       Example: _____

1-25. **Random Assignment of Participants to Experimental Conditions**: _____

       Example: _____

1-26. **Structuralism**: _____

       Example: _____

1-27. **Survey Method**: _____

       Example: _____

CHALLENGE: Develop Your Critical Thinking Skills

Analysis, Induction, and Deduction

As your text points out, one "hidden bonus" of taking introductory psychology is that it will help you develop your critical thinking skills. One important element in critical thinking is the ability to use what you've learned to analyze the world around you. In addition, the ability to go from the specific case exercise to the general (induction) and to go from general principles to specific cases (deduction) are crucial skills for the critical thinker. Practice these skills in the following exercise.

It is sometimes suggested that bright stimulating colors may cause people to eat faster than duller and less stimulating colors. The fact that many fast food restaurants have brightly colored interiors is seen as consistent with this idea. These restaurants supposedly want people to eat quickly and make available space for additional customers.

1-1. What do you think of this possibility? _____

_____

_____

1-2. Can you develop a theory that might explain why such an effect might be produced? _____

_____

_____

1-3. What are some hypotheses suggested by your theory? _____

_____

_____

1-4. Design an experiment to test your hypotheses. You should decide on the experimental conditions (independent variables), dependent variables, need for deception, procedures, and random assignment technique.

_____

_____

_____

_____

_____

_____

1-5. Can you do such an experiment in actual restaurants? Why or why not? _____

_____

_____

1-6. Would there be ethical problems? _____

_____

_____

1-7. Can some of your hypotheses be tested with animals? _____

_____

_____

YOUR NOTES:

CHALLENGE: Making Psychology Part of Your Life

<u>Becoming a Better Consumer</u>

Newspapers, TV, and popular psychology books are filled with claims that may or may not be backed by sound research. One major benefit that you can claim from this course is a heightened sensitivity to the validity of these claims. Your text discusses some of the strengths and pitfalls associated with the various methods of psychological research. This information can make you a better educated consumer. Practice using this knowledge by critically analyzing these claims. They represent the kinds of statements we commonly hear in the media.

1-1.   Beer and soft drink ads commonly claim that those who drink their product "have more fun."

A. Describe the relationships between variables or correlations that are claimed by these ads.

_____

_____

_____

B. Do you think these companies have scientific evidence that back up these claims?

_____

_____

C. Do you think people who watch these ads actually believe that the products will be associated with favorable results?

_____

_____

D. Do you think such advertising is ethical if it is not backed by strong scientific data? Why or why not?

_____

_____

_____

_____

1-2.   You read in the newspaper that recent research suggests that joggers live longer.

A. Does this result imply that running causes increased longevity? (Hint: Remember the pitfalls of inferring causative relationships from correlations?)

_____

_____

_____

B. What alternative explanations might exist for this finding? (Hint: Are there other differences between joggers and non-joggers?)

_____

_____

C. What kind of research would be required to determine whether jogging causes increased longevity?

_____

_____

YOUR NOTES:

CHALLENGE: Review Your Comprehensive Knowledge

SAMPLE TEST QUESTIONS

Once you have worked through the preceding sections, you should be ready for a comprehensive self-test. You can check your answers with those at the end of this section. An additional practice test is given in the supplementary section at the end of this study guide.

1-1.   Psychologists who believed that psychology should focus on analyzing conscious experience into its basic components are called:
    a.   functionalists.   c.   behaviorists.
    b.   structuralists.   d.   experimentalists.

1-2.   Psychologists who felt that psychology should study only observable activities were the:
    a.   functionalists.   c.   behaviorists.
    b.   structuralists.   d.   experimentalists.

1-3.   The founder of behaviorism was:
    a.   Wundt.   c.   Watson.
    b.   James.   d.   Freud.

1-4.   The philosophical view that knowledge can be acquired through observation is known as:
    a.   empiricism.   c.   structuralism.
    b.   behaviorism.   d.   functionalism.

1-5.   Observable behavior is to conscious experience as:
    a.   structuralism is to behaviorism.   c.   behaviorism is to psychoanalysis.
    b.   structuralism is to psychoanalysis.   d.   behaviorism is to structuralism.

1-6.   The common sense approach to psychology often is characterized by:
    a.   contradictory statements.   c.   systematic observations.
    b.   objective evaluations.   d.   direct experimentation.

1-7.   In the 1930s and 1940s, behaviorists were very concerned with the study of:
    a.   development.   c.   physiology.
    b.   learning.   d.   emotion.

1-8.   Psychologists who try to understand how we think and remember are taking a _____ perspective.
    a.   physiological   c.   social-cultural
    b.   psychodynamic   d.   cognitive

1-9.   When the hypothesis behind the study is communicated through the experimental procedures, this may be a _____ characteristic.
    a.   double-blind   c.   random
    b.   survey   d.   demand

1-10.   The method that involves watching animals or humans in natural settings is called:
    a.   survey   c.   introspection
    b.   naturalistic observation   d.   case study

1-11.   Having a large number of individuals complete a questionnaire is called the _____ approach.
    a.   case
    b.   natural observation
    c.   survey
    d.   cognitive

1-12.   Correlations can range from:
    a.   0 to 10
    b.   1 to 10
    c.   1 to 100
    d.   -1 to +1

1-13.   If one wants to know the cause of a behavior, one should use:
    a.   observation.
    b.   correlation.
    c.   experimentation.
    d.   surveys.

1-14.   In an experiment, the factor that is varied is called the _____ variable.
    a.   independent
    b.   dependent
    c.   control
    d.   stimulus

1-15.   In experiments, it is important that the assignment of subjects to the level of an independent variable is:
    a.   systematic.
    b.   natural.
    c.   random.
    d.   biased.

1-16.   In an experiment, all subjects in a noisy condition are tested on Mondays and those in the no noise condition on Wednesdays. The noise and day of week variables are:
    a.   implicated.
    b.   confounded.
    c.   contrived.
    d.   interactive.

1-17.   The most important source of ideas for studies in psychology is:
    a.   literature.
    b.   theory
    c.   common sense.
    d.   mathematics.

1-18.   The main purpose of theories is to:
    a.   explain.
    b.   postdict.
    c.   evaluate.
    d.   summarize.

1-19.   Because it is often necessary to conceal certain aspects of an experiment, experimental psychologists may use the technique of:
    a.   deception.
    b.   projection.
    c.   subliminal stimulation.
    d.   conversion.

1-20.   The humanistic perspective concentrates on:
    a.   remembering.
    b.   biological factors.
    c.   personal growth.
    d.   social and cultural systems.

Answers and Feedback for Sample Test Questions:

1-1.   B   Structuralists focused on analyzing conscious experience into its components. (p. 5)

1-2.   C   Behaviorists believe psychology should focus on the analysis of observable actions. (p. 5)

1-3.   C   Watson is the founder of behaviorist approaches to psychology. (p. 5)

1-4.   A   Empiricism is the philosophical view that assumes knowledge can be acquired through observation. (p. 3)

1-5.   D   Behaviorism focuses on observable behavior and structuralism focuses on conscious experience. (p. 5)

1-6.   A   Common sense often involves contradictory claims, such as "opposites attract" and "birds of a feather flock together." The existence of these claims make a more scientific approach to psychology necessary. (p. 14)

1-7.   B   Learning was the focus of behaviorists during the 1930s and 1940s. (p. 5)

1-8.   D   Cognitive psychologists focus on understanding the processes which underlie memory and thought. (p. 8)

1-9.   D   Demand characteristics exist when the procedures of a study in some way communicate the experimental hypotheses. (p. 24)

1-10.   B   Naturalistic observation is the method of study that involves observation in natural settings. (p. 18)

1-11.   C   A survey involves having a large number of individuals complete a questionnaire. (p. 19)

1-12.   D   Correlations range from -1 (perfect, negative relationship) to +1 (perfect, positive relationship). (p. 21)

1-13.   C   Experimentation is the method that allows us to understand causal relationships. (p. 22)

1-14.   A   We call the variable that is purposely manipulated in a study an independent variable. (p. 22)

1-15.   C   There must be random assignment of subjects in an experiment in order to be sure that manipulated variables, rather than characteristics of subjects, are responsible for the outcomes of the study. (p. 23)

1-16.   B   In this example, the day of the week the testing was done was not held constant. Therefore, noise and day of the week are confounded. (p. 24)

1-17.   B   Theories are the most important sources of research ideas because they represent attempts to understand why events occur. (p. 28)

1-18.   A   The purpose of theories is to explain why events occur. (p. 28)

1-19.   A   Deception is used whenever it is absolutely necessary to conceal certain aspects of a study from participants. It must be used with caution, and only when necessary. (p. 31)

1-20.   C   The humanistic perspective concentrates on personal growth. (p. 8)

Glossary of difficult words and expressions	Definition
Acquainting you...	introducing you
Adamantly	strongly
Bizarre	very unusual
Capsule overview	short summary
Confounding	confusing; changing two variables at the same time
Debriefing	explaining an experiment to participants
Eclectic	having broad interests; knowing a lot
Eminently	remarkable; thought highly of
Flaws	things that are not perfect
Flock together	are seen together
Gloss over	trying to solve a problem in a way that is only temporary
Grapple	have trouble with; hard to figure out
Harsh	not justified; overly critical
Hasten	increase the speed of your actions
High school dropouts	people who do not finish high school
Insurmountable	unable to defeat; difficult
Just around the corner	will happen very soon
Loners	people who are by themselves a lot
Nuisance	something or someone that is annoying
Ominous	creates fear
Overt	out in the open; obvious
Pine away	do poorly, sad
Pitfalls	danger that you are not aware of
Rehashing	repeating several times
Remiss	not fulfilling the expected responsbility
Scrutiny	to examine closely
Span concentration	amount of time that you can pay attention
Stampeded	being made to do something
Stemming from	had its origins from
Stringent	strict

Glossary of difficult words and expressions	Definition
Subtle cues	signals that are not obvious
Tapestry	piece of cloth used for covering walls and furniture; a picture of something
Underpinnings of...	background information
Unfurled	unfolded

YOUR NOTES:

CHAPTER 2
BIOLOGICAL BASES OF BEHAVIOR:
A LOOK BENEATH THE SURFACE

OUTLINE: Develop a Study Plan

Use this outline to help you grasp the organizational structure of the chapter contents. The learning objectives (LOs) for each section are included. Use them as tools for developing your study plan. Space has been provided for you to write any notes or questions that come to mind as you begin your exploration into this material.

Heading:	Learning Objective:	Your Notes:
I. Neurons: Building Blocks of the Nervous System		
A. Neurons: Their Basic Structure	**L.O. 2.1:** Describe the basic structure of the neuron.	
B. Neurons: Their Basic Function	**L.O. 2.2:** Explain how neurons function and how synaptic transmission occurs.	
C. Neurotransmitters: Chemical Keys to the Nervous System	**L.O. 2.3:** Discuss the effects of neurotransmitters.	
II. The Nervous System: Its Basic Structure and Functions		
A. The Nervous System: Its Major Divisions	**L.O. 2.4:** Describe the major divisions of the nervous system.	
B. The Nervous System: How It Is Studied	**L.O. 2.5:** Describe the major techniques for studying the nervous system.	
	L.O. 2.6: Know how imaging techniques have increased our understanding of brain/behavior relationships.	
III. The Brain: Where Consciousness is Manifest		
A. Survival Basics: The Brain Stem	**L.O. 2.7:** Identify the structures and functions of parts of the brain.	

Heading:	Learning Objective:	Your Notes:
B. Emotion and Motivation: The Hypothalamus, Thalamus, and Limbic System		
C. The Cerebral Cortex: The Hub of Complex Thought		
D. Language and the Cerebral Cortex		
IV. Lateralization of the Cerebral Cortex: Two Minds in One Body	**L.O. 2.8:** Describe the different roles of the two hemispheres of the cerebral cortex.	
A. Research With Intact (Noninjured) Persons		
B. Research With Split-Brain Participants: Isolating the Two Hemispheres		
V. The Endocrine System: Chemical Regulators of Bodily Processes	**L.O. 2.9:** Describe how the endocrine system regulates bodily processes.	
A. Hormones and Behavior: Is The Premenstrual Syndrome Real?	**L.O. 2.10:** Identify the various factors that influence the premenstrual syndrome.	
	L.O. 2.11: Discuss the role of biology in the behavior of males and females.	
VI. Heredity and Behavior Differences		
A. Genetics: Some Basic Principles	**L.O. 2.12:** Outline the basic principles of genetics.	
B. Disentangling Genetic and Environmental Effects: Research Strategies	**L.O. 2.13:** Discuss the different research strategies employed to determine the relative importance of genetic and environmental factors in behavior.	

Heading:	Learning Objective:	Your Notes:
VII. Making Psychology Part of Your Life **A.** Traumatic Brain Injury: Using Psychology to Enhance Quality of Life	**L.O. 2.14:** Be able to describe how psychologists have developed rehabilitation programs to help improve the quality of life for TBI victims.	

SURVEY AND QUESTION

This section presents the major topics and ideas from the chapter. Use it as a tool for seeing how the components of the chapter fit together. At the end of each major topic, we have asked you a question that relates to the major learning objectives. If you can answer these questions, you have taken a major step toward mastering this material.

I. Neurons: Building Blocks of the Nervous System

A. Neurons: Their Basic Structure

Biopsychology is concerned with how biological processes are related to behavior, feelings, and cognition. The following sections review what we have learned from this exciting field.

The cells within our bodies that are specialized for the task of receiving, moving, and processing information are neurons. Neurons have three basic parts: cell body, axon, and dendrites. Information is carried to the cell body by the dendrites. It is carried from the cell body by the axon. The axon is covered by a fatty myelin sheath. This sheath is made of glial cells. It is interrupted at several points by small gaps. The axon divides into small branches that end in axon terminals. The region at which these terminals approach other cells is the synapse.

B. Neurons: Their Basic Function

Information travels within a neuron by means of a change in electric charge or action potential. When a neuron is at rest, there are more negatively charged particles inside than outside. The resulting negative charge is called the resting potential. When the neuron is stimulated, the cell membrane lets positively charged ions enter, reducing or eliminating the resting potential. The neuron then pumps the positive ions inside the cell back out, restoring the resting potential. The passage of this action potential along the cell membrane is the basic signal of the nervous system. The action potential occurs in an all-or-none fashion. In neurons with a myelin sheath, the action potential passes openings known as nodes of Ranvier.

The axon terminals contain synaptic vesicles. Arrival of the action potential causes these vesicles to approach the cell membrane and empty their contents into the synapse. These substances -- known as neurotransmitters -- then reach receptors in the membranes of the other cell. The transmitter substances may either have excitatory or inhibitory effects on the neuron. After the transmitter substances have crossed the synapse, they are either taken back into the axon terminals, known as re-uptake, or they are deactivated.

C. Neurotransmitter: Chemical Keys to the Nervous System

There are at least nine universally recognized substances known to function as neurotransmitters; and forty or more peptides appear to function as neurotransmitters. Several transmitters and their functions are summarized in Table 2.1 on p. 50 of your text. The neurotransmitter at most junctions between motor neurons and muscle cells is acetylcholine. Interference with this transmitter can cause paralysis. This transmitter is believed to play a role in attention, arousal, and memory processes. Alzheimer's disease may result from the degeneration of cells producing acetylcholine.

There are special receptor sites in the brain for drugs such as morphine. The brain appears to release naturally occurring substances that resemble this drug in response to pain or vigorous exercise. These substances are known as endorphins. It may be the case that understanding the process of synaptic transmission may be key in developing successful treatements for addictive disorders -- we may be able to alter this transmission through drug therapy.

Questions:

2-1.   What is the basic structure of the neuron? _____

_____

_____

_____

2-2.   How do neurons function, and how does synaptic transmission occur? _____

_____

_____

_____

2-3.   What are endorphins and why was their discovery exciting? [Discuss the practical implications of the existence of such substances.] _____

_____

_____

_____

II. The Nervous System: Its Basic Structure and Functions

A. The Nervous System: Its Major Divisions

Although the nervous system functions as an integrated whole, it is studied by divisions. The nervous system is divided into two major portions -- the central and peripheral nervous system. These systems regulate all of our internal bodily functions and enable us to react to the external world.

The two major parts of the central nervous system are the brain and the spinal cord. The spinal cord runs through bones called vertebrae. One of its functions is to carry sensory information (via afferent nerve fibers) from the receptors to the brain and to conduct information from the brain to muscles and glands (via efferent nerve fibers). Another function of the spinal cord is to regulate reflexes.

The peripheral nervous system consists of bundles of axons or nerves that connect the central nervous system with various parts of the body. Nerves that are attached to the spinal cord and serve the body below the neck are the spinal nerves. Those attached to the brain are the cranial nerves. These nerves serve the neck and the head.

The part of the peripheral system that connects the central nervous system to the voluntary muscles is the somatic nervous system. The part that connects the central system to the glands, internal organs, and involuntary muscles is the autonomic nervous system. The nervous system can be divided further. The autonomic nervous system consists of two distinct parts.

The part of the autonomic system that readies the body for the use of energy is the sympathetic division. The part of the autonomic system which has the opposite effect and stimulates processes that conserve energy is the parasympathetic division. These systems function in a coordinated way.

B. The Nervous System: How It Is Studied

There are several methods for constructing a map that will reveal the brain structures and processes involved in mental activities and behavior. One way is to observe the behavior of persons suffering from brain or nervous system damage. Then, after the person's death, the brain can be examined, and the location of the damage can be identified.

Another method involves introducing minute amounts of drugs directly to produce damage at specific brain sites or inducing drugs to influence neurons. This is known as the psychopharmacological method.

The nervous system is also studied by recording electrical activity within the brain. It can involve measuring the electrical activity of the entire brain, a procedure called electroencephalography or EEG. It can also involve the measurement of single neurons or groups of neurons by tiny electrodes. Further, electric current to certain areas of the brain may be used to investigate their functions.

Magnetic resonance imaging or MRI uses a strong magnetic field to obtain images of the brain. Functional MRI captures detailed images of the brain in action. Superconducting quantum interference device (SQUID) produces images based on its ability to detect tiny changes in magnetic fields. Another method involves the injection of small amounts of radioactive forms of glucose that is absorbed by the most active cells. This is called positron emission tomography or PET.

One application of brain imaging procedures is to scan the brains of normal persons and compare them to those persons with a variety of mental disorders to detect differences in the activity of their brains. Persons suffering from obsessive-compulsive disorder show increased activity in several areas including the frontal cortex. Imaging procedures have also been used to reveal how the brain delegates mental tasks including language processing tasks. When tasks are novel or complex, a greater overall amount of mental effort is required -- especially in the cortex. After a task is mastered, responsibility for the task is shifted from the cortex to more automatic brain regions.

Questions:

2-4.   What are the major divisions of the nervous system? _____

_____

_____

_____

2-5.   What are the major techniques for studying the nervous system? _____

_____

_____

_____

2-6.   How have imaging techniques increased our understanding of brain-behavior relationships? _____

_____

_____

_____

III. The Brain: Where Consciousness Is Manifest

The brain is often divided into three major components: 1) those concerned with bodily functions and survival; 2) those concerned with motivation and emotion; and 3) those concerned with complex activities such as language and reasoning.

A. Survival Basics: The Brain Stem

The portions of the brain that regulate basic bodily processes are located in the brain stem. Two of the structures in the brain stem that are located just above the spinal cord are the medulla and the pons. Major sensory and motor pathways pass through these structures. They also contain the reticular activating system which plays a role in arousal and sleep. The medulla contains collections of neuron cell bodies called nuclei that control vital functions such as breathing, heart rate, and blood pressure. The cerebellum is involved in the regulation of motor activities. The midbrain contains an extension of the reticular activating system and primitive centers for vision and hearing. It also contains structures that play a role in relieving pain and the guidance and control of motor movements by sensory inputs.

B. Emotion and Motivation: The Hypothalamus, Thalamus, and Limbic System

The hypothalamus is a small structure deep within the brain and plays a role in the regulation of the autonomic nervous system. It also helps keep the body's internal environment at an optimal level, known as the process of homeostasis. In addition, it also is involved in the regulation of eating and drinking. Damage to one part of the hypothalamus in animals is related to excessive eating, while damage to another part is related to reduced eating. The hypothalamus also plays a role in mating and aggression, partly by its influence on the release of hormones from the pituitary gland.

The thalamus is located deep within the brain and receives information from all of the senses except olfaction; it transmits this information to other parts of the brain. The thalamus is located above the hypothalamus and has been called the relay station of the brain. The limbic system seems to play an important role in emotion and motivated behavior such as feeing, fleeing, fighting, and sex.

C. The Cerebral Cortex: The Hub of Complex Thought

The cerebral cortex is the thin outer covering of the brain and is involved in our mental or information processing capacities. The cerebral cortex lies on top of two cerebral hemispheres. The two hemispheres are mirror images of one another -- although they differ in function. Each hemisphere is divided into four distinct lobes or regions.

The area of the brain nearest the face is the frontal lobe. It is bounded by a deep central fissure. Along this fissure is the motor cortex that is concerned with the control of bodily movement. Damage to this area causes only partial paralysis because other regions of the brain may take over some of the functions. This feature of the brain is called plasticity.

The parietal lobe is behind the central fissure and contains the somatosensory cortex which deals with information from the skin senses. Damage to the left part of this area may lead to loss of ability to read, write, or locate parts of the body. Damage to the right part leads to lack of awareness of the left side of the body.

The occipital lobe is concerned primarily with vision. Damage to one area may cause individuals to be unable to see part of their visual field. With severe damage to this lobe, a person may report complete loss of vision but be able to respond to stimuli as if they were seen. Damage to the right hemisphere leads to loss of vision in the left visual field whereas damage to the left hemisphere leads to loss of vision in the right visual field.

The temporal lobe is concerned primarily with hearing. Damage to the left hemisphere leads to loss of ability to understand spoken words. Damage to the right side is related to inability to recognize sounds other than speech.

The rest of the cortex (about 75-80%) consists of the association cortex. It plays a role in coordination of sensory systems and complex cognitive activities such as thinking and memory.

D. Language and the Cerebral Cortex

A great deal of research has been directed at understanding how and where the brain processes language. According to the Wernicke-Geschwind model, different areas of the cortex are involved in language. The Wernicke-Geschwind model of speech proposes that information received by the ears goes to the primary auditory cortex. Then it goes to the Wernicke's area where it is comprehended. Information is sent from this area through the accurate fasciculus to Broca's area. When this information is sent to the primary motor cortex, speech occurs.

Research has not supported this model. Little disruption of language results from removal of areas viewed as crucial by this model. CAT scans and the examination of the brains of persons with language-related problems do not find damage in the brain areas predicted by the Wernicke-Geschwind model. The Wernicke-Geschwind model is a serial one, and recent research supports a parallel model. Parallel models suggest that language involves different mechanisms that may occur at the same time, rather than in a sequence. Given the complexity of language, it makes sense that neural information can move along several routes at once and be processed in different ways in different areas of the brain.

Questions:

2-7.   What are the structures and functions of the brain stem? _____

_____

_____

_____

2-8.   What are the roles of the hypothalamus, thalamus and limbic system? _____

_____

_____

_____

2-9.   List the parts of the cerebral cortex and their functions. _____

_____

_____

_____

_____

_____

2-10.   What is the role of the cerebral cortex in language? _____

_____

_____

_____

IV. Lateralization of the Cerebral Cortex: Two Minds In One Body?

The brain shows a considerable degree of lateralization of function -- each hemisphere seems to be specialized for the performance of somewhat different tasks. In most persons, the left side of the brain specializes in verbal activities and analysis of information. For most of us, the right side is concerned with control of motor movements, synthesis, and the comprehension and communication of emotion. Evidence for hemisphere specialization has been obtained from studies of people with intact brains and from research with split-brain individuals.

A. Research With Intact (Noninjured) Persons

Research with noninjured persons has been conducted in order to find out about the functions of the two brain hemispheres. Studies which anesthetize one side of the brain indicate that left hemisphere has more highly developed verbal skills. Studies of brain activity indicate that activity in the left hemisphere increases when individuals work with numbers, but it increases in the right hemisphere when individuals work on perceptual tasks. When one is trying to decide an issue, activity is high in the left hemisphere. Once a decision is made, activity shifts to the right hemisphere, which seems to play a role in global, nonanalytic thought.

B. Research With Split-Brain Participants: Isolating the Two Hemispheres

Some research has examined individuals for whom the connection between the two sides of the brain has been severed in order to relieve some disorder, such as the symptoms of epilepsy. This connection is called the corpus callosum. Research on these individuals has provided evidence on lateralization of brain function. In these participants, stimuli in the left side of the visual field stimulate only the right hemisphere. Stimuli on the right side of the visual field stimulate only the left hemisphere. Stimuli presented to the left hemisphere of split-brain subjects can be named, suggesting that the left hemisphere controls speech. Stimuli presented to the right hemisphere can be pointed out but not named, suggesting that the right hemisphere has seen the stimulus but cannot describe it in words.

Recent research suggests that cooperation between the two sides of the brain is based on efficiency. The brain appears to delegate its resources between the two hemispheres. These ideas form the basis of the multiple resource theory. The brain also delegates its resources within each hemisphere. Therefore, if a person performs two tasks, and if the two tasks use the same cognitive resources, a decrease in performance is unlikely. These results are consistent with multiple resource theory. To summarize, research suggests it is possible to do two things at once -- as long as the tasks do not require the same hemispheric resource.

Questions:

2-11.   What are the different roles of the two hemispheres of the cerebral cortex? _____

_____

_____

_____

2-12.   What does the research on lateralization with intact brain persons suggest about the function of the two hemispheres? _____

_____

_____

_____

2-13.   What does the research on lateralization with split-brain persons suggest about the function of the two hemispheres? [Be sure you can describe the logic of these studies' procedures.] _____

_____

_____

_____

2-14.   Describe the multiple resource theory. _____

_____

_____

_____

V. The Endocrine System: Chemical Regulators of Bodily Processes

The hypothalamus plays a role in regulating the endocrine glands. The endocrine glands secrete hormones directly into the blood stream. These hormones exert far-reaching effects on bodily processes and behavior. Hormones that interact with and affect the nervous system are neurohormones. Their influence on neural activity is slower, but often more long-lasting, than the influence of neurotransmitters.

The endocrine glands are controlled by the hypothalamus through its influence on the pituitary gland (sometimes called the master gland). The pituitary is comprised of the posterior and the anterior pituitary. The posterior pituitary releases hormones that regulate reabsorption of water by the kidneys and, in females, the production and release of milk. The anterior pituitary releases hormones that regulate the activity of other endocrine glands. The hormones secreted influence sexual development, metabolism, excretion, and other bodily functions. For example, if the adrenal glands of genetic females produce too much adrenal androgen, they may be born with male-like sexual organs. This is called the andrenogenital syndrome. When genetic males lack receptors for androgens, they develop the androgenic insensitivity syndrome. They develop females genitals but have no ovaries and other internal female organs. The major endocrine glands and their effects are shown in Table 2.2 in your text.

A. Hormones and Behavior: Is the Premenstrual Syndrome Real?

In general, the endocrine system functions similarly in men and women. The exception to this is in the gonadal hormone levels: they're fairly stable in males but change in females. Gonadal hormone levels vary with the female menstrual cycle and are related to shifts in fertility. The change in moods, energy, and sexual desire prior to menstruation is known as the premenstrual syndrome. While these effects may be related to hormones, they also appear to be influenced by beliefs about such changes. Research has found that females who strongly believe in PMS over-report symptoms and mood shifts prior to menstruation.

The perspectives on diversity section discusses the biological basis of gender differences. Although changes in social and cultural forces have reduced sex-related differences, recent findings suggest that sex-related differences in certain cognitive processes and behaviors still remain. For example, men tend to score higher on tests of spatial ability, such as the ability to rotate 3-dimensional figures, and show greater language lateralization (hemispheric specialization) for processing verbal material than women. Women tend to hold a slight advantage on certain verbal tasks. One possible reason for these differences is the size of their brains, including the corpus callosum. In one study, the areas of the corpus callosum (reported to be larger in women than in men) was positively related to the women's scores on a verbal test -- a test on which women typically score higher. In contrast, the areas reported to be larger in men than in women were negatively related to the women's scores on a language lateralization task -- a task on which men typically score higher. Sex differences in brain structure may be due to basic biological processes that occur very early in development.

Recent evidence suggests that hormones may play a significant role in important aspects of human development, such as gender-related behavior, even before birth. The genetically based disorder of CAS, which appears to produce in girls behavior patterns more typical of boys, due to high levels of adrenal androgens may be an example of this kind of influence.

Questions:

2-15. How does the endocrine system regulate bodily processes? _____

_____

_____

_____

2-16. What are the various factors that influence the premenstrual syndrome? _____

_____

_____

_____

2-17. What is the role of biology in the behavior of males and females? _____

_____

_____

_____

VI. Heredity and Behavior

A. Genetics: Some Basic Principles

Each cell contains a biological blueprint that enables it to perform its essential functions. This information is contained in chromosomes, which are composed of the substance DNA. Most cells contain 46 chromosomes. Chromosomes also contain genes that contain thousands of segments of DNA. Genes, in conjunction with environmental forces, determine many aspects of our biological makeup.

Progress has been made in detecting genetic involvement in a variety of physical and mental disorders. Recently, researchers have identified a gene responsible for Huntington's Disease -- a rare, progressive neuromuscular disorder. Most human traits, however, are determined by more than one gene. Further, the possession of a gene does not insure that a specific effect will occur. Genes influence behavior only indirectly through their influence on chemical reactions in the brain or other organs. Therefore, these reactions may depend on certain environmental influences. For example, phenylketonuria (PKU) is a genetically-based disorder in which persons lack an enzyme to break down a substance (phenylalanine) present in many foods, leading to a build-up of this substance in their bodies and to mental retardation, seizures, and hyperactivity. Children placed on a diet low in phenylalanine do not develop the symptoms of PKU.

B. Disentangling Genetic and Environmental Effects: Research Strategies

The concern with the relative importance of genetic versus environmental factors in behavior is the nature-nurture controversy. A way to address this issue is to study identical or monozygotic twins.

Comparisons can be made between identical twins who are separated early in life and raised in contrasting environments. Because these twins have identical genes, any differences between them have to be due to contrasting experiences (an environmental factor). Similarities, in the face of contrasting environments, reflect the contribution of genetics. Support for genetic influences comes from findings that identical twins reared in very different environments show remarkable similarities. For example, research using this kind of procedures has found evidence that genetic factors may play a role in job satisfaction and sexual preference. However, it should be noted that environmental factors exert important effects on these processes.

Questions:

2-18.   What are the basic principles of genetics? _____

_____

_____

_____

2-19.   What are the research strategies employed to determine the relative importance of genetic and environmental factors in behavior? _____

_____

_____

_____

VII. Making Psychology Part of Your Life

A. Traumatic Brain Injury: Using Psychology To Enhance Quality of Life

Injuries to the brain often produce major physical and psychological problems. Severe instances of head injury, called traumatic brain injury (TBI) involve damage due to extreme forces applied to the skull. Research in biopsychology has led to the establishment of effective rehabilitation programs that focus on creating flexible environments that help TBI victims deal with their disabilities. Two ingredients for success are: (1) arranging environments in a way that reduces frustration and, (2) beginning treatment early.

Question:

2-20. Can you apply what you have learned to think of other factors that would be helpful in helping TBI victims? _____

_____

_____

_____

MAKING PSYCHOLOGY PART OF YOUR LIFE: Key Terms and Concepts

Knowing the important concepts and key terms contained in this chapter is a very important part of mastering the material. We have presented a sample of these concepts below. Define each concept and check your definition with that presented in the chapter. It will also be beneficial for you to think of an example of each concept. Whenever possible, use your own personal experience to provide an example of each term below.

2- 1. **Action Potential:** _____

2- 2. **Agonist:** _____

2- 3. **Antagonist:** _____

2- 4. **Autonomic Nervous System:** _____

2- 5. **Axon:** _____

2- 6. **Axon Terminals:** _____

2- 7. **Biopsychology:** _____

2- 8. **Central Nervous System:** _____

2- 9. **Cerebellum:** _____

2-10. **Cerebral Cortex:** _____

2-11. **Chromosomes:** _____

2-12. **Computerized Axial Tomography (CAT):** _____

2-13. **Corpus Callosum:** _____

2-14. **Dendrites:** _____

2-15. **Electroencephalography (EEG):** _____

2-16. **Endocrine Glands:** _____

2-17. **Frontal Lobe:** _____

2-18. **Genes:** _____

2-19. **Genetic Linkage Analysis:** _____

2-20. **Glial Cells:** _____

2-21. **Graded Potential:** _____

2-22. **Heredity:** _____

2-23. **Hormones:** _____

2-24. **Huntington's Disease:** _____

2-25. **Hypothalamus:** _____

2-26. **Lateralization of Function:** _____

2-27. **Limbic System:** _____

2-28. **Magnetic Resonance Imaging:** _____

2-29. **Medulla:** _____

2-30. **Midbrain:** _____

2-31. **Mitosis:** _____

2-32. **Nervous System:** _____

2-33. **Neurons:** _____

2-34. **Neurotransmitters (Transmitter Substances):** _____

2-35. **Nodes of Ranvier:** _____

2-36. **Occipital Lobe:** _____

2-37. **Parasympathetic Nervous System:** _____

2-38. **Parietal Lobe:** _____

2-40. **Peripheral Nervous System:** _____

2-41. **Phenylketonuria (PKU):** _____

2-42. **Pituitary Gland:** _____

2-43. **Pons:** _____

2-44. **Positron Emission Tomography (PET):** _____

2-45. **Reticular Activating System:** _____

2-46. **Somatic Nervous System:** _____

2-47. **SQUID:** _____

2-48. **Sympathetic Nervous System:** _____

2-49. **Synaptic Vesicles:** _____

2-50. **Synapse:** _____

2-51. **Temporal Lobe:** _____

2-52. **Thalamus:** _____

2-53. **Traumatic Brain Injury (TBI)**: _____

2-54. **Wernicke-Geschwind Theory**: _____

YOUR NOTES:

CHALLENGE: Develop Your Critical Thinking Skills

Seeing Two Sides of Issues

One of the most important elements in critical thinking is the ability to see two sides of an issue. Clearly, one controversial argument concerns whether a person's sexual orientation is determined by genes or by environmental influences. Can you apply critical thinking skills to this issue?

2-1. The basic theme of this chapter is that behavior results from complex biological processes within our bodies. Thus, it makes sense that much of our behavior is determined by hereditary factors. At the same time, it is clear that experience and the environment plays a major role in determining behavior. Using what you have learned, provide an argument for how biological factors may play a role in determining sexual preference.

_____

_____

_____

_____

_____

2-2. Provide an argument for how environmental factors would influence sexual preference. _____

_____

_____

_____

_____

_____

2- 3. Can you develop an analysis that integrates both biological and environmental influences on the development of sexual preference? _____

_____

_____

_____

_____

_____

_____

CHALLENGE: Making Psychology Part of Your Life

Diagnosis: Playing the Part of a Neuroscientist

For this exercise, let's stretch a bit and engage in role-playing. Pretend that you are a neuroscientist and that you consult with various doctors when they're having problems with a diagnosis. In each of the following cases, a M.D. has come to you with a list of symptoms. Make a diagnosis of where you believe brain damage has occurred. This will help you clarify your understanding of brain structure and function. Check your answers with those at the end of this section.

2-1. A fifty-year old woman has suffered a minor stroke. The stroke seems to have done little damage, but she seems to have lost interest in everything around her. She is losing weight rapidly and shows no interest in either food or drink.

Your diagnosis: _____

Note the basis for your diagnosis: _____

2-2. A 12-year-old boy fell from a tree. His collar-bone is broken, but more disturbingly, he seems to have lost control over fine muscle movements, especially of the fingers.

Your diagnosis: _____

Note the basis for your diagnosis: _____

2-3. After a car accident, a young woman reports that she seems to have a "hole" in her field of vision. She can't see objects in a particular location, but the rest of her vision seems normal.

Your diagnosis: _____

Note the basis for your diagnosis: _____

2-4. After a stroke, an older gentleman seems to have lost his ability to understand spoken words, but he can recognize melodies.

Your diagnosis: _____

Note the basis for your diagnosis: _____

2-5. A woman comes to the doctor concerned that her husband routinely forgets to shave the left side of his face. She is puzzled and is concerned that he may need a CAT Scan.

Your diagnosis: _____

Note the basis for your diagnosis: _____

Feedback Answers to Making Psychology a Part of Your Life Challenge

2-1. Damage to the lateral hypothalamus.

2-2. Damage to the motor cortex. Given his age, your estimate of his recovery probability is high; plasticity is greater when brain damage occurs early in life.

2-3. Damage to the occipital lobe of the cerebral cortex.

2-4. Damage to the left hemisphere of the temporal lobe within the cerebral cortex.

2-5. Possible lesion in the right hemisphere of the parietal lobe.

YOUR NOTES:

CHALLENGE: Review Your Comprehensive Knowledge

SAMPLE TEST QUESTIONS

Once you have worked through the preceding sections, you should be ready for a comprehensive self-test. You can check your answers with those at the end of this section. An additional practice test is given in the supplementary section at the end of this study guide.

2-1.   The three basic parts of the neurons are:
  a. vesicles, gray matter, and the synapse.
  b. telodendria, nodes of Ranvier, and synaptic terminals.
  c. cell body, axon, and dendrites.
  d. myelin sheath, cell body, and dendrites.

2-2.   The stage at which the neuron has a slightly negative charge is called the:
  a. dynamic state.   c. action potential.
  b. steady-state stage.   d. resting potential.

2-3.   Naturally occurring substances in the brain that resemble the effects of opiates are called:
  a. serotonin.   c. endorphins.
  b. dopamine.   d. norepinephrine.

2-4.   Drugs seem to affect our behavior and cognitive processes primarily by changing:
  a. thalamic structures.   c. the shape of the axons.
  b. synaptic transmission.   d. the number of axon terminals.

2-5.   Which of the following is not one of the functions of the spinal cord?
  a. regulates reflexes
  b. conducts information from receptors to the brain
  c. conducts information from the brain to the muscles
  d. connects the central nervous system to the involuntary muscles

2-6.   The part of the peripheral system that connects the central nervous system to the voluntary muscles is the _____
        system.
  a. central   c. parasympathetic
  b. sympathetic   d. somatic

2-7.   A procedure for measuring the electrical activity of the entire brain is called:
  a. superconducting quantum interference device or SQUID.
  b. positron emission tomography or PET.
  c. high-tech snooper or HTS.
  d. electroencephalography or EEG.

2-8.   The part of the brain that is involved in regulating motor activity is:
  a. brain stem.   c. cerebellum.
  b. medulla.   d. pons.

2-9.   Primitive centers for vision and hearing are in the:
  a. brain stem.   c. cerebellum.
  b. midbrain.   d. pons.

2-10.   This part of the brain regulates the autonomic nervous system.
a. hypothalamus   c. midbrain
b. thalamus   d. medulla

2-11.   Damage to the motor cortex leads to:
a. complete paralysis.
b. partial paralysis and loss of control over fine movements.
c. loss of vision in the left visual field.
d. loss of the ability to read and write.

2-12.   The lobe concerned with vision is:
a. occipital.   c. frontal.
b. temporal.   d. parietal.

2-13.   The lobe concerned with hearing is:
a. occipital.   c. frontal.
b. temporal.   d. parietal.

2-14.   The Wernicke-Geschwind Model is a _____ model explaining language processing.
a. parallel   c. olfaction
b. serial   d. hormonal

2-15.   Research has found that during the making of a decision the _____ hemisphere is active; once the decision is made, the _____ hemisphere is active.
a. left, left   c. right, right
b. left, right   d. right, left

2-16.   Most cells contain _____ chromosomes.
a. 23   c. 31
b. 46   d. 43

2-17.   This structure connects the two sides of the brain.
a. temporal lobe   c. limbic system
b. corpus callosum   d. midbrain

2-18.   This gland releases hormones that regulate the activity of other endocrine glands.
a. thyroid   c. anterior pituitary
b. adrenal   d. gonadal

2-19.   Men tend to score higher on _____ tests whereas women tend to score higher on certain _____ tests.
a. verbal ability, spatial ability   c. spatial ability, verbal ability
b. language lateralization, verbal ability   d. verbal ability, language lateralization

2-20.   Which statement is not true about genes?
a. They contain thousands of segments of DNA.
b. Most human traits are determined by more than one gene.
c. Genes influence behavior directly.
d. There is evidence for genetic involvement in a variety of physical and mental disorders.

Answers and Feedback for Sample Test Questions:

2-1.   C   The three basic parts are the cell body, axon, and dendrites. (p. 45)

2-2.   D   When a neuron is at rest, there are more negatively charged particles inside than outside. The resulting negative charge is called the resting potential. (p. 46)

2-3.   C   Endorphins are the brain substances that resemble the effects of opiates. (p. 50)

2-4.   B   Drugs affect our feelings or behavior by altering the process of synaptic transmission. (p. 50)

2-5.   D   Answers A - C are functions of the spinal cord. Option D is not a function of the spinal cord. The autonomic nervous system, a part of the peripheral system, connects the central nervous system with involuntary muscles, glands, and internal organs. The spinal cord is a part of the central nervous system. (p. 51)

2-6.   D   The somatic nervous system is the part of the peripheral system that connects the central nervous system to voluntary muscles. (p. 52)

2-7.   D   EEG is the procedure for measuring the electrical activity of the entire brain. (p. 54)

2-8.   C   The cerebellum is involved in the regulation of motor activity. (p. 57)

2-9.   B   The midbrain contains primitive centers for vision and hearing. (p. 58)

2-10.   A   The hypothalamus regulates the autonomic nervous system. (p. 58)

2-11.   B   Damage to the motor cortex leads to partial paralysis because other regions of the brain may take over some of the functions. (p. 59)

2-12.   A   The occipital lobe is concerned primarily with vision. (p. 60)

2-13.   B   The temporal lobe is concerned primarily with hearing. (p. 60)

2-14.   B   The Wernicke-Geschwind model is a serial model concerned with language. This has been a basis for criticizing this model. Parallel models are more plausible. (p. 61)

2-15.   B   When a person is trying to decide an issue, activity is high in the left hemisphere. Once a decision is made, activity shifts to the right hemisphere. (p. 64)

2-16.   B   Most cells contain 46 chromosomes or 23 <u>pairs</u> of chromosomes. (p. 72)

2-17.   B   The corpus callosum connects the two sides of the brain. (p. 64)

2-18.   C   The anterior pituitary gland releases hormones that regulate the activity of other endocrine glands. (p. 66)

2-19.   C   Men tend to score higher on spatial ability tests; women tend to score higher on certain verbal ability tests. These gender differences have been related to differences in the size of regions in the corpus callosum. (p. 69)

2-20.   C   Genes influence behavior **indirectly** through their influence on chemical reactions in the brain or other organs. (p. 71)

Glossary of difficult words and expressions	Definition
Compelling	convincing, persuasive, a good argument
Culprits	people who have done wrong; person who is responsible
Cumulative	add up; successive addition that increase
Cyclicity	regular and predictable patterns
Distraught	extremely upset, extremely annoyed
Dissipate	disappear; reduce
Enhanced	improved, to make better
Fleeing	running or hurrying away from
Foresight	can see the future
Heightened activity	increased activity
Hollow	Scopped out; without a center
Immutable	will not change
Intricate	complex; complicated
Jittery	nervous, anxious
Offset	balance, compensate for
Reared	raised; brought-up
Secrete	release
Seizures	physical attacks
Shedding light	making it clearer, making it more understandable
Shedding of	getting rid of
Snoop	inquiring; be a curious person
Source	starting point; the person or agent that began something
Sparked	be the immediate cause of
"Take up the slack"	do extra work that someone else has not completed
Tenant	person who pays rent for a room
The onset	the beginning
Threshold	a level that must be attained for an activity or process to start or occur
"Tomboy"	girl who likes rough noisy games and play
Triggered	started; caused to happen

CHAPTER 3
SENSATION AND PERCEPTION:
MAKING CONTACT WITH THE WORLD AROUND US

OUTLINE: Develop a Study Plan

Use this outline to help you grasp the organizational structure of the chapter contents. The learning objectives (LOs) for each section are included. Use them as tools for developing your study plan. Space has been provided for you to write any notes or questions that come to mind as you explore this material.

Heading:	Learning Objective:	Your Notes:
I. Sensation: The Raw Materials of Understanding	**L.O. 3.1:** Distinguish between sensation and perception.	
A. Sensory Thresholds: How Much Stimulation is Enough?	**L.O. 3.2:** Describe how researchers study sensory thresholds and the factors that influence sensory thresholds.	
B. Sensory Adaptation: "It Feels Great Once You Get Used To It"		
II. Vision		
A. The Eye: Its Basic Structure	**L.O. 3.3:** Describe the basic structure of the eye and the properties of light.	
B. Light: The Physical Stimulus for Vision		
C. Basic Functions of the Visual System: Acuity, Dark Adaptation, and Eye Movements	**L.O. 3.4:** Describe how the visual system works and how we process visual information.	
D. Color Vision		
E. Vision and the Brain: Processing Visual Information		
III. Hearing		
A. The Ear: Its Basic Structure	**L.O. 3.5:** Describe the basic structure of the ear and the characteristics of sound.	
B. Sound: The Physical Stimulus for Hearing		

Heading:	Learning Objective:	Your Notes:
C. Pitch Perception	**L.O. 3.6:** Describe two theories of pitch perception.	
D. Sound localization	**L.O. 3.7:** Know how we are able to localize sound.	
IV. Touch and Other Skin Senses	**L.O. 3.8:** Discuss the nature of the skin senses.	
A. Pain: Its Nature and Control	**L.O. 3.9:** Describe the implications of the gate control theory of pain.	
	L.O. 3.10: Know how culture influences our perception of pain.	
V. Smell and Taste: The Chemical Senses		
A. Smell and Taste: How They Operate	**L.O. 3.11:** Explain the nature of the sensory systems involved in our senses -- smell and taste.	
B. Smell and Taste: Some Interesting Findings		
VI. Kinesthesis and Vestibular Sense	**L.O. 3.12:** Explain the nature of the sensory systems involved in our sense of balance and body movements.	
VII. Perception: Putting It All Together		
A. Perception: The Focus Of Our Attention	**L.O. 3.13:** Explain the functions of selective attention processes.	
B. Perception: Some Organizing Principles	**L.O. 3.14:** Describe the ways in which Gestalt principles of perceptual organization help structure the input from sensory receptors.	
C. Constancies and Illusions: When Perception Succeeds and Fails	**L.O. 3.15:** List the major perceptual constancies and illusions.	

Heading:	Learning Objective:	Your Notes:
D. Some Key Perceptual Processes: Pattern and Distance	**L.O. 3.16:** Discuss the various pattern recognition theories and the cues we use to perceive depth and distance.	
VIII. The Plasticity of Perception: To What Extent Is It Innate or Learned?		
A. Perception: Evidence That It's Innate	**L.O. 3.17:** Discuss the evidence that suggests that perception is innate or learned.	
B. Perception: Evidence That It's Learned		
C. Must We Resolve the Nature-Nurture Controversy?		
IX. Extrasensory Perception: Perception Without Sensation?	**L.O. 3.18:** List the different types of extrasensory perception and describe the evidence for and against the existence of Psi.	
A. Psi: What Is It?		
B. Psi: Does It Really Exist?		
X. Making Psychology Part of Your Life		
A. The Danger of Stereo Headsets: Let's Turn Down the Volume	**L.O. 3.19:** Be able to discuss the dangers of wearing stereo headsets and know how to use these products safely.	

SURVEY AND QUESTION

This section presents the major topics and ideas from the chapter. Use it as a tool for seeing how the components of the chapter fit together. At the end of each major topic, we have asked you a question that relates to the major learning objectives. If you can answer these questions, you have taken a major step toward mastering this material.

I.   Sensation: The Raw Materials of Understanding

Psychological research has found that we do not know or understand the external world in a simple, automatic way. The topic of sensation is concerned with the information brought to us by our senses. Perception refers to the process through which we interpret and organize information.

A.   Sensory Thresholds: How Much Stimulation Is Enough?

Sensory receptors code information. The task of changing the many forms of energy in the world to signals for our nervous system is called transduction. When we are deprived of all sensory input we experience sensory deprivation and our bodies often produce hallucinations to fill in the void. To determine the level of sensitivity in each sensory system, psychologists use psychophysical methods. The amount of physical stimulation necessary to experience a sensation is called the absolute threshold. For most aspects of sensation, this threshold is quite low. These thresholds have been explored by using the method of constant stimuli. Since our sensitivity varies from moment to moment, the absolute threshold is usually defined as the magnitude of physical energy we can detect 50 percent of the time.

Several factors complicate the determination of absolute thresholds. Aspects of our bodily functions are constantly changing in order to maintain our body's internal environment at an optimal level -- a state termed homeostasis. Other factors include our level of motivation and the rewards and costs related to the detection process. These last factors are taken into consideration by signal detection theory.

Difference thresholds refer to the amount of change required to produce a just noticeable difference (JND) in stimulus intensity. Our ability to detect differences in stimulus intensity depends on the magnitude (strength) of the original stimulus. For example, we easily detect differences in weak stimuli.

Subliminal perception has been a source of controversy. Are we affected by stimuli that are outside our awareness? Research has explored this issue. In one study, subjects were not aware of stimuli; nevertheless, they responded as if they were. The results of several studies have indicated that subliminal messages in self-help materials do not improve performance. Rather, improvement appears to be related to other factors, such as motivation and expectations.

B.   Sensory Adaptation: It Feels Great Once You Get Used To It!

Sensory adaptation refers to the fact that sensitivity to an unchanging stimulus declines over time. This can be beneficial because it allows us not to be distracted by the many sensations we constantly experience. However, it can be detrimental in that we can become less sensitive to toxic stimuli, like smoke or harmful chemicals.

Questions:

3-1. What is the difference between "sensation" and "perception." _Initial contact_

Sensation is the input about the physical world provided by our sensory receptors while perception is the process we select, organize and interpret input from our sensory receptors.

3-2. How do researchers study sensory thresholds and what factors influence sensory thresholds?

Researchers study sensory threshold by using variety of procedures called psychophysical methods. There are two factors that influence sensory threshold o/c are absolute threshold and difference threshold.

3-3. What does research suggest about subliminal perception? _____

_____

_____

_____

3-4. What is the definition and function of sensory adaptation? _____

_____

_____

_____

II. Vision

A. The Eye: Its Basic Structure

Light passes through the cornea and enters the eye through the pupil. The size of the pupil is controlled by the iris. Next, the light rays pass through the lens which allows us to focus on objects at various distances. The sensory receptors are found in the retina at the back of the eye. Cones are the light receptors that function best in bright light. They are involved in color vision and our ability to notice fine detail. Rods are light receptors that are most important under low levels of illumination. Information is carried from the rods and cones to the brain by the optic nerve. A spot exists in our visual field at this place in the eye because there are no receptors.

B. Light: The Physical Stimulus For Vision

Visible light is only a small part of the entire electromagnetic spectrum. The distance between successive peaks and valleys of light energy is wavelength. This is related to perception of hue or color. The amount of energy or intensity of light is related to brightness. The fewer the number of wavelengths mixed together, the more saturated a color appears.

C.   Basic Functions of the Visual System: Acuity, Dark Adaptation, and Eye Movements

The ability to see fine details is acuity. Our ability to discriminate different objects when they are stationary is called static visual acuity. Dynamic visual acuity is our ability to resolve detail when objects (or us) are moving. A recognition acuity test (like the eye chart test at a doctor's office) is a way of measuring static visual acuity. Our ability to discriminate objects decreases as angular velocity increases. Angular velocity refers to the speed at which an object's image moves across the retina.

If your eyeball is too long, you may suffer from near-sightedness. You see near objects clearly but distant objects appear blurry. If your eyeball is too short, you may suffer from far-sightedness and you cannot see near objects clearly.

The increase in sensitivity that occurs when we move from brightly to dimly lit environments is called dark adaptation. During the adaptation process the cones reach their peak sensitivity in about five minutes. The rods begin to adapt in about ten minutes.

Eye movement is another important aspect of visual acuity. There are two types: (1) version movements occur when the eyes move together in the same direction, (2) vergence movements occur when our eyes converge or diverge. Vergence movements influence our ability to perceive distance and depth. Three types of version movements are involuntary, saccadic and pursuit movement. Involuntary movements occur without conscious control. Eye movements that are characterized by the eye jumping from one fixation point to another are called saccadic movements. The movement that tracks moving objects is called pursuit movement.

D.   Color Vision

People who have some insensitivity to red-green and yellow-blue have color weakness. Those who see only varying shades of white, black and gray are color blind. The theory of color vision that suggests that there are three different types of cones (which are primarily sensitive to red, green, or blue) is the trichromatic theory. Research suggests that there are three different types of receptors in the retina, but they overlap in sensitivity to the three colors. This research supports the trichromatic theory.

This trichromatic theory has difficulty explaining the perception of the many different colors and negative afterimages. [Negative afterimages are the occurrence of complementary colors that occur after staring at a particular color.] Thse can be explained by opponent process theory. This theory proposes that there are six kinds of cells above the retina. Two handle red and green, two deal with yellow and blue, and two handle black and white. For each pair, one cell is stimulated by one of the colors and inhibited by the other. It is now believed that both theories are necessary to explain color vision. According to this view, trichromatic coding occurs at the level of the cones and opponent processing occurs at higher neural levels.

E.   Vision and the Brain: Processing Visual Information

Research by Hubel and Wiesel has found that there are neurons in the visual system that respond only to stimuli possessing certain features. Cells that respond only to bars or lines in certain orientations are simple cells. Those that respond to moving stimuli are complex cells. Cells that respond to features such as length, width and shape are called hypercomplex. This research suggests that the visual system is highly selective and that these cells serve as the basis for complex visual abilities. Further, it suggests that the brain processes visual information hierarchically. Additional research supporting the idea that information is processed hierarchically comes from studying persons with visual disorders like prosopagnosia -- a condition in which persons can no longer recognize faces but still retain relatively normal vision in other respects.

Questions:

3-5.   What is the basic structure of the eye and the properties of light? _____

_____

_____

_____

3-6.   How does the visual system work? [Include a discussion of acuity, dark adaptation, and eye movements.] _____

_____

_____

_____

3-7   Compare and contrast the trichromatic theory and the opponent-process theory of color vision. What is the current thinking concerning these theories? _____

_____

_____

_____

3-8.   How does the brain process visual information? [Be sure to include a discussion of feature detectors.] _____

_____

_____

_____

III.   Hearing

A.   The Ear: Its Basic Structure

The part of the ear that responds to sound waves is the eardrum. Its movement in response to sound waves causes tiny bones within the middle ear to vibrate. One of these three bones is attached to the oval window, which covers the cochlea (a portion of the inner ear containing the sensory receptors for sound). Movement of the fluid triggers nerve cells to send messages to the brain through the auditory nerve.

B.   Sound: The Physical Stimulus for Hearing

Sound waves consist of compressions and expansions of air. The faster these alternate, the higher the pitch. This speed of alternation or frequency is measured in hertz. The greater the amplitude of these sound waves, the greater the loudness. The quality of sound is related to its timbre. Timbre is the characteristic that helps us distinguish the sound of a flute from the sound of a saxophone.

C.   Pitch Perception

Pitch perception involves our ability to perceive fine distinctions in sound. Place theory and frequency theory help explain how we perceive pitch.

Place theory (or traveling wave theory) suggests that differences in pitch can be detected because sounds of different frequency cause different portions of the basilar membrane to vibrate. However, no portion of the basilar membrane is sensitive to low frequency sounds. In addition, place theory does not account for our ability to discriminate sounds that differ by as little as 1 or 2 Hz.

Frequency theory suggests that sounds of different pitch cause different rates of neural firing. Since neurons can only fire up to 1000 cycles per second, sounds with high frequency may generate successive firings or volleys.

D.   Sound Localization

Several factors play a role in localization or our ability to detect the source of a given sound. Our head creates a sound shadow, a barrier that reduces the intensity of sound received by the ear on the side of the head opposite the source. The placement of our ears also increases the time it takes sound to travel to the shadowed ear. We have difficulty in determining the source of sound that is directly in front or behind us.

Questions:

3-9.   What is the basic structure of the ear? _As the eardrum vibrates from sound, the sound waves causes three tiny bones to vibrate within the middle ear. One of the three bones is attached to the cochlea. Movement of the fluid triggers nerve cells to send messages to the brain through the auditory nerve._

3-10.   What are the characteristics of sound? _____

_____

_____

_____

3-11.   What are the two theories of pitch perception? _____

_____

_____

_____

3-12. How do we localize sound? _____

_____

_____

_____

IV.   Touch and Other Skin Senses

There are several skin senses: touch, warmth, cold and pain. These properties are not sensed by specific sensory receptors, but by the total patterns of nerve impulses. Touch is perceived by stretching or pressure against the skin. Passive touch occurs when objects are placed against the skin. Active touch involves individuals bringing their body parts into contact with an object. We are most accurate in identifying objects through active touch, in part because of the feedback we receive from the movement of our body.

A.   Pain: Its Nature and Control

Pain plays an important adaptive role in protecting us from severe injury. Pain originates in free nerve endings. Damage to the body releases chemical substances that stimulate these neurons. Pain sensitivity varies from one body region to another body region. Sharp and quick pain is carried by large myelinated sensory nerve fibers. Dull, throbbing pain is carried by small unmyelinated fibers that conduct impulses more slowly. These two receptors are the basis for the gate-control theory of pain perception. This theory proposes that neural mechanisms in the spinal cord can close and prevent pain signals from reaching the brain. Pain messages from the large fibers can activate these gates while those from the small ones cannot. Techniques such as acupuncture and ice packs may reduce pain by stimulating large nerve fibers and closing the spinal "gate."

Mechanisms in the brain can also affect pain perception by transmitting messages that open or close the spinal "gate." This may account for the influence of emotional states on pain perception. The brain may also produce endorphins which reduce pain perception. Changing our thoughts and feelings, as well as our overt responses before, during, and after painful episodes, can influence our perceptions of pain.

There are large cultural differences in the interpretation and expression of pain. These differences appear to be perceptual and not physical in nature.

Questions:

3-13. What is the nature of the skin senses? _____

_____

_____

_____

3-14) How does culture influence our perception of pain? _In general, pain expression is automatic but other cultures believe that the difference of pain perception seem to result from the powerful effects of social learning and not from physical differences._

V.   Smell and Taste: The Chemical Senses

A.   Smell and Taste: How They Operate

Smell is stimulated by molecules in the air that come into contact with receptor cells in the olfactory epithelium. Our olfactory senses are restricted to a specific range of stimuli. To be smelled, substances must have molecular weights between 15 and 300. The stereochemical theory suggests that substances differ in smell because they have different molecular shapes. However, substances with nearly identical molecular structures often do not have identical smells. Receptors for taste are located in papillae on the tongue. These contain taste buds that have receptor cells responsible for taste sensations. There appear to be four basic tastes: sweet, salty, sour and bitter.

B.   Smell and Taste: Some Interesting Facts

Smell and taste have received less attention from researchers than vision and hearing. In this section, a few interesting facts are discussed. We are poor at identifying different odors. Although we may recognize a smell, we may not be able to name the odor in question -- the "tip-of-the-nose" phenomenon. However, our ability to remember specific odors is good. Although little evidence exists, some practitioners in a field called aromatherapy claim that fragrance can have positive therapeutic results. Fragrance has been shown to influence behavior. In job interviews, wearing a fragrance appears to influence ratings of the candidate. Pleasant fragrances (or ambiant fragrance) have also been associated with increased confidence in task ability, positive moods, and willingness to help other persons. These findings suggest that pleasant fragrances enhance people's current moods -- therefore, they exert a wide range of effects on behavior.

Questions:

3-15. What are the basic principles and findings relating to the chemical senses -- smell and taste?

_____

_____

_____

3-16. How can our sense of smell have practical implications? _____

_____

_____

_____

VI.   Kinesthesis and Vestibular Sense

Kinesthesia is the sense that gives us information about the location of our body parts with respect to each other and allows us to perform movements. Kinesthetic information comes from many different sources: It comes from receptors in our joints, ligaments, and muscle fibers, as well as from our other senses. Our vestibular sense gives us information about body position in movement and acceleration -- factors that help maintain a sense of balance. The sensory organs for the vestibular sense are located in the inner ear. The two vestibular sacs provide information about the position of our head and body's axes with respect to the earth by tracking changes in linear movement. The three semi-circular canals provide information about rotational acceleration of the head and body along three principle axis. The vestibular system is designed to detect changes in motion.

Question:

3-17. What is the nature of the sensory systems involved in our sense of balance and body movement?

Sensory systems involved in our sense of balance and body movement is the responsibility of the vestibular sacs w/c provide information about the position of our head and body's axes w/ respect to the earth by tracking changes in linear movement.

VII. Perception: Putting It All Together

A.   Perception: The Focus of Our Attention

The process by which we select, organize and interpret information from our immediate surroundings is called perception. It is clear that we are not capable of absorbing all the available sensory information in our environment. We selectively attend to certain aspects of the environment and ignore other aspects. This process allows us to maximize information gained from the object of our attention, while reducing sensory interference from irrelevant stimuli. The cocktail party phenomenon illustrates that unattended information does have an influence on the focus of our attention. Our attention shifts, for example, when we hear our name mentioned by someone at a party even though we were not previously aware of the content of that person's conversation. Other characteristics of stimuli can cause our attention to shift; for example, features such as contrast, stimulus intensity, color, novelty, and sudden change attract our attention. Our attentional focus is also affected by higher-level cognitive processes such as expectancy and motivation. Attentional processes play an important role in our survival. Research on this topic has been applied to the development of effective warnings.

Some persons have argued that the excessive use of warnings may cause people to ignore warnings altogether. Furthermore, using warnings that are rarely associated with aversive outcomes (low-risk hazards or those that are unlikely to occur) may teach people to ignore warnings. Concerns like these have led to the establishment of standards for the development and use of warnings -- these include content, type size, style, font, and placement.

The effectiveness of a warning depends upon sensation, which involves the warning's physical features, and perception (which involves the way in which the warning is presented).

B.   Perception: Some Organizing Principles

The process by which we structure the input from our sensory receptors is called perceptual organization. The first psychologists to study this aspect of perception were known as Gestalt psychologists. They identified several principles of organization. In perception, we tend to divide the world into parts. Those that have definite shape and location in space are figure, and those that do not have definite shape are ground. This principle is called the figure-ground relationship.

The Gestaltists also pointed out a number of laws of grouping. The tendency to group similar objects together is the law of similarity. The tendency to perceive a space enclosed by a line as a simple, enclosed figure is the law of closure. When elements are grouped because they are close together, it shows the law of proximity.

Elements that are seen as going in a particular direction illustrate the law of good continuation. When elements are grouped because they occupy the same place within a plane, we see the law of common region. The tendency to perceive complex patterns in terms of simpler shapes reflects the law of simplicity. Examples of these laws are seen on p. 107. Whether these laws are innate or learned is still being debated.

C.   Constancies and Illusions: When Perception Succeeds -- and Fails

This section discusses two important perceptual phenomena: constancies and illusions. Size constancy refers to perceiving objects to be of similar size even though they are at different distances. This may be due to the fact that we take distance into account in determining size. This is the principle of size-distance invariance. When we determine size by comparison with an object whose size is known, we are using the principle of relative size.

The principle of shape constancy refers to the fact that we perceive an object as having a constant shape even when the image it casts on the retina changes. Brightness constancy is shown when we see objects as similarly bright under different lighting conditions. These and other perceptual consistencies refer to the fact that our perception of the world does not change as much as variations in the sensory information would lead us to expect.

Incorrect perceptions are known as illusions. Some illusions seem to be caused by the inappropriate application of the size constancy principle. It has also been found that illusions are affected by learning. The moon illusion is an example of how size consistency can lead us astray in perceptions of shape or area. For example, the Muller-Lyer illusion may be a result of learning. The Poggendorf illusion involves misperceptions of the positions of angled lines disappearing behind a solid figure. Illusions are not limited to visual processes; there are examples of illusions in other sense modalities, such as touch and audition.

D.   Some Key Perceptual Processes: Pattern and Distance

Perception is a practical process that provides organisms with important information about what is in their environment. Pattern recognition is the process by which we identify what is in our environment. The template matching theory of pattern recognition suggests that we store exact representations of each pattern in memory and match visual stimuli to these patterns. This theory does not account for our ability to recognize variations in visual patterns. The prototype matching theory overcomes this problem by assuming that abstract representations of stimuli are stored in memory. Prototypes are general patterns of stimuli. In either view, recognition depends upon a match between visual stimuli and stored representations.

Bottom-up theories propose that pattern recognition is built from the organization of simple perceptual abilities, such as feature detectors. Perceptions are also determined by our expectations; this is the basis for top-down theories. Evidence suggests that both processes may play a role in pattern recognition. Bottom-up processes may be used in unfamiliar situations; top-down processes may be used in familiar situations.

Distance perception depends on cues that involve the use of only one eye (monocular) or both eyes (binocular). We will briefly review these. The larger the image on the retina, the larger and closer the object appears: size cue. The more parallel lines converge in the distance, the farther objects appear: linear perspective. Texture appears to be smoother as distance increases: texture gradient. Farther objects are seen less distinctly: atmospheric perspective. An object overlapping another is seen as closer: overlap or interposition. For objects below the horizon, lower ones are seen as closer. For those above the horizon, the higher ones are seen as closer. These are height cues or aerial perspectives. Cues provided by light and shadow are shading. A binocular cue described by the inward movement of the eyes as objects come closer is called convergence. The differences between the images provided by the two eyes is retinal disparity.

Questions:

3-18. What are the functions of selective attention processes? _____

_____

_____

_____

3-19 What are the ways in which Gestalt principles of perceptual organization help structure the input from sensory receptors? *Gestalt principles are figure-ground relationship where the objects w/ shapes @ focus are figure, and all others are ground. Laws of grouping — law of similarity, law of good continuation, closure, proximity, common region, simplicity.*

3-20. What are the major perceptual constancies and illusions? *size constancy — perceive a physical object as having a constant size.*

_____

_____

3-21. What are the various pattern recognition theories and what are the cues used to perceive depth and distance? _____

_____

_____

_____

VIII.   The Plasticity of Perception: To What Extent Is It Innate Or Learned?

A.   Perception: Evidence That It's Innate

There is some controversy about whether perception is innate or learned. The innate position gains support from evidence that when sight is gained by individuals who were born blind, they can make sense of their visual world. Research with three day old infants indicates that they do have a preference for color stimuli. Exposure of newborn female infants to certain odors led to preference for these odors. This research supports the innate perspective on perception.

B.   Perception: Evidence That It's Learned

There is some evidence for the role of learning in perception. In one study, kittens were raised in darkness except for exposure to either horizontal or vertical stripes. Upon release from darkness, kittens tended to respond only to objects exposed in the same position as the stripes. These deficits were permanent. One can conclude that both innate factors and experience are important in perception.

C.   Must We Try to Resolve the Nature -- Nurture Controversy?

Confronted with mixed evidence, most psychologists believe that perception is influenced by innate as well as learned factors. From this, Baron concludes that we do not need to resolve the nature-nurture issue. Learning and biology both play critical roles in perception.

Questions:

3-22.   What evidence suggests that perception is innate? _____

_____

_____

_____

3-23.   What evidence suggests that perception is learned? _____

_____

_____

_____

3-24.   Why do most psychologists believe that both innate and experiential factors influence perception?

_____

_____

_____

IX.   Extrasensory Perception: Perception Without Sensation

Extrasensory perception (ESP) involves perception without sensation. Psi refers to unusual processes of information or energy transfer that are currently unexplained in terms of known physical or biological mechanisms. Those who study this are called parapsychologists. The ability to foretell the future is known as precognition. The ability to perceive events that do not directly stimulate the sense organs is clairvoyance. Direct transmission of thoughts from one person to another is telepathy. The ability to move objects by thought is psychokinesis. Psi has been difficult to reproduce reliably in the laboratory. These is no known physical basis for psi and much of the support for psi comes from persons who believe in its existence.

Questions:

3-25. What are the different types of extrasensory perception? *precognition - foretell future events, clairvoyance - to perceive objects / events that dont directly stimulate our sensory organ, telepathy - mind readers - direct transmission of thought from one person to the next, psychokinesis - affect physical world purely through thought*

3-26. What is the evidence for and against the existence of psi? _____

_____

_____

_____

X.   Making Psychology Part of Your Life

A.   The Danger of Stereo Headsets: Let's Turn Down the Volume

Noise has become a pervasive part of everyday living. There is increasing evidence that noise pollution affects our health, performance, and social behavior. Many of these sources of noise pollution are outside of our control but we can control our use of headsets. Stereo headsets can produce sounds intense enough to cause hearing loss. Evidence exists that the habitual use of headsets at high volume result in perceptual auditory threshold shifts and tinnitus-ringing of the ears; they increase the risk of permanent hearing loss. Be sure and keep the volume of your headset turned down; the hearing you save may be your own.

In this section, Baron also describes three types of hearing loss. These are: 1) temporary threshold shifts: short-term reversible elevation of the level at which sound is detected, 2) permanent threshold shift -- nonreversible hearing loss from long-term exposure to noise; and 3) acoustic trauma -- permanent hearing loss from an extremely loud noise.

Question:

3-27. What are the dangers associated with exposure to noise? _____

_____

_____

_____

MAKING PSYCHOLOGY PART OF YOUR LIFE: Key Terms and Concepts

Knowing the important concepts and key terms contained in this chapter is a very important part of mastering the material. We have presented a sample of these concepts below. Define each concept and check your definition with that presented in the chapter. It will also be beneficial for you to think of an example of each concept. Whenever possible, use your own personal experience to provide an example of each term below.

3-1.   **Absolute Threshold:** _____

       Example: _____

3-2.   **Acuity:** _____

       Example: _____

3-3.   **Binocular Cues:** _____

       Example: _____

3-4.   **Blind Spot:** _____

       Example: _____

3-5.   **Braille Alphabet:** _____

3-6.   **Brightness:** _____

3-7.   **Brightness Constancy:** _____

       Example: _____

3-8.   **Cochlea:** _____

3-9.   **Complex Cells:** _____

3-10.   **Cones:** _____

3-11.   **Constancies:** _____

       Example: _____

3-12.   **Cornea**: _____

3-13.   **Dark Adaptation**: _____

      Example: _____

3-14.   **Difference Threshold**: _____

      Example: _____

3-15.   **Farsightedness**: _____

3-16.   **Feature Detectors**: _____

3-17.   **Figure-Ground Relationship**: _____

      Example: _____

3-18.   **Fovea**: _____

3-19.   **Frequency Theory**: _____

3-20.   **Gate-Control Theory**: _____

3-21.   **Gestalt Psychologists**: _____

3-22.   **Hue**: _____

      Example: _____

3-23.   **Hypercomplex Cells**: _____

3-24.   **Illusions**: _____

      Example: _____

3-25.   **Iris**: _____

3-26.   **Just Noticeable Difference (jnd):** _____

Example: _____

3-27.   **Kinesthesia:**   _____

3-28.   **Laws of Grouping:**   _____

Example: _____

3-29.   **Lens:**   _____

3-30.   **Localization:**   _____

Example: _____

3-31.   **Monocular Cues:**   _____

Example: _____

3-32.   **Nearsightedness:**   _____

3-33.   **Negative Afterimage:**   _____

Example: _____

3-34.   **Opponent Process Theory:**   _____

3-35.   **Optic Nerve:**   _____

3-36.   **Parapsychologists:**   _____

3-37.   **Perception:**   _____

Example: _____

3-38.   **Pinna:**   _____

3-39.   **Pitch:**   _____

3-40.   **Place Theory:** _____

3-41.   **Prosopagnosia:** _____

3-42.   **Prototypes:** _____

        Example: _____

3-43.   **Psi:** _____

        Example: _____

3-44.   **Pupil:** _____

3-45.   **Relative Size:** _____

        Example: _____

3-46.   **Retina:** _____

3-47.   **Rods:** _____

3-48.   **Saccadic Movement:** _____

3-49.   **Saturation:** _____

3-50.   **Semi-circular Canals:** _____

3-51.   **Sensation:** _____

        Example: _____

3-52.   **Sensory Adaptation:** _____

        Example: _____

3-53.   **Sensory Receptors:** _____

3-54.   **Shape Constancy:** _____

Example: _____

3-55.   **Signal Detection Theory:** _____

3-56.   **Simple Cells:** _____

3-57.   **Size Constancy:** _____

Example: _____

3-58.   **Subliminal Perception:** _____

3-59.   **Templates:** _____

3-60.   **Timbre:** _____

3-61.   **Transduction:** _____

Example: _____

3-62.   **Trichromatic Theory:** _____

3-63.   **Vestibular Sacs:** _____

CHALLENGE: Develop Your Critical Thinking Skills

Imagining Possibilities

Critical thinking involves the ability to "play with ideas" and imagine possibilities. In this exercise, practice this skill and stretch your imagination. Imagine that a person who has been blind from birth suddenly can see. What will this person see? Will his visual world be the same as yours? As your text points out, this is an intriguing question that has often served as the basis for exploring the nature-nurture controversy. Explore this question for yourself and answer the following questions in light of what you've learned.

3-1.∪ Take the position that perception is innate. That is, that experience is unnecessary for the development of perception. What would the person be able to perceive if this is the case? _____

_____

_____

_____

_____

_____

_____

_____

3-2✓ Take the position that visual experience is necessary for visual development. What would the person be able to perceive? _____

_____

_____

_____

_____

_____

_____

_____

3-3.   What does the evidence suggest concerning this nature-nurture controversy? _____

_____

_____

_____

_____

_____

_____

_____

3-4. ✓   Baron suggests that we need not resolve the "nature-nurture" controversy. Why does he take this position?
    What are your thoughts concerning this issue? _____

_____

_____

_____

_____

3-5.   Can you think of a way to integrate both innate and experiential factors in an analysis of how perceptual
    development occurs? _____

_____

_____

_____

_____

CHALLENGE: Making Psychology Part of Your Life

<u>Everyday Sensation and Perception</u>

There are many ways in which the material in this chapter can be applied to your lives. Many dramatic examples could be provided. But the impact of the processes discussed in this chapter on our everyday behavior may be even more fascinating. Below, we present you with several situations that occur to all of us at one time or another. Practice using your knowledge of sensation and perception by analyzing these events. Check your answers with those presented at the end of this section.

3-1.   Normally, you sleep through the alarm clock and have to be dragged out of bed. But today, you have an important date and wake-up at the first buzz of your clock.

What happened? _____

_____

_____

_____

_____

3-2.   You notice even the slightest change in volume when the volume of your TV is low. But when the volume is high, changes in the sound are not as noticeable.

Why? _____

_____

_____

_____

_____

3-3.   Your little sister is happily coloring on the porch. Since you're babysitting, you'd like to let her play happily for as long as possible. But as the sun sets and the porch becomes darker, she begins to cry because she can't see the colors in the dim light.

Why? _____

_____

_____

_____

_____

3-4.   Sitting in the dentist chair, I'm acutely aware of the drill and feel the discomfort of the tooth-capping procedure. I start thinking about my recent trip to the beach and feel better.

Why? _____

_____

_____

_____

_____

3-5.   At a party, you're having an interesting conversation with a friend. You're oblivious to everyone else around you until, suddenly, you hear someone mention your name. Now you turn your attention to this conversation.

What happened? _____

_____

_____

_____

_____

3-6.   As you stand on the deck at night, you wonder at how huge the moon looks as it hangs above the horizon.

Why? _____

_____

_____

_____

_____

Answers to Making Psychology Part of Your Life Challenge

3-1.   According to signal detection theory, the costs and rewards associated with detecting stimuli affect our perceptions. The cost of oversleeping and missing an important event increased your detection of the clock.

3-2.   You're experiencing changes in difference thresholds. Our ability to detect differences in stimulus intensity depends on the magnitude of the initial stimulus. At low intensities, small changes are more noticeable then at louder intensities.

3-3.   As the porch light becomes dim, she has dark-adapted to the setting. In dim light, her rods are most effective. But rods do not register information about color. Therefore, she is frustrated because she can't see her crayons.

3-4.   Pain perception stems from both physical and psychological causes. I have used a form of cognitive-behavioral treatment to change my perception of pain by changing my thoughts.

3-5.   You've experienced what is often called "the cocktail party" phenomenon. Certain characteristics of stimuli often capture our attention. In addition, higher level cognitive processes determine what we attend to. Our name is meaningful to us; therefore, we focus attention on environmental stimuli that incorporate this meaningful stimulus.

3-6.   You're experiencing the moon illusion. When the moon is near the horizon, we can see it is farther away than trees and other objects. Such cues are lacking when the moon is overhead. This is an example of the influence of size constancy.

Now it's your turn to provide some examples of the everyday occurrences of perceptual phenomena. In the following section, write out an instance in which you have experienced each of these phenomenon.

3-1.   Figure-ground relationship: _____

_____

3-2.   Laws of grouping: _____

_____

3-3.   Size constancy: _____

_____

3-4.   Monocular cues in distance perception: _____

_____

3-5.   The influence of expectancies in shaping perception: _____

_____

CHALLENGE: Review Your Comprehensive Knowledge

SAMPLE TEST QUESTIONS

Once you have worked through the preceding sections, you should be ready for a comprehensive self-test. You can check your answers with those at the end of this section. An additional practice test is given in the supplementary section at the end of this study guide.

3-1.   The definition of perception involves:
    a.   transduction.
    b.   interpretation.
    c.   simplicity.
    d.   direct sensation.

3-2.   The definition of sensation involves:
    a.   knowledge.
    b.   interpretation.
    c.   the senses.
    d.   simplicity.

3-3.   For most aspects of sensation our threshold is:
    a.   low.
    b.   high.
    c.   strong.
    d.   weak.

3-4.   The absolute threshold is usually defined as the magnitude of physical energy one can detect _____% of the time.
    a.   10
    b.   30
    c.   50
    d.   75

3-5.   These are most important under low levels of illumination.
    a.   rods
    b.   cones
    c.   lens
    d.   feature detectors

3-6.   The sensory receptors in the eye are found in the:
    a.   pupil.
    b.   lens.
    c.   iris.
    d.   retina.

3-7.   The distance between successive peaks and valleys of light energy are related to the perception of:
    a.   saturation.
    b.   brightness.
    c.   hue.
    d.   complexity.

3-8.   The theory of color vision that holds that there are six types of nerve cells which are stimulated by one type of stimulus and inhibited by another is:
    a.   trichromatic theory.
    b.   opponent process theory.
    c.   complementary theory.
    d.   saccadic theory.

3-9.   Fluid movement that stimulates hair cells in the ear occurs in the:
    a.   oval.
    b.   eardrum.
    c.   auditory nerve.
    d.   cochlea.

3-10.   Which of the following theories suggests that sounds of different pitch cause different rates of neural firing?
    a.   place theory
    b.   frequency theory
    c.   matching theory
    d.   gate-control theory

3-11.   The tendency to shift the focus of our attention toward meaningful, unattended information is known as the:
    a.   risky-shift effect.
    b.   cocktail party phenomenon.
    c.   template-matching effect.
    d.   prototype-matching phenomenon.

3-12.   Which of the following has not been found with regard to smell?
   a.   We are poor at identifying different odors.
   b.   Linguistic processing plays a central role in our ability to recognize odors.
   c.   Recognition of past odors is quite accurate.
   d.   Loss of smell is anosmia.

3-13.   The figure-ground relationship is of interest to _____ psychologists.
   a.   Gestalt   c.   clinical
   b.   behavioral   d.   humanist

3-14.   Basic ways in which we group items together perceptually are known as the:
   a.   proximity principle.   c.   closure laws.
   b.   good continuation rule.   d.   laws of grouping.

3-15.   The ability to perceive stability in the face of change defines:
   a.   perceptual illusions.   c.   size-distance variances.
   b.   perceptual constancies.   d.   the Muller-Myer illusion.

3-16.   Theories that propose that perceptions may be determined by our expectations are:
   a.   prototype.   c.   bottom-up.
   b.   top-down.   d.   feature.

3-17.   The binocular cue derived from the inward movement of the eyes as objects come closer is:
   a.   overlap.   c.   parallel perspective.
   b.   retinal disparity.   d.   convergence.

3-18.   Overt transmission of thoughts from one person to another is:
   a.   telepathy.   c.   precognition.
   b.   clairvoyance.   d.   psychokinesis.

3-19.   Exact representations of stimuli stored in memory are called:
   a.   features.   c.   prototypes.
   b.   binocular cues.   d.   templates.

3-20.   Which of the following theories takes into consideration that rewards and costs affect our ability to detect environmental stimulation?
   a.   discrimination theory   c.   Place Theory
   b.   threshold analysis   d.   signal detection theory

Answers and Feedback to Sample Test Questions:

3-1.   B   Perception refers to the process through which we interpret and organize information. (p. 80)

3-2.   C   Sensation is concerned with the information brought to us by our senses. (p. 80)

3-3.   A   For most aspects of sensation, our sensory thresholds are quite low, meaning that we are sensitive to relatively small amounts of sensory stimulation. (p. 81

3-4.   C   Absolute thresholds are defined as the magnitude of physical energy we can detect 50% of the time. (p. 81)

3-5.   A   Rods are most effective with low levels of illumination. (p. 86)

3-6.   D   The retina contains our sensory receptors. (p. 86)

3-7.   C   The perception of hue or color is related to the distance between successive peaks and valleys (wavelengths) of light energy. (p. 86)

3-8.   B   Opponent process theory suggests that six kinds of cells above the retina play a role in color vision. Two handle red and green, two handle yellow and blue, and two handle black and white. For each pair, one is stimulated by one of the colors and inhibited by the other. (p. 89)

3-9.   D   Movement of the fluid in the cochlea cause hair cells to transmit messages to the brain through the auditory nerve. (p. 91)

3-10.   B   Frequency theory suggests that sounds of different pitch cause different rates of neural firing. (p. 93)

3-11.   B   The cocktail party phenomenon occurs when we shift the focus of our attention toward meaningful unattended information, such as when we hear someone say our name at a party. (p. 104)

3-12.   B   In contrast to other senses, linguistic processing does not seem to play a role in the recognition of odors. (p. 100)

3-13.   A   Gestalt psychologists are interested in the laws of perceptual organization, such as figure-ground relationships. (p. 105)

3-14.   D   Laws of grouping refer to the basic ways we perceptually group stimuli. (p. 105)

3-15.   B   The ability to perceive stability in the face of change is referred to as perceptual constancy. (p. 106)

3-16.   B   Top-down theories describe the role that cognitive factors such as expectancies, plays in perception. (p. 111)

3-17.   D   Binocular (two-eye) cues are used for distance-perception. In order to see close objects, our eyes turn inward, toward one another. The greater the movement, the closer the objects. This is called convergence. (p. 113)

3-18.   A   Telepathy refers to direct transmission of thoughts from one person to another. (p. 115)

3-19.   D   Templates are exact representations of stimuli stored in memory. Template matching is one way of understanding pattern recognition. (p. 111)

3-20.   D   Signal detection theory considers how rewards and costs affect perception. (p. 82)

Glossary of difficult words and expressions	Definition
Acuity	ability to see fine details
Ailments	illness, affliction, disorder
Amiss	missing, out of place
Aversive	unpleasant, negative
Babble	meaningless talk, unable to be understood
Bassinet	type of cradle for a baby
Cast an image	to project a picture
Clamor of	loud noise
Coaxed down a path of	persuaded to take a particular stance or direction
Converge	to move toward each other
Dangle	to hang
Ellipse	a flattened circle
Embedded	implanted, inside
Faint spot	area in which details are difficult to see
Feats	accomplishments, deeds, achievements
Frowning	expression to show displeasure
Fuss	bother, commotion
Gauze pad	A sterile bandage used to protect open wounds
Gaze	to look at something intensively
Goggles	glasses worn to protect eyes
Gossip	rumors
Grittiness	grainy
Hoax	trick or prank
Hoisted	lifted, raised
Hue	color
Lead us astray	to lead to believe something that is not true
Lukewarm	barely warm
Murky	obscure, muddy
Pervasive	to spread through every part of
Porpoises	sea animal resembling a dolphin

Glossary of difficult words and expressions	Definition
Riveted	to focus attention on something
Sever	to cut, to terminate, to break
Smattering	to scatter a small quantity
Snipped	to cut
Stoic	dispassionate, detached, brave
Swirl	to move something in circles
Thrive	to succeed, to do well
Throbbing	pulsating
Transduce	to change
Trigger	to cause, to be responsible for something
Wintry	characteristic of a winter season

CHAPTER 4
CONSCIOUSNESS:
AWARENESS OF OURSELVES AND THE EXTERNAL WORLD

OUTLINE: Develop a Study Plan

Use this outline to help you grasp the organizational structure of the chapter contents. The learning objectives (LOs) for each section are included. Use them as tools for developing your study plan. Space has been provided for you to write any notes or questions that come to mind as you begin your exploration into this material.

Heading:	Learning Objective:	Your Notes:
I. Biological Rhythms: Tides of Life -- and Conscious Experience		
A. Circadian Rhythms: Their Basic Nature	**L.O. 4.1:** Describe the basic nature of circadian rhythms and the mechanisms that are thought to underlie them.	
B. Circadian Rhythms: What Mechanisms Underlie Them?		
C. Individual Differences in Circadian Rhythms: Of Larks and Owls		
D. Disturbances in Circadian Rhythms: Jet Lag and Shift Work		
II. Waking States of Consciousness: Everyday Experience		
A. Controlled and Automatic Processing: The Limits of Attention	**L.O. 4.2:** Compare and contrast automatic and controlled processing.	
B. Daydreams and Fantasies: Self-Induced Shifts in Consciousness	**L.O. 4.3:** List the major themes involved in daydreams and fantasies and the functions of these states of consciousness.	
C. Self-Consciousness: Some Effects of Looking Inward	**L.O. 4.4:** Know the various ways in which self-consciousness affects behavior and be able to discuss the control theory of self-awareness.	

Heading:	Learning Objective:	Your Notes:
III. Sleep: The Pause That Refreshes?		
A. Sleep: How It Is Studied		
B. Sleep: Its Basic Nature	**L.O. 4.5:** Describe the basic nature of sleep and how it is studied, and the potential function of sleep.	
C. Sleep: What Functions Does It Serve?		
D. Sleep Disorders: No Rest For The Weary	**L.O. 4.6:** Describe the sleep disorders.	
E. Dreams: Stimulation In The Midst of Sleep	**L.O. 4.7:** Survey the basic facts about dreams and discuss their nature from the psychoanalytic, cognitive, and physiological viewpoints.	
IV. Hypnosis: Altered State of Consciousness or Social Role-Playing?		
A. Hypnosis: What Is It and Who Is Susceptible To It		
B. Hypnosis: Contrasting Views About Its Nature	**L.O. 4.8:** Describe hypnosis and compare and contrast the views on the nature of hypnosis.	
V. Consciousness-Altering Drugs: What They Are And What They Do		
A. Consciousness-Altering Drugs: Some Basic Concepts	**L.O. 4.9:** Describe what consciousness-altering drugs are and what they do.	
B. Psychological Mechanisms Underlying Drug Abuse: Contrasting Views	**L.O. 4.10:** Compare and contrast the different perspectives on why people abuse drugs.	

Heading:	Learning Objective:	Your Notes:
C. Consciousness-Altering Drugs: An Overview	**L.O. 4.11:** List the characteristics of depressants, stimulants, opiates, and hallucinogens.	
D. A Note On the Psychology of Drugs Effects		
VI. Making Psychology Part of Your Life		
A. A Technique for Inducing Potentially Beneficial Shifts in Consciousness	**L.O. 4.12:** Know how you can practice transcendental meditation and its potential benefits.	

SURVEY AND QUESTION

This section presents the major topics and ideas from the chapter. Use it as a tool for seeing how the components of the chapter fit together. At the end of each major topic, we have asked you a question that relates to the major learning objectives. If you can answer these questions, you have taken a major step toward mastering this material.

I.   Biological Rhythms: Tides of Life and Conscious Experience

Throughout a day, we are aware of ourselves and the world around us in different ways. These contrasting levels of awareness are examples of distinct states of consciousness. Although the study of consciousness is an important topic area, it was rejected by behavioral psychologists. It has now reemerged as an important topic of study.

We are most alert and energetic at certain times of the day. These regular fluctuations in our bodily processes (and consciousness) over time are called biological rhythms. These fluctuations can take place over different periods of time. If they occur over the course of a single day, they are termed circadian rhythms. If they occur over the course of two or three hours, they are termed ultradian rhythms. Some biological rhythms can occur over longer periods of time.

A.   Circadian Rhythms: Their Basic Nature

Many bodily processes show daily, cyclical changes such as the production of various hormones. For many persons, core body temperature and blood pressure are highest in the late afternoon or evening. Cyclic fluctuations influence performance on many tasks. Simple cognitive tasks and those requiring physical activity are performed best when cyclic fluctuations are at or near their peaks. The link between circadian rhythms and performance on cognitive tasks weakens as the complexity of the task increases.

B.   Circadian Rhythms: What Mechanism Underlies Them?

A biological clock is an internal biological mechanism that regulates various circadian rhythms. There is some evidence that a portion of the hypothalamus (suprachiasmatic nucleus) is sensitive to visual input and stimulates or inhibits activity in the pineal gland, which in turn secretes a hormone termed melatonin. Exposure to intense light decreases the secretion of melatonin. When the level of melatonin is high, people experience fatigue. During the winter when people do not experience much sunlight they may become depressed. This reaction is termed seasonal affective disorder.

C.   Individual Differences in Circadian Rhythms: Of Larks and Owls

There are individual differences in circadian rhythms. For example, compared to "evening people" (owls), "morning people" (larks) seem to have a higher level of activation. Compared to evening people, morning people seem to have a higher body temperature early in the day and a lower body temperature at night.

D.   Disturbances in Circadian Rhythms: Jet Lag and Shift Work

There are circumstances in which circadian rhythms may get badly out of phase with our daily activities. Modern travel and shift work are examples of these circumstances.

When we travel across time zones, we often experience problems in adjusting. Our internal biological clock is set for one type of activity, while the external world calls for another type. Gradually, the adverse effect of this change goes away.

Shift work is another example. In many cases, individuals must work at times when they normally sleep or must change their working schedule from week to week. The constant re-setting of a person's biological clock may lead to adverse effects including fatigue, sleep disorders, ulcers, heart disease, and increased use of alcohol and other drugs. Our knowledge about these rhythms suggest simple steps to help shift workers. For example, it is easier to reset your clock if you work on a particular shift for a longer period of time vs. having several days between shifts. It is also easier to shift to a later, rather than earlier shift.

Questions:

4-1   What are the different types of biological rhythms? _____

_____

_____

_____

4-2.   What are the influences of circadian rhythms on performance? _____

_____

_____

_____

4-3   Discuss the basic nature of circadian rhythms and the mechanism thought to underlie them.

_____

_____

_____

4-4.   Discuss the individual differences in circadian rhythms and the consequences of disturbances in their normal cycles. _____

_____

_____

_____

II.   Waking States of Consciousness: Everyday Experience

A.   Controlled and Automatic Processing: The Limits of Attention

Our attentional capacities are limited. How do we manage to perform two or more tasks at once? There appear to be two levels of attention or conscious control over our behavior. The initiation and performance of an activity with little conscious awareness is called automatic processing. Because this requires very little attentional capacity, several of these activities can occur at the same time. Activities that require more effort and conscious control are controlled processing. This type of processing does consume attentional capacity. Automatic processing is faster than controlled processing. Automatic processing, however, is less flexible than controlled processing. Automatic and controlled processing are not hard-and-fast categories; they represent ends of a continuum.

B.   Daydreams and Fantasies: Self-Induced Shifts in Consciousness

The frequency and intensity of daydreams varies greatly across persons. Some of the most common fantasy themes of daydreams include success or failure, aggression, sex, guilt, and problem-solving.

Daydreams have many functions. They may serve as a way to escape from boredom and as a way to alter one's mood in a positive direction. They may also provide a way to find a solution to a problem and a way to regulate behavior.

C.   Self-Consciousness: Some Effects of Looking Inward

Self-consciousness occurs when your thoughts are focused on yourself. We can be privately or publicly self-conscious. According to the control theory of self-consciousness, when we focus attention on ourselves, we compare our current state with important goals or values. If we observe a discrepancy between reality and our goals or values, we attempt to reduce the discrepancy by making adjustments in our behavior.

Looking into a mirror, mood states, and being familiar with the environment are circumstances that result in heightened self-consciousness. Some persons spend more time thinking about themselves than others. These persons score high on the private self-consciousness scale.

Individuals often perform worse when they are under pressure. According to some writers, this may occur because pressure increases self-consciousness. This change in self-consciousness increases the amount of attention people devote to task performance. This change in attention can decrease performance because it interferes with a person's ability to perform a task in an automatic way. On the positive side, a state of increased self-awareness may sometimes lead to enhanced self-insight. Although thinking about ourself too much can lead to confusion at times, self-reflection can be an important ingredient for self-knowledge.

Questions:

4-5.   How does automatic processing compare to controlled processing? _____

_____

_____

_____

4-6.   What are the major themes involved in daydreams and fantasies, and what are their functions?

_____

_____

_____

49. What are the ways in which self-consciousness affects behavior and what is the control theory of self-awareness? _____

_____

_____

_____

III. Sleep: The Pause That Refreshes

A.   Sleep: How It Is Studied

Changes in brain activity during sleep can be measured by means of electroencephalograms or EEGs. Researchers also measure other changes in bodily functions such as respiration, muscle tone, heart rate, and blood pressure.

B.   Sleep: Its Basic Nature

When we are awake, our EEGs contain many high frequency and low voltage beta waves. During a resting state, these are replaced by slower but higher voltage alpha waves. During this phase, neurons are firing individually. As we fall asleep, these alpha waves are replaced by even slower, higher voltage delta waves. This reflects the fact that increasing numbers of neurons are firing together.

Sleep onset is sudden and can be divided into four stages. These stages are associated with a slowing of bodily functions and increased frequency of delta waves. Transition from wakefulness to sleep occurs in Stage 1. Stage 2 is marked by sleep spindles -- short bursts of rapid, high-voltage brain waves. In Stages 3 and 4, we see the appearance of more slow, high-voltage delta waves and a further slowing of all major bodily functions. After about 90 minutes, we enter REM sleep. At this time, our brain resembles a wakeful but resting state. Delta waves disappear and low voltage activity returns. There are rapid eye movements and almost total muscular relaxation. There may also be some evidence of changes in sexual organs which are related to increased arousal. Because of this, REM sleep has been called paradoxical.

During REM sleep, individuals dream. REM sleep alternates with other stages throughout the period of sleep, with the length of REM sleep increasing toward morning.

C.   Sleep: What Functions Does It Serve?

What benefits are gained by sleeping? One possibility is that sleep has a restorative function. Research does not offer strong support that sleep serves primarily a restorative function. A second possibility is that sleep serves a circadian function. That is, sleep is merely the neural mechanism which evolved to encourage various species to remain inactive during periods of the day. A third possibility is that only certain components of sleep, like REM, are essential. Results are mixed; most sleep researchers believe sleep serves both a restorative function and a circadian function.

D.   Sleep Disorders: No Rest for the Weary

Problems of falling or staying asleep are known as insomnia. These problems increase with age. Complaints of insomnia may be related to the quality of sleep, rather than its length. Reading before sleeping, regular bedtimes, and relaxing activities aid sleep onset. Sleeping pills appear not to be helpful in the long run.

Sleepwalking or somnambulism occurs in about 25 percent of children. Another disorder of arousal is night terrors -- individuals awaken from deep sleep with intense arousal and fear without recollecting dreams. These occur primarily at stage 4. Nightmares occur during REM and involve dreams. A disturbance that involves stopping of breathing while sleeping is called apnea. Twitching while sleeping or while falling to sleep is called nocturnal myoclonus. Sleeping too much is hypersomnia. One form of hypersomnia in which individuals fall asleep in the midst of waking activities is called narcolepsy.

There is some evidence that there is a relationship between the regulation of body temperature and sleep; temperature declines as we fall asleep. Persons suffering from insomnia have relatively high body temperatures during sleep. Sleep disorders may also involve disturbances of the biological clock within the hypothalamus.

E.   Dreams: Stimulation in the Midst of Sleep

Dreams are the most dramatic aspects of sleep. Baron presents you with several basic facts we know about dreams. We summarize these below:

1)   Everyone dreams, although not everyone remembers their dreams.

2)   Dreams do run on "real-time," in contrast to occurring in an instant.

3)   External events can be encorporated into dreams.

4)   Physiological signs of sexual arousal during sleep do not mean that a person is having a sexy dream.

Several explanations for the occurence of dreams have been offered. Freud believed dreams reflect suppressed thoughts, impulses, and wishes. There is little evidence supporting Freud's view. A physiological view argues that dreams are our subjective experience of random brain activity. According to this view, dreams are generated by spontaneous activity. A cognitive view assumes that neural activity forms the basis for the imagery and thought of dreams. However, this activity is not meaningless in that it reflects aspects of our memories and waking experiences.

Cross-cultural research suggests that the content and meaning of dreams are affected by culture and that dreams can sometimes function as an outlet for expressing unacceptable impulses. But research does not support Freud's view that dream content, such as Oedipus complex themes, are universal.

Questions:

4-8.   How is sleep studied? _____

_____

_____

_____

✓

4-9)   What is the basic nature of sleep? _____

_____

_____

_____

4-10. What are the potential functions of sleep? _____

_____

_____

_____

4-11. What are the various sleep disorders? _____

_____

_____

_____

4-12. What are the basic facts about dreams? _____

_____

_____

_____

4-13. Compare and contrast the psychoanalytic, physiological, and cognitive viewpoints concerning dreams. _____

_____

_____

_____

_____

IV. Hypnosis: Altered States of Consciousness or Social Role-Playing?

A. Hypnosis: What Is It and Who Is Susceptible To It

Hypnosis involves a state in which individuals are highly susceptible to the suggestions of others. Standard hypnotic inductions usually involve either suggestions by the hypnotist that the person being hypnotized feels relaxed, is getting sleepy, and is unable to keep his or her eyes open or a suggestion by the hypnotist that the person being hypnotized concentrate on a small object.

About 15 percent of individuals are very susceptible to hypnosis; 10 percent are highly resistant to hypnosis. Individuals prone to fantasies are easily hypnotized. Those individuals who tend to become deeply involve in sensory or imaginative experiences tend to be high in hypnotic susceptibility. In addition, individuals who are dependent on others, those who seek direction, and those who expect to respond to hypnotic suggestions are also quite susceptible.

B. Hypnosis: Contrasting Views About Its Nature

Systematic research has led to the formulation of two major theories about hypnosis. The social-cognitive (role-playing) view assumes that hypnotized persons are playing a social role in which they expect to lose control over their own behavior and be unable to resist suggestions. The neodissociation theory assumes that there is a split in consciousness. One part accepts suggestions from the hypnotist, while another part is a hidden observer. Of the two explanations, most psychologists believe that the social-cognitive view is more accurate. The results of recent studies suggest that hypnosis does not produce actual changes in memory -- it simply suggests to people what they should remember. Evidence also suggests that hypnotism cannot produce changes in what people perceive. Evidence does support the idea that hypnotism is best understood in terms of processes such as influence and demand characteristics.

Questions:

4-14. How is hypnosis performed and is everyone susceptible to it? _____

_____

_____

_____

4-15. What are the two major views concerning the nature of hypnosis? _____

_____

_____

_____

V.   Consciousness-Altering Drugs: What They Are and What They Do

A.   Consciousness-Altering Drugs: Some Basic Concepts

Drugs are chemical compounds that change the structure or function of biological systems. When drugs produce a change in consciousness, they are called consciousness-altering drugs. When taken on a regular basis, individuals often become dependent on their use. Physiological dependence occurs when the need is biological in nature. Psychological dependence occurs when individuals desire to continue using a drug even though there is not a physiological need. These two dependencies often occur together. Drug tolerance is a by-product of prolonged use. In some cases, use of one drug can increase tolerance for another drug. This is termed cross-tolerance.

B.   Psychological Mechanisms Underlying Drug Abuse: Contrasting Views

There are several views on the nature of drug abuse. According to the learning perspective, people take drugs because they expect that positive outcomes will be associated with drug use and/or they expect drug use to decrease negative outcomes. Anxiety reduction is an important cause of drug use from the psychodynamic approach. Drug use can be understood in terms of social factors from the social perspective. From the cognitive perspective, drug use can be viewed as an automatic behavior which can be initiated by internal or external cues, even in the absence of strong urges to consume the drug.

C.   Consciousness-Altering Drugs: An Overview

There are four major categories of consciousness-altering drugs: depressants, stimulants, opiates, and hallucinogens.

Drugs that reduce the activity in the central nervous system are depressants. The most frequently used is alcohol. One of the effects of alcohol is to lower our inhibitions. Alcohol may have its effects by acting on the cell membrane of neurons.

Sleeping pills and relaxants contain barbiturates, which is another type of depressant. These drugs reduce overall mental alertness. Barbiturates may reduce the release of excitatory transmitter substances at the synapses.

Drugs that increase arousal and feelings of energy are stimulants. Amphetamines and cocaine inhibit the re-uptake of transmitter substances at the synapse. They may produce a short period of pleasurable sensations followed by feelings of anxiety and depression. Continued use of cocaine can lead to psychological disorders. Caffeine and nicotine are also stimulants.

Heroin and morphine are called opiates. These produce dramatic slowing of bodily functions. They may produce very pleasurable sensations, but they are highly addictive, and withdrawal is painful. Opiates may cause the brain to stop producing endorphins. Therefore, individuals may loose their natural pain reducing mechanism.

LSD is an hallucinogen. These produce strong shifts in consciousness. For example, LSD may lead to a blending of sensory experiences known as synesthesia. They may also produce strong negative effects such as sorrow and fear. The effects are quite unpredictable. Marijuana produces a mild increase in arousal, a perceived increase in the intensity of various stimuli, a distortion in the sense of time, and a reduced ability to judge distances. Some persons report that it reduces inhibitions, increases sexual pleasures, and increases feelings of relaxation.

D.   A Note on the Psychology of Drug Effects

The impact of a drug is strongly affected by the user's expectations concerning the drug's effect. Its impact may also depend upon the user's physical state, on the user's previous experiences with these substances, and whether the user is or is not taking other drugs.

Questions:

4-16.   What is the basic information relating to consciousness-altering drugs and their use? _____

_____

_____

_____

4-17.   What are the different explanations for drug abuse? _____

_____

_____

_____

4-18.   What are the characteristics of depressants, stimulants, opiates, and hallucinogens? _____

_____

_____

_____

4-19)   What factors influence a drugs' impact? _____

_____

_____

_____

VI.   Making Psychology Part of Your Life

A.   Meditation: A Technique for Inducing Potentially Beneficial Shifts in Consciousness

Meditation is a procedure designed to alter consciousness and reduce awareness of the external world. It has been found to produce positive changes in biological processes, such as relaxation and reduced tension.

Baron provides you with several steps that are part of transcendental meditation procedure.   We summarize these below, but refer to page 151-152 for details.

1)   Find a quiet, isolated location.
2)   Choose an appropriate mantra.
3)   Meditate.
4)   Continue meditating for 15-20 minutes.

MAKING PSYCHOLOGY PART OF YOUR LIFE: Key Terms and Concepts

Knowing the important concepts and key terms contained in this chapter is a very important part of mastering the material. We have presented a sample of these concepts below. Define each concept and check your definition with that presented in the chapter. It will also be beneficial for you to think of an example of each concept. Whenever possible, use your own personal experience to provide an example of each term below.

4-1.   **Alpha Waves:** _____

4-2.   **Amphetamines:** _____

4-3.   **Automatic Processing:** _____

Example: _____

4-4.   **Barbiturates:** _____

4-5.   **Biological Rhythms:** _____

Example: _____

4-6.   **Choking Under Pressure:** _____

Example: _____

4-7.   **Circadian Rhythms:** _____

4-8.   **Cocaine:** _____

4-9.   **Control Theory of Self-Consciousness:** _____

4-10.   **Controlled Processing:** _____

Example: _____

4-11.   **Crack:** _____

4-12.   **Cross-Tolerance:** _____

Example: _____

4-13.   **Daydreams:** _____

　　　　　Example: _____

4-14.   **Delta Waves:** _____

4-15.   **Dependence:** _____

　　　　　Example: _____

4-16.   **Depressants:** _____

　　　　　Example: _____

4-17.   **Dreams:** _____

　　　　　Example: _____

4-18.   **Dreams of Absent-Minded Transgression:** _____

　　　　　Example: _____

4-19.   **Drugs:** _____

　　　　　Example: _____

4-20.   **Drug Abuse:** _____

4-21.   **Electroencephalogram (EEG):** _____

4-22.   **Fantasies:** _____

　　　　　Example: _____

4-23.   **Hallucinogens:** _____

4-24.   **Hallucinations:** _____

　　　　　Example: _____

4-25.   **Hypnosis**: _____

       Example: _____

4-26.   **Hypersomnias**: _____

       Example: _____

4-27.   **Insomnias**: _____

       Example: _____

4-28.   **Latent Content**: _____

       Example: _____

4-29.   **LSD**: _____

       Example: _____

4-30.   **Manifest Content**: _____

       Example: _____

4-31.   **Narcolepsy**: _____

       Example: _____

4-32.   **Neodissociation Theory of Hypnosis**: _____

4-33.   **Night Terrors**: _____

       Example: _____

4-34.   **Opiates**: _____

       Example: _____

4-35.   **Physiological Dependence**: _____

       Example: _____

4-36.   **Psychedelics:** _____

      Example: _____

4-37.   **Psychological Dependence:** _____

      Example: _____

4-38.   **REM Sleep:** _____

4-39.   **Seasonal Affective Disorder (SAD):** _____

      Example: _____

4-40.   **Self-Consciousness:** _____

      Example: _____

4-41.   **Sleep:** _____

4-42.   **Somnambulism:** _____

      Example: _____

4-43.   **States of Consciousness:** _____

      Example: _____

4-44.   **Stimulants:** _____

      Example: _____

4-45.   **Suprachiasmatic Nucleus:** _____

4-46.   **Tolerance:** _____

      Example: _____

CHALLENGE: Develop Your Critical Thinking Skills

Critical thinking is an important skill in our complex world. Practice expanding your critical thinking skills by completing these exercises which deal with hypnosis.

<u>Thinking Critically About Hypnosis</u>

4-1.   **Telling Fact From Fiction**

Baron discusses important research on the nature of hypnosis in the "Evidence for the Social-Cognitive View of Hypnosis" section (see pp. 143-144). One issue concerns whether hypnosis can improve the memories of eyewitnesses to crimes or whether the extra details recalled by eyewitnesses under hypnosis reflects <u>distortions in memory</u> rather than <u>improved recall</u>. What are the implications of these two contrasting possibilities?

_____

_____

_____

_____

_____

_____

_____

_____

4-2.   Assume that we find that a hypnotized person **can** distinguish between hypnotist-induced suggestions and what they actually saw or heard. Compare and contrast what proponents of the social-cognitive and neodissociation theories of hypnosis would say about this finding.

_____

_____

_____

_____

_____

_____

_____

_____

CHALLENGE: Making Psychology Part of Your Life

Dream Diary

Dreams are fascinating. And, as your book points out, there are many contrasting views concerning their nature and function. The content of dreams often includes important life events and can also incorporate noises that occur during sleep (e.g., thunderstorms). Although some people do not remember their dreams, research suggests that everyone experiences REM sleep (the stage of sleep during which we dream). We are more likely to remember our dreams when we first wake up. A fun exercise is to keep a dream diary for a week or two. Copy our "Dream Diary" form and keep it near your bed at night. Record your dream immediately after waking...don't jump out of bed and into the shower as soon as you wake up. Rather, lie quietly for a few minutes and try to remember your dreams. After you've recorded several of your dreams, complete the "Dream Exercise" and explore what your dreams may tell you. You may want to discuss your experiences with classmates who have also completed this exercise.

DREAM DIARY

Date: _____

Have you had this dream before?   Yes   No

Was your dream in color?   Yes   No

How long do you think your dream lasted? _____

Describe your dream as clearly as possible. _____

_____

_____

_____

_____

_____

_____

_____

_____

_____

_____

_____

Are you aware of any connection between your dream and anything that is currently happening in your life? If so, please discuss this connection below.

_____

_____

_____

_____

_____

_____

Are you aware of any connection between your dream and anything that was going on around you as you slept (e.g., telephone ringing, storms)? If so, please discuss this below.

_____

_____

_____

_____

_____

_____

List the persons that were in your dream. Label those whom you know personally, and describe those whom you do not know.

_____

_____

_____

_____

_____

DREAM EXERCISE SUMMARY: What Did You Learn?

4-1.   Do you see any recurring themes in your dreams? If so, please explain.

_____

_____

_____

_____

_____

4-2.   Can you relate any of your dreams or dream themes to any changes that you are currently attempting to make in your life? If so, please explain.

_____

_____

_____

_____

_____

4-3.   If you answered "yes" to question #2, you may have experienced DAMIT dreams (dreams of absent-minded transgression). Go back and review the feelings you noted about these dreams. Which view of dreams do these experiences best support? Discuss below.

_____

_____

_____

_____

_____

4-4. Relate your experiences in your dream diary to the basic facts about dreams discussed in your text. Do they fit?

_____

_____

_____

_____

_____

_____

4-5. Discuss how the physiological view of dreams would interpret your experiences.

_____

_____

_____

_____

_____

_____

4-6. How would the cognitive view interpret your experiences?

_____

_____

_____

_____

_____

_____

4-7.   How would the psychodynamic view interpret your experiences?

_____

_____

_____

_____

_____

4-8.   Discuss what you learned from keeping a dream diary.

_____

_____

_____

_____

_____

CHALLENGE: Review Your Comprehensive Knowledge

SAMPLE TEST QUESTIONS

Once you have worked through the preceding sections, you should be ready for a comprehensive self-test. You can check your answers with those at the end of this section. An additional practice test is given in the supplementary section at the end of this study guide.

4-1.   A disturbance that involves stopping of breathing while sleeping is:
   a.   hypersomnia.
   b.   apnea.
   c.   night terrors.
   d.   somnambulism.

4-2.   When we are awake our EEGs contain many high frequency and low voltage:
   a.   beta waves.
   b.   alpha waves.
   c.   delta waves.
   d.   zeta waves.

4-3.   Sleep can be divided into _____ stages.
   a.   two
   b.   three
   c.   four
   d.   five

4-4.   LSD has been associated with all but one of the following effects:
   a.   predictable effects.
   b.   synesthesia.
   c.   sorrow.
   d.   fear.

4-5.   Research examining sleep disorders suggests that there may be a relationship between these disorders and areas of the brain which regulate:
   a.   controlled processing.
   b.   body temperature.
   c.   automatic processing.
   d.   eating and drinking behavior.

4-6.   According to the psychodynamic perspective, the hidden meaning of a dream is known as:
   a.   latent content.
   b.   manifest content.
   c.   associative content.
   d.   disassociational content.

4-7.   Individuals who are easily hypnotized tend to:
   a.   be old.
   b.   have negative attitudes about hypnotism.
   c.   be prone to fantasies.
   d.   be independent.

4-8.   The drugs that may stop the brain from producing endorphins are:
   a.   opiates.
   b.   amphetamines.
   c.   hallucinogens.
   d.   barbiturates.

4-9.   Research on automatic processing suggests that:
   a.   it requires a lot of attention.
   b.   it is more flexible than controlled processing.
   c.   it is slower than controlled processing.
   d.   it requires little conscious awareness.

4-10. Which of the following is not a correct statement about daydreams?
   a.   They serve as a way to escape from boredom.
   b.   They serve as a way to regulate behavior.
   c.   Dreams concerned with future events seem to increase with age.
   d.   The frequency and intensity of daydreams varies greatly.

4-11.   A hormone that seems to influence circadian rhythm is:
a.   adrenalin.   c.   melatonin.
b.   endorphins.   d.   testosterone.

4-12.   Alcohol is classified as a(n):
a.   stimulant.   c.   opiate.
b.   depressant.   d.   hallucinogen.

4-13.   Rapid, low amplitude brain waves that occur when individuals are in a relaxed, waking state are called:
a.   beta waves.   c.   REMs.
b.   delta waves.   d.   alpha waves.

4-14.   About _____ percent of individuals are very susceptible to hypnosis.
a.   15   c.   50
b.   40   d.   70

4-15.   Which of the following is not a correct statement about stimulants?
a.   They increase arousal.   c.   They inhibit the re-uptake of transmitter substances.
b.   Cocaine is a stimulant.   d.   Alcohol is a stimulant.

4-16.   Which of the following can influence the impact of a drug on its user?
a.   the user's expectations   c.   drug interactions
b.   the user's physical state   d.   all of the above

4-17.   The view that people take drugs because they expect that positive outcomes will be associated with drug use is the:
a.   humanistic perspective.   c.   biological perspective.
b.   psychodynamic perspective.   d.   learning perspective.

4-18.   Self-awareness can decrease performance because it interferes with a person's ability to perform a task in a(n) _____ way.
a.   controlled   c.   self-aware
b.   automatic   d.   conscious

4-19.   Which of the following involves the least use of attention capacity?
a.   controlled processing   c.   hypnosis
b.   automatic processing   d.   transcendental

4-20.   Which of the following is **not** a correct statement about opiates?
a.   Heroin is an opiate.
b.   The pain reducing ability of the user may be reduced.
c.   Their use produces dramatic slowing of bodily functions.
d.   They may cause an increase in endorphins production in the brain.

Answers and Feedback to Sample Test Questions:

4-1.   B   Apnea is a sleep disorder in which people stop breathing while asleep. (p. 136)

4-2.   A   Beta waves are relatively high frequency (14 to 30 Hz) and have low voltage and they occur when we are awake. (p. 132)

4-3.   C   There are four stages of sleep. (p. 132)

4-4.   A   The effects of LSD are unpredictable. It may yield pleasant or unpleasant effects. (p. 149)

4-5.   B   In persons suffering from insomnia, internal mechanisms that regulate body temperature fail to operate normally, with the result that their body temperatures remain relatively high. (p. 137)

4-6.   A   Latent dream content refers to the hidden content of a dream, according to Freud. (p. 138)

4-7.   C   Persons who are highly susceptible to hypnosis tend to have vivid, frequent fantasies. (p. 141)

4-8.   A   Regular users of opiates may overload endorphine receptors within the brain. As a result, the brain ceases production of these substances. (p. 148)

4-9.   D   Automatic processing makes little demand upon our consciousness and attentional capacity. (p. 127)

4-10. C   Dreams concerned with future events do not increase with age. (p. 129)

4-11. C   Melatonin is the hormone that seems to influence circadian rhythms. (p. 124)

4-12. B   Alcohol is a depressant. (p. 146)

4-13. D   Alpha waves occur when people are awake, but relaxed, and are rapid, low-amplitude brain waves. (p. 132)

4-14. A   Individual differences in hypnosis exist; about 15% of adults are highly susceptible to hypnosis, while 10% are highly resistant. The rest are somewhere in between. (p. 141)

4-15. D   Alcohol is not a stimulant -- it is a depressant. (p. 146)

4-16. D   The user's expectations and physical state as well as other drugs the user takes influence the impact of a drug. (p. 149)

4-17. D   The learning perspective assumes that person's expectations that positive outcomes will be associated with drug use and/or that drug use will decrease negative outcomes underlie drug abuse. (p. 145)

4-18. B   Self-awareness can decrease performance because it produces changes in attention that may interfere with a person's ability to perform a task in an automatic fashion. (p. 131)

4-19. B   Automatic processing makes the least demands on attentional capacity. (p. 127)

4-20. D   Opiates may cause the brain to cease its production of endorphins. (p. 148)

Glossary of difficult words and expressions	Definition
Automatic pilot	performing activities without awareness
Blotting out	blocking out
Choke	perform at a lower level than usual
Compress	get smaller, reduce in size
Cravings for	having a strong desire for
Diligently	showing care and effort
Dimly lit	not bright
Early classes are a drag	difficult; requiring effort to go to
Enacting	performing, doing, carrying out
Feats	something difficult done well
Grooming	activities involved in looking and being clean
Hailed as	labeled as, identified as
Havoc	widespread damage; destruction
Jumbled	mixed-up, not at all clear
Mock robbery	fake robbery
Nature's way	natural process; how something would occur naturally
Onset	beginning, start
Out of sorts	irritable; in a bad mood
Perchance	to occur by accident or chance
Puzzling behavior	difficult to understand behavior
Realm of	boundaries of
Reemerged	started or began a second time
Recent decades	in the last 20-30 years
Safety valve	a release; allowing pressure to escape
Slurred speech	confusing speech
"Shady" topic	a sinister or evil or socially unacceptable topic
Staggering	walk or move unsteadily
Swings of emotion	changes of emotion
They...dull the senses	detract sensibility from the senses

Glossary of difficult words and expressions	Definition
Thoughts a thousand miles away	Not thinking about what you're doing; thinking about something else
Time slots	times available for a meeting
Tossing and turning	moving uneasily and continuously
Trance	condition-like sleep
Turmoil	based on disagreement, confusion
Twitch	sudden quick movement or a muscle

CHAPTER 5
LEARNING: HOW WE'RE CHANGED BY EXPERIENCE

OUTLINE: Develop a Study Plan

Use this outline to help you grasp the organizational structure of the chapter contents. The learning objectives (LOs) for each section are included. Use them as tools for developing your study plan. Space has been provided for you to write any notes or questions that come to mind as you begin your exploration into this material.

Heading:	Learning Objective:	Your Notes:
I. Classical Conditioning: Learning that Some Stimuli Signal Others	**L.O. 5.1:** Describe classical conditioning and survey the basic principles of classical conditioning.	
A. Pavlov's Early Work on Classical Conditioning: Does This Ring a Bell?		
B. Classical Conditioning: Some Basic Principles		
C. Classical Conditioning: Exceptions to the Rules	**L.O. 5.2:** Discuss what the research on acquired taste aversion has told us about the traditional principles of classical conditioning.	
D. Classical Conditioning: A Cognitive Perspective	**L.O. 5.3:** Describe the cognitive perspective of classical conditioning.	
E. Classical Conditioning: Turning Principles Into Action	**L.O. 5.4:** Discuss the ways in which classical conditioning can be used in therapy.	
II. Operant Conditioning: Learning Based on Consequences	**L.O. 5.5:** Explain the basic nature and principles of operant conditioning.	
A. The Nature of Operant Conditioning: Consequential Operations	**L.O. 5.6:** List the various schedules of reinforcement and define their effects.	
C. Operant Conditioning: A Cognitive Perspective	**L.O. 5.7:** Describe the research that supports the cognitive perspective of operant conditioning.	

Heading:	Learning Objective:	Your Notes:
D. Applying Operant Conditioning: Can We Make a Difference?	**L.O. 5.8:** List the various ways operant conditioning has been applied to practical problems.	
III. Observational Learning: Learning From the Behavior and Outcomes of Others **A.** Observational Learning: Some Basic Principles	**L.O. 5.9:** Define observational learning and discuss common instances of its occurrence.	
B. Observational Learning and Aggression	**L.O. 5.10:** Discuss how observational learning can be used to prepare employees for cross-cultural assignments.	
IV. Making Psychology Part of Your Life **A.** Getting in Shape: Applying Psychology to Get Fit and Stay Fit	**L.O. 5.11:** Be able to describe how you can use what you've learned to get fit and stay fit.	

SURVEY AND QUESTION

This section presents the major topics and ideas from the chapter. Use it as a tool for seeing how the components of the chapter fit together. At the end of each major topic, we have asked you a question that relates to the major learning objectives. If you can answer these questions, you have taken a major step toward mastering this material.

I.   Classical Conditioning: Learning That Some Stimuli Signal Others

Any relatively permanent change in behavior or behavior potential produced by experience is called learning. This experience can be direct as well as indirect through observation.

Classical, operant and observational learning are three forms of learning. In classical conditioning, a stimulus can acquire the ability to elicit a response by pairing it with another stimulus that already elicits this response. This first section deals with this form of learning.

A.   Pavlov's Early Work on Classical Conditioning: Does This Ring a Bell?

Classical conditioning was first studied by Pavlov, who studied salivation in dogs. He used an unconditioned stimulus (UCS), such as meat powder, that already elicited salivation. He preceded this by a neutral stimulus, such as a bell, that did not elicit salivation. After repeated pairing(s) or conditioning trials, the bell elicited salivation. The salivation produced by the bell was termed the conditioned response (CR). The salivation produced by the meat powder was termed the unconditioned response (UCR).

B.   Classical Conditioning: Some Basic Principles

Acquisition is the process in which a conditioned stimulus gradually acquires the capacity to elicit a conditioned response. At first, conditioning proceeds rapidly. Later, it slows down and finally levels off.

Conditioning is determined by the number of conditioned-unconditioned stimulus pairings. It is also influenced by timing. Forward conditioning refers to situations in which the conditioned stimulus always precedes the unconditioned stimulus. Delayed and trace conditioning are examples of forward conditioning. In backward conditioning the unconditioned stimulus precedes the conditioned stimulus whereas in simultaneous conditioning they begin and end at the same time.

In addition to number and timing, conditioning also depends on the time interval between the conditioned and unconditioned stimulus, on the intensity of either the conditioned or unconditioned stimulus and on familiarity. The optimal time interval is .2 to 2 seconds in most situations. Conditioning improves as the intensity of either the conditioned or unconditioned stimulus increases. It is not, however, the absolute intensity that is important to the conditioning process. At least for the conditioned stimulus, it is the intensity of the CS relative to other background stimuli that is important for the process.

Finally, familiarity may influence conditioning by influencing the predictive power of a conditioned stimulus. The eventual decline and disappearance of a conditioned response in the absence of an unconditioned stimulus is known as extinction. The conditioned response to the conditioned stimulus can return very quickly if the CR is again paired with the conditioned stimulus. This is termed reconditioning. Once extinction occurs, the CR can spontaneously recover if there is a time delay between the last extinction trial and the presentation of the conditioned stimulus.

The tendency of stimuli that are similar to the conditioned stimulus to produce conditioned reactions is called stimulus generalization. This process allows us to apply what we have learned to other situations. Stimulus discrimination occurs when stimuli similar to the conditioned stimulus do not produce reactions that are similar to those produced by the conditioned stimulus.

C.   Classical Conditioning: Exceptions to the Rules

It appears that all responses or associations are not learned with equal ease. Studies by Garcia and Koelling found that learned aversion to taste was less easily learned by using shock as an unconditioned stimulus than a nausea producing injection. This work also contradicted the belief that conditioning can occur only if the time interval between the conditioned and unconditioned stimulus is very short.

Species differ in the relative ease with which various types of conditioning occur. These are called biological constraints. Most instances of conditioning require a conditioned stimulus-unconditioned stimulus interval of a few seconds. Conditioned taste aversions can occur with a conditioned-unconditioned stimulus interval of a few hours. They can also be acquired in a single CS-UCS pairing and are difficult to extinguish.

D.   Classical Conditioning: A Cognitive Perspective

The cognitive perspective suggests that classical conditioning is based on the development of an expectation that the conditioned stimulus will be followed by the unconditioned stimulus. This view is supported by the fact that conditioning will not occur if the pairing of the conditioned and unconditioned stimuli occurs in a random manner. Also, once a conditioned stimulus has been learned, it is difficult to condition another stimulus since it provides no new information. This phenomenon is known as blocking.

Stimulus generalization may also involve cognitive processes. According to one theory, memory and active comparison processes play an important role in stimulus generalization -- a phenomenon that was once thought to be automatic.

E.   Classical Conditioning: Turning Principles Into Action

Knowledge about classical conditioning has been put to practical use. One of the most practical uses has been in reducing phobias -- intense, irrational fears of objects or events. When fear-provoking thoughts are not too painful to deal with, techniques like flooding have been used to reduce fear. In flooding, a person is forced to confront the fear-eliciting stimulus without an avenue of escape. Systematic desensitization as a progressive technique designed to replace anxiety with a relaxation response. It has also been found to reduce fear. First, a person is asked to describe the least aversive situation; then when the person learns to relax in this situation, the person is asked to describe another situation which is the next most aversive. This sequence continues until the person learns to relax to the most aversive situation.

Conditioning may also be involved in instances of drug overdose. For certain addictive drugs, the conditioned response can be just the opposite of the unconditioned response. For example, conditioned stimuli may signal the body to prepare for morphine by suppressing the response to morphine. When these conditioned stimuli are present, the influence of the drug may be less severe than when they are absent.

Questions:

5-1.   How is learning defined and what are the three basic forms of learning? _____

_____

_____

_____

5-2.   What are the general characteristics of classical conditioning? _____

_____

_____

_____

5-3.   How did Pavlov research classical conditioning?_____

_____

_____

_____

5-4.   What are the basic components of the classical conditioning procedure? _____

_____

_____

_____

5-5.   What are the basic principles of classical conditioning? _____

_____

_____

_____

5-6.   How can a conditioned stimulus gradually cease to elicit a conditioned response through extinction and how can it regain this ability? _____

_____

_____

_____

5-7.   How does stimulus generalization differ from stimulus discrimination? _____

_____

_____

_____

5-8.   Why is the work of Garcia and his colleagues important for an understanding of classical conditioning? _____

_____

_____

_____

5-9.   What does the research on acquired taste aversion tell us about the traditional principles of classical conditioning? _____

_____

_____

_____

5-10.   How does the cognitive approach to classical conditioning differ from the more traditional approach? _____

_____

_____

_____

5-11.   What are the practical implications of classical conditioning? _____

_____

_____

_____

II.   Operant Conditioning: Learning Based on Consequences

A.   The Nature of Operant Conditioning: Consequential Operations

In operant conditioning, organisms learn the relationships between certain behaviors and consequences. In this form of learning, the probability that a given response will occur changes depending upon the consequences that follow the response. Stimuli that strengthen responses that precede them are positive reinforcers. Ones that are related to biological needs are primary reinforcers (e.g., food). Objects or events that acquire their reinforcing quality by association with primary reinforcers are conditioned reinforcers (e.g., money). Stimuli that strengthen responses related to escape or avoidance are negative reinforcers. When preferred activities reinforce behavior, the Premack Principle is in effect. This principle suggests that preferred activities can be used to reinforce less preferred activities.

Punishment involves learning to refrain from doing an action that is followed by an unpleasant event. Omission training involves learning to refrain from doing an action that is followed by the removal of something pleasant. Thus, positive and negative reinforcers increase the likelihood that a behavior will occur, but punishment and omission training decrease the likelihood that a behavior will occur.

B.   Operant Conditioning: Some Basic Principles

These are two primary differences between classical and operant conditioning: (1) In classical conditioning, organisms learn associations between stimuli whereas in operant conditioning organisms learn associations between particular behaviors and the consequences that follow them; (2) In classical conditioning, responses performed are generally involuntary and are elicited by a specific UCS whereas in operant conditioning responses are more voluntary and are emitted by organisms in a given environment. To understand operant conditioning, we need to find out why certain behaviors are emitted in the first place and what determines the frequency with which these behaviors are repeated.   The following sections address these issues.

Most research on operant conditioning studies animals in Skinner boxes using spontaneous behaviors. In the case of nonspontaneous behaviors, the technique of shaping can be used. This involves reinforcing subjects for behaviors that resemble the desired behavior. Gradually, greater and greater resemblance to desired responses is required to receive reinforcement. Chaining usually begins by shaping the final response in a sequence of behaviors. This technique is used to teach complex sequences of behavior.

Operant conditioning is subject to biological constraints. For example, animals that have been shaped to do unusual behaviors may return to more natural behaviors after a time. This is called instinctual drift.

Operant conditioning is influenced by perceptions of reward magnitude and reward delay. In most instances, operant conditioning proceeds faster with increments in reward magnitude and decrements in the delay of reinforcement.

Rules for the delivery of reinforcements are called schedules. With a continuous reinforcement schedule (CRF), a reward is given after every response. When a reward is given only after a specific period of time, a fixed interval (FI) schedule is being used. This schedule leads to low rates of responding immediately after the presentation of the reward. When the time for reward is near, high rates of responding are observed. In variable-interval schedules (VI), the period of time which must elapse before the reward is presented varies around some average value. This leads to a fairly steady level of responding. If reinforcement is provided only after a number of responses have been performed, a fixed-ratio schedule (FR) is being used. This leads to a high rate of responding with a brief pause after each reinforcement.

With variable-ratio schedules, (VR) the reinforcement occurs after completion of a variable number of responses. This typically leads to consistently high response rates. Behaviors acquired by this schedule are usually very resistant to extinction. This is known as the partial reinforcement effect.

Stimuli that have been associated with reinforcement come to serve as signals for behavior. This is known as stimulus control. When an event signals the availability of rewards, the stimulus is called a discriminative stimulus.

C.   Operant Conditioning: A Cognitive Perspective

Cognitive factors such as expectancies play a role in operant conditioning. Expectations may be involved in developing learned helplessness. When subjects are exposed to situations in which it is not possible to attain reinforcement or avoid negative events, organisms may develop "learned helplessness." In these situations, people may become helpless and may not respond even when the situation changes. This occurs in both animals and humans and may result in depression.

In addition to expectancies, other cognitive factors also play a role in operant conditioning. Belief is a second factor. In fact, several studies have found that beliefs about schedules of reinforcement may be more influential than the actual schedules. Another cognitive factor is the evaluation of the reward. A positive contrast effect occurs when subjects are shifted from a small to a large reward. In this situation, there is an increase in performance to a level greater than that of subjects receiving the large reward only. Positive and negative contrast effects provide evidence that behavior is influenced not by the absolute level of obtained (or expected) reward but also by the relative level of reward.

D.   Applying Operant Conditioning: Can We Make a Difference?

There are many practical applications of operant conditioning. It is used in precision teaching where the teacher performs as a coach. It is used in computer assisted instruction and it can aid in the treatment of psychological problems like anorexia nervosa. Operant conditioning has been used to solve socially significant issues and to improve performance in the work place.

Questions:

5-12.   What is the basic nature of operant conditioning? _____

_____

_____

_____

5-13.   How do punishment and omission training differ? How does operant conditioning differ from classical conditioning? _____

_____

_____

_____

5-14.   What are the procedures involved in shaping and chaining? _____

_____

_____

_____

5-15.   What is the connection between instinctual drift and biological constraints on learning? _____

_____

_____

_____

5-16. What role does the size and timing of reinforcement play in operant or instrumental conditioning?

_____

_____

_____

5-17. What are the different schedules of reinforcement and what are their defining characteristics?

_____

_____

_____

5-18. What is stimulus control and why is it important? _____

_____

_____

_____

5-19. What are the cognitive factors that seem to be involved in operant conditioning? What findings support the belief that cognitive factors are involved in operant conditioning? _____

_____

_____

_____

5-20. How has operant conditioning been applied to practical problems? _____

_____

_____

_____

III. Observational Learning: Learning From the Behavior and Outcomes of Others

A.   Observational Learning: Some Basic Principles

Acquiring new forms of behavior and information from exposure to others and the consequences they experience is observational learning. This can occur by merely watching others. According to Bandura, observational learning requires that we attend to models (other persons peforming an activity). We tend to focus on attractive and knowledgeable models. We also need to remember what the models have done. It is necessary to transform the observations into behavior. This is affected by our physical abilities and our capacity to match our performance with that of the model. One must also be motivated to reproduce the behavior.

B.   Observational Learning and Aggression

There is evidence that children and adults exposed to media violence tend to acquire aggressive behaviors. Media violence may also convey the message that violence is acceptable. It may also make violence less upsetting to an observer.

Observational learning has been used in an attempt to prepare employees for cross-cultural assignments. One approach is the experiential approach; it involves behavioral modeling in which trainees first watch a model perform the correct behaviors. Then, they are put in a roleplay setting and act out the modelled behavior. Finally, they receive constructive feedback. The results of several studies indicate that the experiential approach as well as others based on observational learning seem effective in cross-cultural training.

Questions:

5-21.   What is observational learning and what are some instances of observational learning? _____

_____

_____

_____

5-22.   According to Bandura, what factors influence observational learning? _____

_____

_____

_____

5-23.   What are the effects of exposure to media on aggression and other kinds of behavior? _____

_____

_____

_____

5-24.   How has observational learning been used to prepare employees for cross-cultural assignments?

_____

_____

_____

IV.   Making Psychology Part of Your Life

A.   Getting in Shape: Applying Psychology to Get Fit and Stay Fit

You can use the basic principles you have learned in this chapter to establish your personal fitness program. Baron offers you five suggestions.

1)   Set your sights realistically.
2)   Take advantage of shaping techniques by setting yourself up for small wins.
3)   Specify and write down the amount and intensity of the exercise you will do -- and write it down.
4)   Use the principles of stimulus control to set the stage for healthy responses.
5)   Take advantage of observational learning by identifying people with desirable skills and traits.

Question:

5-25.   Discuss how you might use these suggestions to develop your own fitness program. What other ideas can you apply from this chapter to your program? _____

_____

_____

_____

MAKING PSYCHOLOGY PART OF YOUR LIFE: Key Terms and Concepts

Knowing the important concepts and key terms contained in this chapter is a very important part of mastering the material. We have presented a sample of these concepts below. Define each concept and check your definition with that presented in the chapter. It will also be beneficial for you to think of an example of each concept. Use your own personal experience to provide an example of each term below.

5-1.   **Acquisition**: _____

       Example: _____

5-2.   **Backward Conditioning**: _____

       Example: _____

5-3.   **Biological Constraints on Learning**: _____

       Example: _____

5-4.   **Chaining**: _____

       Example: _____

5-5.   **Classical Conditioning**: _____

       Example: _____

5-6.   **Conditioned Response (CR)**: _____

       Example: _____

5-7.   **Conditioned Stimulus (CS)**: _____

       Example: _____

5-8.   **Conditioned Taste Aversion**: _____

       Example: _____

5-9.   **Continuous Reinforcement Schedule**: _____

       Example: _____

5-10.   **Delayed Conditioning**: _____

Example: _____

5-11.   **Discriminative Stimulus**: _____

Example: _____

5-12.   **Extinction**: _____

Example: _____

5-13.   **Fixed-Interval Schedule**: _____

Example: _____

5-14.   **Fixed-Ratio Schedule**: _____

Example: _____

5-15.   **Flooding**: _____

Example: _____

5-16.   **Learning**: _____

Example: _____

5-17.   **Negative Reinforcers**: _____

Example: _____

5-18.   **Observational Learning**: _____

Example: _____

5-19.   **Omission Training**: _____

Example: _____

5-20.   **Operant Conditioning**: _____

Example: _____

5-21. **Phobia**: _____

Example: _____

5-22. **Positive Reinforcers**: _____

Example: _____

5-23. **Premack Principle**: _____

Example: _____

5-24. **Punishment**: _____

Example: _____

5-25. **Reconditioning**: _____

Example: _____

5-26. **Reinforcement**: _____

Example: _____

5-27. **Schedules of Reinforcement**: _____

Example: _____

5-28. **Shaping**: _____

Example: _____

5-29. **Simultaneous Conditioning**: _____

Example: _____

5-30. **Stimulus**: _____

Example: _____

5-31. **Spontaneous Recovery**: _____

Example: _____

5-32. **Stimulus Control**: _____

    Example: _____

5-33. **Stimulus Discrimination**: _____

    Example: _____

5-34. **Stimulus Generalization**: _____

    Example: _____

5-35. **Trace Conditioning**: _____

    Example: _____

5-36. **Unconditioned Response (UCR)**: _____

    Example: _____

5-37. **Unconditioned Stimulus (UCS)**: _____

    Example: _____

5-38. **Variable-Interval Schedule**: _____

    Example: _____

5-39. **Variable-Ratio Schedule**: _____

    Example: _____

CHALLENGE: Develop Your Critical Thinking Skills

Critical thinking is an important skill in our complex world. Practice expanding your critical thinking skills by analyzing the following learning situations. Your task is to identify the principle of learning that may be involved. [Please refer to the answers at the end after you complete the exercise.]

5-1.   Mary's boss yells at her every time she returns late from lunch. Now she is always prompt...she returns on time.

Learning principle: _____

5-2.   After seeing the joy that his parents feel when they give to charity, Johnny is more likely to share his toys with his friends.

Learning principle: _____

5-3.   A salesperson is paid a commission for every car sold.

What kind of reinforcement schedule is this? _____

5-4.   A worker is paid a weekly salary.

What kind of reinforcement schedule is this? _____

5-5.   Susan had a bad case of the stomach flu the first night she ate feta-cheese pizza. Now she feels nauseated every time she sees feta cheese.

What type of learning is involved? _____

5-6.   Carol was attacked by a bluebird when she was very young and she became afraid of bluebirds. Now, she feels afraid when she sees any bird.

What type of learning is involved? _____

5-7.   Referring to the situation above, assume that Carol is now 30 years old and she finds that she is no longer afraid of birds at all.

What principle of learning is involved here? _____

Answers to Critical Thinking Exercises

5-1.   Negative reinforcement
       Explanation: The probability of the response "returning from lunch on time" is increased because it avoids the negative consequence of her "boss yelling."

5-2.   Observational learning
       Explanation: Exposure to his parents' behavior, and the consequences that follow, has taught Johnny to engage in a conceptually similar kind of behavior (sharing with others).

5-3.   Fixed-ratio schedule
       Explanation: Fixed-ratio schedules involve giving reinforcement after a set number of responses have been emitted. Paying this salesperson on the basis of the response of "selling a car" involves giving reinforcement based upon the emission of a response.

5-4.   Fixed-interval schedule
       Explanation: Fixed-interval schedules involve giving reinforcement after a specific interval of time has passed. Paying a worker a salary at the end of a week fits this requirement.

5-5.   Conditioned taste aversion
       Explanation: The internal cues (UCS) associated with the flu (e.g., nausea) occurred after Susan ate a novel food (the CS). This led to a strong CS-UCS pairing in a single trial.

5-6.   Stimulus generalization
       Explanation: Stimulus generalization refers to the tendency for stimuli similar to a conditioned stimulus to elicit similar conditioned responses.   Carol's initial fear of bluebirds was acquired by classical conditioning in her early years. Now, it has spread to all members of the bird category.

5-7.   Extinction
       Explanation: Extinction is the process through which a conditioned stimulus gradually loses its ability to evoke conditioned responses when it is no longer followed by the unconditioned stimulus. If Carol has been in the presence of birds and has not been attacked for a number of years, she may lose her fear through this process.

CHALLENGE: Making Psychology Part of Your Life

Doing well on tests is great! But in order for this material to be really useful, you should be able to apply psychology to your life. Try applying what you've learned to the following situation:

Situation

Many of us have experienced both the pleasure and pain of getting a new puppy. The pleasure of a puppy includes the "tail-wagging" joy that greets you when your charge sees you walk in the door...and the fun of teaching him or her new tricks. And the "pain" often includes house-breaking. Imagine that you just got a new puppy...named Bruno. See if you can apply what you've learned to his training.

Application Question

5-1.   What operant conditioning principles might you use in his training? (Hint: How would you arrange rewards such as dog-treats, in order to increase the probability of desired responses?)

5-2.   Could you use observational learning to increase the speed of training? (Hint: Would it help if you had an older dog to teach him how to behave?)

5-3.   Do you think it might be more difficult to teach your new puppy new skills at 2 or 3 weeks of age vs. 10 to 12 weeks? Why or why not? (Hint: Refer to the research on biological constraints on learning.)

5-4.   Could you make use of classical conditioning procedures? (Hint: Are there some reflexes that you might build upon to elicit desirable responses?)

CHALLENGE: Review Your Comprehensive Knowledge

SAMPLE TEST QUESTIONS

Once you have worked through the preceding sections, you should be ready for a comprehensive self-test. You can check your answers with those at the end of this section. An additional practice test is given in the supplementary section at the end of this study guide.

5-1.   Classical conditioning was first examined by:
a. Freud.
b. Watson.
c. Pavlov.
d. Bandura.

5-2.   A stimulus that is paired with another stimulus that already elicits a response is called a(n):
a. stimulus intensity.
b. unconditioned stimulus.
c. conditioned stimulus.
d. evoking stimulus.

5-3.   When the unconditioned stimulus no longer follows the conditioned stimulus, _____ occurs.
a. spontaneous recovery
b. extinction
c. classical conditioning
d. operant conditioning

5-4.   The salivation produced by meat powder is termed a(n):
a. learned response.
b. reinforcer.
c. conditioned response.
d. unconditioned response.

5-5.   Which of the following is not a factor that influences the acquisition of classical conditioning?
a. timing
b. familiarity
c. intensity
d. implosion

5-6.   The therapeutic technique that involves the extinction of classically conditioned fears is called:
a. operationalization.
b. defusing.
c. flooding.
d. psychoanalysis.

5-7.   Stimuli that strengthen the responses related to their escape and avoidance are:
a. negative reinforcers.
b. positive reinforcers.
c. primary reinforcers.
d. secondary reinforcers.

5-8.   The process of acquiring new behaviors or information from others is called _____ learning.
a. conformity
b. instigation
c. empathy
d. observational

5-9.   Negative reinforcement is to punishment as:
a. response decrease is to response increase.
b. response increase is to response decrease.
c. response decrease is to response decrease.
d. response increase is to response increase.

5-10.   Individuals who are paid on a piecework basis are operating on a _____ schedule.
a. fixed-interval
b. variable-interval
c. variable-ratio
d. fixed-ratio

5-11.   Behaviors acquired by the _____ schedule are the most resistant to extinction.
a. fixed-interval
b. fixed-ratio
c. variable-interval
d. variable-ratio

5-12.   Which of the following is false?
a. Conditioning improves as the intensity of either the conditioned or unconditioned stimulus increases.
b. All responses or associations are learned with equal ease.
c. Taste aversion research shows that classical conditioning can occur with a relatively long interval between the conditioned stimulus and the unconditioned stimulus.
d. Chaining usually begins by shaping the final response in a sequence of behaviors.

5-13.   Exposure to conditions in which it is not possible to attain reinforcement or avoid negative events may result in:
a. enhanced avoidance.   c. learned helplessness.
b. extinction of avoidance.   d. enhanced escape.

5-14.   The process by which organisms learn to respond to certain stimuli and to not respond to others is called:
a. stimulus generalization.   c. punishment.
b. flooding.   d. stimulus discrimination.

5-15.   Stimulus generalization:
a. is the tendency of stimuli dissimilar to the conditioned stimulus to produce conditioned responses.
b. is identical to stimulus discrimination.
c. is the tendency of stimuli similar to the conditioned stimulus to produce conditioned reactions.
d. occurs when the UCS and CS are no longer paired.

5-16.   The schedule of reinforcement that leads to low rates of responding immediately after the presentation of the reward but a high rate of responding when the time for reward is near is called:
a. fixed-ratio.   c. variable-ratio.
b. fixed-interval.   d. variable-interval.

5-17.   Animals that have been shaped to do unusual behavior may return to more natural behavior. This is called:
a. extinction.   c. instinctual drift.
b. acquisition.   d. shaping.

5-18.   Television violence has been shown to be related to all but one of the following:
a. aggressive behavior   c. lessened emotional reactions to violence
b. improved work performance   d. acceptance of violence

5-19.   Conditioned taste aversions
a. are easy to extinguish.
b. require many conditioned stimulus-unconditioned stimulus pairings.
c. are difficult to extinguish.
d. occur with animals, but not with people.

5-20.   A positive contrast effect occurs when subjects are shifted from a _____ to a _____ reward.
a. small, large   c. large, large
b. large, small   d. small, small

Answers and Feedback to Sample Test Questions:

5-1.   C Pavlov was the Russian psychologist who first examined classical conditioning. (p. 159)

5-2.   C A previously neutral stimulus that acquires the ability to evoke a response after its repeated pairing with another stimulus (unconditioned stimulus) that already elicits a response is called a conditioned stimulus. (p. 160)

5-3.   B Extinction (the gradual decline and disappearance of a conditioned response) occurs when the unconditioned stimulus no longer is paired with the conditioned stimulus. (p. 164)

5-4.   D Salivation is an example of a reflex or unconditioned response that naturally occurs when meat powder is placed in the mouth. (p. 160)

5-5.   D Timing, familiarity, and stimulus intensity influence classical conditioning. Implosion is a type of behavioral therapy that doesn't relate to classical conditioning acquisition. (p. 162)

5-6.   C Flooding is a therapeutic technique involving confronting the fear-eliciting stimulus. (p. 169)

5-7.   A Negative reinforcers strengthen responses that lead to the avoidance or escape of aversive stimuli. (p. 172)

5-8.   D Acquiring new behaviors by observing models is observational learning. (p. 185)

5-9.   B Negative reinforcers increase responses; punishment decreases response rates. (p. 172)

5-10.   D Piece-work involves being paid per unit produced and is an example of a fixed ratio schedule of reinforcement. (p. 177)

5-11.   D Variable-ratio schedules produce behaviors that are very resistant to extinction. (p. 177)

5-12.   B Acquisition of a conditioned response does not occur with equal ease for different stimuli. (p. 165)

5-13.   C Learned helplessness can occur when it is not possible to obtain reinforcement or avoid negative events. (p. 180)

5-14.   D Stimulus discrimination is the process by which organisms learn to respond to certain stimuli and not to respond to others. (p. 164)

5-15.   C The tendency of stimuli similar to the conditioned stimulus to produce conditioned responses is called stimulus generalization. (p. 164)

5-16.   B Fixed interval schedules lead to low rates of responding immediately after reward presentation and high rates just prior to reward. (p. 177)

5-17.   C The tendency for animals that have been trained to do unusual behaviors to return to more natural patterns of behavior is called instinctual drift. (p. 176)

5-18.   B TV violence has not been related to improved work performance. (p. 187)

5-19.   C Conditioned taste aversions are hard to extinguish. (p. 166)

5-20.   A Positive contrast effects occur when subjects are shifted from small to large rewards. (p. 181)

Glossary of difficult words and expressions	Definition
A food pellet	a little bit of food
Antics	devices used to procure a desired response
Begin to feel dreadful	start to be afraid
Bland foods	foods that have little taste
Blurts out	says something spontaneously
Cozy	secure, relaxed
Cram for tests	study at the last minute
Dingy	unclean
Forthcoming	something that will happen in the future
…has chewed you out	has verbally scolded you
Hectic	very busy
Losing a bundle	losing a large amount
Media blitz	multiple reports on tv, news, and radio
Metronome	instrument that keep time with clicking noises
Noteworthy	worth remembering
Stings	injury from a bee
Tantrums	outburst of anger
The breed of the dog	the type of dog
Unsettling	disturbing
Urban slums	poor neighborhood in a big city
Uttered	spoke
Vicarious	to experience something through the experience of another

CHAPTER 6
MEMORY: OF THINGS REMEMBERED...AND FORGOTTEN

OUTLINE: Develop a Study Plan

Use this outline to help you grasp the organizational structure of the chapter contents. The learning objectives (LOs) for each section are included. Use them as tools for developing your study plan. Space has been provided for you to write any notes or questions that come to mind as you begin your exploration into this material.

Heading:	Learning Objective:	Your Notes:
I. Human Memory: The Information-Processing Approach	L.O. 6.1: Explain why the information processing approach uses the computer as a model for human memory.	
A. Human Memory: One Influential Model -- And An Emerging, New Approach	L.O. 6.2: List the basic components of the modal model of memory. L.O. 6.3: Compare and contrast the modal model with the parallel distributed processing perspective.	
B. Types of Information in Memory	L.O. 6.4: List the characteristics of three types of information stored in memory.	
II. Sensory Memory: Gateway to Consciousness	L.O. 6.5: Explain the characteristics and functions of sensory memory.	
III. Short-Term Memory: The Workbench of Consciousness		
A. Evidence For the Existence of Short-Term Memory	L.O. 6.6: Describe the evidence for the existence of a short-term memory system.	
IV. Long-Term Memory: The Storehouse of Consciousness		
A. Long-Term Memory: Its Basic Operation	L.O. 6.7: Explain the operation of long-term memory.	

Heading:	Learning Objective:	Your Notes:
V. Forgetting From Long-Term Memory		
A. The Trace Decay Hypothesis: Forgetting with The Passage of Time	**L.O. 6.8:** Compare and contrast the trace decay hypothesis and the interference view of forgetting.	
B. Prospective Memory: Forgetting To Do What We're Supposed To Do	**L.O. 6.9:** Discuss the factors that influence prospective memory.	
VI. Memory in Natural Contexts		
A. Autobiographical Memory: Remembering The Events of Our Own Lives	**L.O. 6.10:** Discuss the operation of autobiographical memory and how it is studied.	
	L.O. 6.11: Describe the nature of infantile amnesia.	
	L.O. 6.12: Discuss the evidence for and against the existence of flash bulb memories.	
B. Distortion and Construction in Memory for Natural Events	**L.O. 6.13:** Explain how schemas influence memory distortion and memory constructions.	
VII. The Biological Bases of Memory: How the Brain Stores Knowledge		
A. Amnesia and Other Memory Disorders: Keys to Understanding the Nature of Memory	**L.O. 6.14:** Discuss the biological bases of amnesia and other memory disorders.	
B. Memory and the Brain: A Modern View	**L.O. 6.15:** Discuss the modern view on the storage and processing of information within the brain.	
VIII. Making Psychology Part of Your Life		
A. Improving Your Memory: Some Useful Steps	**L.O. 6.16:** List the ways in which you can improve your memory.	

SURVEY AND QUESTION

This section presents the major topics and ideas from the chapter. Use it as a tool for seeing how the components of the chapter fit together. At the end of each major topic, we have asked you a question that relates to the major learning objectives. If you can answer these questions, you have taken a major step toward mastering this material.

I.   Human Memory: The Information Processing Approach

The earliest systematic study of memory was done by Ebbinghaus. He used lists of nonsense syllables and himself as a subject. Some of his findings are valid today. For example, he found that forgetting proceeds rapidly at first and then proceeds more slowly.

Today, memory is understood from an information processing perspective. Note, however, that although human memory and computer memory share similarities, they are definitely not identical. The way information is entered into memory is termed encoding. The way it is retained in memory is called storage. The procedure involved in locating and using information in memory is termed retrieval.

A.   Human Memory: One Influential Model -- And An Emerging New Approach

According to the modal model of memory, memory consists of three different systems. The information from our senses is held by sensory memory. It can hold much information, but it retains information for a brief time. The part of memory that holds information we are currently using for a brief period is called short-term memory. The part of memory that holds large quantities of information for long periods of time is long-term memory.

Information moves from one system to another by means of active control processes. Information goes from sensory memory to short-term memory when we attend to it. It moves from short-term memory to long-term by means of elaborative rehearsal.

The parallel distributed processing model is an alternative perspective to the Atkinson-Shiffrin model. It suggests that information is not processed in a step-by-step manner. Rather, this model suggests that information is actually processed simultaneously in several different parts of our total memory system.

B.   Types of Information In Memory

There are several types of information stored in memory. Our general abstract knowledge about the world is known as semantic memory. Our memory for the specific events we have experienced in our lives is known as episodic memory. Our knowledge of how to perform various tasks, such as driving a car, is known as procedural memory.

Questions:

6-1.   Why does the information-processing approach use the computer as a model for human memory? _____

_____

_____

6-2.   What are the basic components of the modal model of memory? _____

_____

_____

_____

6-3.   How does the modal model compare with the parallel distributed processing perspective?

_____

_____

_____

6-4.   What are the three types of information stored in memory? _____

_____

_____

_____

II.   Sensory Memory: Gateway to Consciousness

The capacity of sensory memory appears to be quite large. It holds fleeting representations of everything we see, hear, taste, smell or feel. However, it can only hold information for a very brief period of time. Visual sensory memory lasts for less than a second. Acoustic sensory memory lasts for no more than a few seconds. Thus, representations in sensory memory are broad in scope but last a very short period of time.

Question:

6-5.   What are the characteristics of sensory memory? _____

_____

_____

_____

III.   Short-Term Memory: The Workbench of Consciousness

Experiences such as forgetting phone numbers immediately after dialing directory assistance suggest the existence of a short-term memory system. Because this system is also thought to hold information we are actively processing at the moment, this system is also known as working memory.

A.   Evidence of the Existence of Short-Term Memory

Formal evidence exists suggesting the presence of short-term memory (STM). One source of evidence is found in the pattern of ordered memory shown for unrelated words. Individuals are more likely to remember words at the beginning and end of a word list. This effect is known as the serial position curve. You are presumed to remember the words at the end of the list well because they are in short-term memory. Words at the beginning of the test are presumed to be retrieved from long-term memory.

One feature that distinguishes the different memory systems is the way information is represented in each system. Sensory memory represents information in a form similar to that reported by our senses. It is suggested that STM stores information acoustically whereas information is entered into long-term memory primarily in terms of its meaning.

B.   Short-term Memory: Its Basic Operation

Short-term memory can hold about 7 to 9 separate items. Each of these items can represent several other pieces of information. This is called chunking. Information is retained in short-term memory by means of rehearsal. When rehearsal is prevented, information is almost totally gone within twenty seconds. STM is thought to be the workbench of consciousness -- it temporarily stores the information you are using at the present.

Questions:

6-6.   What are the characteristics and functions of sensory memory? _____

_____

_____

_____

6-7.   What is the evidence for the existence of a short-term memory system? _____

_____

_____

_____

6-8.   What are the basic features of short-term memory? _____

_____

_____

_____

IV.   Long-Term Memory: The Storehouse of Consciousness

LTM can store huge quantities of information for long periods of time. But the information in LTM can be difficult to locate (i.e., there can be retrieval problems). These sections describe what we know about its operation.

A.   Long-Term Memory: Its Basic Operation

Information enters long-term memory from short-term memory by means of rehearsal. The type of rehearsal required is called elaborative rehearsal. This involves thinking about the meaning of new information and relating it to information in memory. Factors, such as alcohol consumption, that interfere with rehearsal interfere with long-term memory.

According to a levels of processing view, information can be processed at different levels. This can range from shallow processing to deep processing. Apparently, the deeper the processing during the exposure to materials, the better the memory. For example, in one study it was found that thinking about the meaning of words (deep processing) aided memory more than thinking about how they looked or rhymed (shallow or moderate processing). This view is known as the levels of processing approach. It has been suggested that deeper or more effortful processing promotes the encoding of more features of the item, making it easier to locate in the memory system later. There are problems, however, associated with this view. First, it is difficult to determine what constitutes deep and shallow processing. Second, it is difficult to speak about discrete levels of processing when several forms of processing may occur at once.

B.   Retrieval: Locating Information in Long-Term Memory

The process of getting information out of long-term memory is called retrieval. Retrieval is related to the form in which information is entered into memory or storage. The more organized this information, the easier the retrieval.

Stimuli that are associated with information stored in memory and that help us retrieve it are called retrieval cues. Research indicates that words learned in a particular environment were remembered better in the same than in a different environment. This is known as context dependent memory. Several studies have found that internal states can serve as retrieval cues. This is known as state-dependent retrieval. Exactly which cue is used and which is most helpful as a retrieval cue depends on what is entered into memory at the time of encoding. This is called the encoding specificity principle.

Questions:

6-9.   What is the basic operation of long-term memory? _____

_____

_____

_____

6-10.   How does the levels of processing perspective provide an alternative to a structural view of memory like the modal model? _____

_____

_____

_____

6-11.   What are the factors that influence retrieval information from long-term memory? _____

_____

_____

_____

V.   Forgetting From Long-Term Memory

A.   The Trace Decay Hypothesis: Forgetting With the Passage of Time

We are most typically aware of memory when it fails. The classic research by Ebbinghaus studied the rate of forgetting; he found that forgetting is rapid at first and then slows down with the passage of time. Recent research confirms his findings. Research has also found that discrete skills are subject to a great amount of forgetting

The simplest view of forgetting suggests that information is lost from LTM because of the mere passage of time; this is the trace decay hypothesis. This view is not supported by research.

B.   Forgetting As a Result of Interference

Forgetting appears to result from interference among information stored in memory. This can take two forms: retroactive and proactive interference. For example, if learning the rules of a new game causes you to forget the rules of an old game, this is termed retroactive interference. If information you know about the board game causes you to have problems learning the information about the new board game, this is termed proactive interference. You can remember this distinction by recognizing that the label refers to whether interference is acting forward in time, which would be proactive interference, or is having an influence on material that has already been learned. The latter would be called retroactive interference.

C.   Repression: Do We Sometimes Forget Because We Want to Forget?

Repression refers to the idea that we forget some information and experiences because we find them too frightening or threatening to bear. Although repression may occur, there is little scientific evidence for its existence. Most support comes from case studies. Accounts of repression may be "invented" in that, in some cases, therapists or the media may lead some persons into reporting memories that do not exist.

D.   Prospective Memory: Forgetting to Do What We're Supposed to Do

Prospective memory involves remembering things that we are supposed to do at a certain time. Forgetting of this type appears to be closely related to motivation. In addition, like other forms of memory, it is influenced by retrieval cues. Some of these cues are internal.

Questions:

6-12.   What is the trace delay hypothesis, the interference view, and the repression view of forgetting?

_____

_____

_____

6-13.   What factors influence prospective memory? _____

_____

_____

_____

VI.   Memory in Natural Contexts

A.   Autobiographical Memory: Remembering the Events of Our Own Lives

Our memory for the events of our lives is called autobiographical memory. A useful technique to study this form of memory is the autobiographical memory schedule in which individuals are systematically questioned about different periods of their lives.

Another technique is the diary method in which individuals attempt to keep detailed diaries of events in their own lives. An extensive diary study has found that autobiographical memory is affected by many of the same variables that affect memory for abstract information under controlled conditions. However, because this research is observational in nature it cannot establish cause-and-effect relationships.

The fact that we are able to keep track of time is an important aspect of autobiographical memory. It appears that we are able to do this by examining events in the context of all of the other information about our lives. This is possible because we associate an event in memory with general contextual information and with other events.

Few individuals have accurate memories for events occurring before their third or fourth birthday. This is known as infantile amnesia. Until recently, there have been two accepted explanations for infantile amnesia. According to one explanation, brain structures are not sufficiently developed before this time, and this fact may account for a lack of early memories. According to the second explanation, the absence of language skills prior to this time accounts for infantile amnesia. Both of these accounts assume that children do not have well-developed memory abilities.

Recent findings, however, suggest that neither of these explanations is entirely accurate -- infants do appear to have well-developed memory abilities. According to a new interpretation, we cannot remember events from our first few years of life because we have not yet developed a clear self-concept.

Our memories for highly unusual events that are accompanied with the subjective impression that we can remember exactly what we were doing at the time the event occurred are called flashbulb memories. Research on this topic indicates that this form of memory is inaccurate. These findings may be due to the role that emotion plays in encoding unusual events.

B.   Distortion and Construction in Memory for Natural Events

Schemas are cognitive frameworks developed through experience which help structure the processing and storing of new information. It appears that information that is consistent with well-developed schemas are encoded more readily than information inconsistent with our schemas. Schemas may lead to distortions of memory. Research suggests that we are likely to notice and remember information that is consistent with well-formed schemas. However, when a schema is initially being formed, we are likely to notice and remember inconsistent information.

We may "fill in details" of natural events, or remember experiences we never had to make our memories more complete or sensible. This is called construction. When we enter information into memory, we may store the information itself, but not the details about the context in which it occurred. This contributes to construction.

C.   Eyewitness Testimony: How Accurate Is It? What Factors Affect It?

Contrary to popular belief, research indicates that eyewitnesses to crimes are often not nearly as accurate as the legal system generally assumes. It appears that the accuracy of eyewitness testimony can be enhanced by using techniques that are based on current information of how our memory operates. Several techniques have been developed. One asks witnesses to report everything. A second asking them to describe the events from several different perspectives. A third involves asking them to imagine themselves back at the scene and to reconstruct as many details as possible. In addition, giving eyewitnesses repeated opportunities to recall the events sometimes helps.

It appears that hypnosis can improve memory retrieval under highly specific conditions. In general, however, it appears that it is not an effective eyewitness testimony technique. Alcohol consumption reduces the accuracy of eyewitness testimony. It seems to impair memory by interfering with the accurate encoding of information.

Questions:

6-14.   How does autobiographical memory operate, and how is it studied? _____

_____

_____

_____

6-15.   What is the nature of infantile amnesia? _____

_____

_____

_____

6-16.   What is the evidence for and against the existence of flashbulb memories? _____

_____

_____

_____

6-17.   How do schemas influence memory distortions and constructions? _____

_____

_____

_____

6-18.   How accurate is eyewitness testimony?   What factors affect the accuracy of eyewitness testimony? _____

_____

_____

_____

VII.   The Biological Bases of Memory: How the Brain Stores Knowledge

A.   Amnesia and Other Memory Disorders: Keys to Understanding the Nature of Memory

The study of various memory disorders has provided important insights into the biological bases of memory. Loss of memory as a result of injuries or illness is called amnesia. Loss of memory for events after an accident is anterograde amnesia. Loss of memory for events prior to an accident is called retrograde amnesia. The case study of H. M. suggests that portions of the temporal lobes play a crucial role in memory. Specifically, these structures appear to be crucial in the consolidation of memories or shifting new information from STM to LTM. Subsequent research has confirmed this conclusion and suggests that it is the hippocampus, a portion of the temporal lobes, that plays a key role in our memory systems.

Research indicates that we possess at least two distinct memory systems and that different portions of the brain play a key role in each. A declarative or explicit memory system brings information that we know into consciousness and, if necessary, describes it. An implicit or procedural memory system may retain information that is not directly accessible to consciousness. The hippocampus appears to play a key role in the declarative or explicit memory system, but not the procedural or implicit memory system. The hippocampus binds together distributed activation sites in the neocortex with activation in other regions. These connections appear to be necessary for the formation of memories.

When individuals abuse alcohol for many years, they sometimes develop Korsakoff's syndrome. These persons report that they cannot remember many of the events that took place before the onset of their illness. Medical examinations reveal that these individuals experienced extensive damage to portions of the diencephalon, especially to the thalamus and hypothalamus. This suggests that these portions of the brain play a key role in LTM.

An illness that afflicts about 5% of all people over the age of 65 and progresses to the point that there is almost a total loss of memory is known as Alzheimer's disease. Careful study of the brains of deceased patients reveal that, in most cases, they contain bundles of amyloid beta protein which may cause damage to neurons that transmit information through the neurotransmitter acetylcholine. Individuals who suffer from Alzheimer's disease show a decrease in acetylcholine in their brains.

B.   Memory and the Brain: A Modern View

Modern views of the relationship between brain and memory suggests that memories are stored in different locations in the brain and that our brains process and store information simultaneously at several different locations. It appears that the formation of long-term memories involves alterations in the rate of production or release of specific neurotransmitters. It may also involve changes in the actual structure of neurons.

Questions:

6-19.   What is the link between declarative or explicit memory and the hippocampus? _____

_____

_____

_____

6-20.   How can amnesia result from alcohol and Alzheimer's disease? _____

_____

_____

_____

6-21.   What is the modern view on the storage and processing of information within the brain?

_____

_____

_____

VII.   Making Psychology Part of Your Life

A.   Improving Your Memory: Some Useful Steps

Memory research offers several practical suggestions for improving our memory. These include the following:

1)   Really think about what you want to remember.
2)   Pay attention.
3)   Use visual imagery.
4)   Give yourself extra retrieval cues.
5)   Develop your own shorthand codes.
6)   Develop your own cognitive scaffolds.

Questions:

6-22.   How can you use what you have learned about memory to improve your memory?

_____

_____

_____

6-23.   Describe how you might use what you have learned about memory to improve your own memory. _____

_____

_____

_____

6-24.   Now might be a good time to review your study strategy for this class. How can you encorporate the steps listed in your textbook into your study habits? _____

_____

_____

_____

MAKING PSYCHOLOGY PART OF YOUR LIFE: Key Terms and Concepts

Knowing the important concepts and key terms contained in this chapter is a very important part of mastering the material. We have presented a sample of these concepts below. Define each concept and check your definition with that presented in the chapter. It will also be beneficial for you to think of an example of each concept. Whenever possible, use your own personal experience to provide an example of each term below.

6-1.   **Alzheimer's Disease:** _____

        Example: _____

6-2.   **Amnesia:** _____

        Example: _____

6-3.   **Anterograde Amnesia:** _____

        Example: _____

6-4.   **Chunk:** _____

        Example: _____

6-5.   **Consolidation (of memory):** _____

        Example: _____

6-6.   **Context-Dependent Memory:** _____

        Example: _____

6-7.   **Elaborative Rehearsal:** _____

        Example: _____

6-8.   **Encoding:** _____

        Example: _____

6-9.   **Encoding Specificity Principle:** _____

        Example: _____

6-10.   **Episodic Memory:** _____

      Example: _____

6-11.   **Explicit Memory:** _____

      Example: _____

6-12.   **Eyewitness Testimony:** _____

      Example: _____

6-13.   **Flashbulb Memories:** _____

      Example: _____

6-14.   **Implicit Memory:** _____

      Example: _____

6-15.   **Infantile Amnesia:** _____

      Example: _____

6-16.   **Information-Processing Approach:** _____

      Example: _____

6-17.   **Korsakoff's Syndrome:** _____

      Example: _____

6-18.   **Levels of Processing View:** _____

      Example: _____

6-19.   **Long-Term Memory:** _____

      Example: _____

6-20.   **Memory:** _____

      Example: _____

6-21. **Parallel Distributed Processing Model:** _____

6-22. **Phonological Loop Model:** _____

6-23. **Proactive Interference:** _____

Example: _____

6-24. **Procedural Memory:** _____

Example: _____

6-25. **Prospective Memory:** _____

Example: _____

6-26. **Repression (Theory of Forgetting):** _____

Example: _____

6-27. **Retrieval:** _____

Example: _____

6-28. **Retrieval Cues:** _____

Example: _____

6-29. **Retroactive Interference:** _____

Example: _____

6-30. **Retrograde Amnesia:** _____

Example: _____

6-31. **Schemas:** _____

Example: _____

6-32.   **Selective Attention:** _____

Example: _____

6-33.   **Semantic Memory:** _____

Example: _____

6-34.   **Sensory Memory:** _____

Example: _____

6-35.   **Serial Position Curve:** _____

Example: _____

6-36.   **Short-Term Memory:** _____

Example: _____

6-37.   **State-Dependent Retrieval:** _____

Example: _____

6-38.   **Storage:** _____

Example: _____

6-39.   **Tip-of-the-Tongue-Phenomenon:** _____

Example: _____

CHALLENGE: Develop Your Critical Thinking Skills

Metacognition: Improving Your Study Skills

Critical thinking requires knowledge about what types of strategies to use for different types of situations. One practical benefit of developing these skills is that it increases your ability to plan and improve your study skills. Below, we provide you examples of typical problems students have with their studies. The material in this chapter should help you identify the problem and formulate a strategy for dealing with the problem. Check your answers with those provided at the end of this section.

6-1.   Cathy is taking a French class. She tries to memorize the vocabulary by repeating the words over and over again. She isn't doing well in the class.

   Problem: _____

   _____

   Solution: _____

   _____

6-2.   John has an American literature class right before his English literature class. He finds that he confuses American authors with British authors on his exams in English literature.

   Problem: _____

   _____

   Solution: _____

   _____

6-3.   Sherry is taking a class in biology. She is unfamiliar with the material and tries to write down everything the professor says. She isn't understanding the material.

   Problem: _____

   _____

   Solution: _____

   _____

<u>Answers to Critical Thinking Exercises</u>:

6-1.   Cathy is trying to learn French by using **rote rehearsal** strategies. She should use **elaborative rehearsal**, such as thinking about the meaning of the words.

6-2.   John is experiencing **proactive interference**. He should try to schedule his classes so that classes with different content follow another.

6-3.   Sherry is straining her attentional capacity. She should attend to her professor, think about what she says, and summarize the relevant material in her notes. She needs to develop a framework for assimilating the information.

CHALLENGE: Making Psychology Part of Your Life

<u>Eye-Witness Memory</u>

We rely on our memory systems in thousands of ways. But, just like our cars, we don't notice its importance until it fails us. The material in this chapter should provide you with a greater appreciation of how your memory system operates. Practice applying this knowledge to an important domain -- eye-witness memory.

<u>Situation</u>

Assume that as you were driving home from school one day, you saw a car run through a red light and hit a pedestrian. Being a "good citizen," you left your name with the police at the scene and told him/her that you saw what happened. Now, a year has passed, and the driver is appearing in court to face charges. The driver claims that the pedestrian walked in front of his/her car and was crossing against the light.

Given the knowledge you have acquired concerning the factors that are important for accurate eyewitness testimony:

<u>Analysis</u>

6-1.   How would you prepare yourself for your account of what happened?

6-2.   What factors would you look for in the manner of questioning that might influence your memory?

6-3.   What kinds of events are you likely to forget?

6-4.   What kinds of events are you likely to remember?

6-5.   How might your past experiences influence your memory for these events?

6-6.   Speculate on the kinds of distortions and constructions that are likely to affect your memory.

CHALLENGE: Review Your Comprehensive Knowledge

SAMPLE TEST QUESTIONS

Once you have worked through the preceding sections, you should be ready for a comprehensive self-test. You can check your answers with those at the end of this section. An additional practice test is given in the supplementary section at the end of this study guide.

6-1.   The way information is entered into memory is called:
    a. retrieval.   c. storage.
    b. encoding.   d. programming.

6-2.   Sensory memory can hold:
    a. little information.   c. 5-9 chunks.
    b. much information.   d. 7-10 chunks.

6-3.   According to the modal model, there is(are) _____ kind(s) of memory systems.
    a. 2   c. 1
    b. 3   d. 5

6-4.   Information goes from sensory memory to short-term memory when we:
    a. attend to it.   c. ignore it.
    b. rehearse it.   d. retrieve it.

6-5.   The first memory structure involved in the encoding of information is:
    a. sensory memory.   c. LTM.
    b. STM.   d. procedural memory.

6-6.   Short-term memory can hold _____ separate items.
    a. 2 to 3   c. 7 to 9
    b. 4 to 5   d. 8 to 10

6-7.   Few individuals have accurate memories for events occurring before their third or fourth birthdays. This is called:
    a. retroactive interference.   c. repression.
    b. proactive interference.   d. infantile amnesia.

6-8.   Research on the influence of alcohol on long-term memory indicates that it:
    a. enhances memory.   c. interferes only with acoustic memory.
    b. interferes with memory.   d. interferences only with semantic memory.

6-9.   Memory for the events of our lives is called _____ memory.
    a. semantic   c. personal
    b. procedural   d. autobiographical

6-10.   The view that suggests that a memory cue's effectiveness depends upon what is entered into memory at the time of learning is called:
    a. encoding specificity.   c. context-dependent memory.
    b. state-dependent retrieval.   d. levels of processing.

6-11. When we fill in details of events to make memories more complete, we are using:
a. association.
c. construction.
b. shallow processing.
d. distortion.

6-12. Information that is _____ with well-developed schemas are encoded more readily than information that is _____ with our schemas.
a. inconsistent, consistent
c. consistent, inconsistent
b. not associated, associated
d. none of the above

6-13. Research on the levels of processing indicates that memory is better with _____ processing.
a. deep
c. moderate
b. shallow
d. rote

6-14. Stimuli that are associated with information stored in memory and aid retrieval are called:
a. loci.
c. cues.
b. state-dependents.
d. phonological loops.

6-15. Susan cannot remember what happened the week before she was in a serious car accident. This is an example of:
a. anterograde amnesia.
c. phobic amnesia.
b. retrograde amnesia.
d. Korsakoff's syndrome.

6-16. The most important factor in forgetting appears to be:
a. attention.
c. interference.
b. emotion.
d. decay.

6-17. Our memory of our first date is an example of:
a. episodic.
c. univariate.
b. semantic.
d. associationistic.

6-18. You are having problems learning the rules of a new board game. The problem seems to be in confusing the rules of chess with this new game. You are experiencing:
a. reactive interference.
c. proactive interference.
b. retroactive interference.
d. anticipatory interference.

6-19. Our memory for things we are supposed to do in the future is:
a. retrospective memory.
c. procedural memory.
b. ruturistic memory.
d. prospective memory.

6-20. Research on flashbulb memory indicates that:
a. it increases over time.
c. it is accurate.
b. it decreases over time.
d. it is not accurate.

Answers and Feedback to Sample Test Questions:

6-1.   B   Encoding is the process responsible for entering information into memory. (p. 195)

6-2.   B   In contrast with STM, sensory memory is unlimited and holds a great deal of information for a very brief period of time. (p. 198)

6-3.   B   The modal model of memory proposes three kinds of memory systems: sensory memory, STM, and LTM. (p. 195)

6-4.   A   Attending to information transfers it from sensory memory to STM. (p. 196)

6-5.   A   Sensory memory is the first memory structure in the information processing sequence. (p. 195)

6-6.   C   STM holds between seven to nine chunks of information. [Remember: The magic number 7 plus or minus 2.] (p. 201)

6-7.   D   This loss of autobiographical memory for early life events is called infantile amnesia. (p. 212)

6-8.   B   Alcohol interferes with memory. (p. 222)

6-9.   D   Autobiographical memory is the term used for our memory of our own life events. (p. 210)

6-10.   A   Encoding specificity is the general principle that says that a memory cue's effectiveness depends upon what is encoded into memory at the time of learning. (p. 205)

6-11.   C   Construction refers to filling in details of an event to make our memories more complete. (p. 218)

6-12.   C   Consistent information is encoded more easily than inconsistent information. (p. 215)

6-13.   A   Deeper levels of processing (e.g., semantic processing) leads to good memory, according to the levels of processing approach. (p. 204)

6-14.   C   "Cues" fit this definition. (p. 205)

6-15.   B   Loss of memory for events that happened before an accident is called retrograde amnesia. (p. 220)

6-16.   C   Interference among information stored in memory is thought to produce forgetting. (p. 207)

6-17.   A   Memory for specific times or places is called episodic memory. (p. 197)

6-18.   C   Proactive interference refers to problems in acquiring new information due to the influence of previously learned material. (p. 208)

6-19.   D   Prospective memory refers to our memory for things we are suppose to do in the future. (p. 210)

6-20.   D   Despite our impressions, research indicates that flashbulb memories are not accurate. (p. 214)

Glossary of difficult words and expressions	Definition
Acronyms	words formed from the initial letters of the name
Array of	variety of
Blazingly hot	extremely hot
Converging	coming towards each other and meeting at a point
Culprits	guilty party
Detrimnetal	harmful
Effortful	involving a lot of effort
Errands	short journeys to take or get something
Evoke	call up; bring out
Fleeting	lasting for a short time
Flooding back	coming back rapidly
Fruitful	producing good results
Gaze	to look at something intensively
Groaning	making a deep sound forced out by pain
Hazardous	dangerous, not beneficial
Infallible	incapable of making a mistake or doing wrong
Jumble	things mixed in a confusing way
"Mental scaffolds"	mental frameworks
Molested	intentionally hurt
Omitted	disregraded; not included
Onset	beginning, starting point
Ostensible	apparent, revealing
Probings	procedures or methods of
Refrain	stop yourself
Rehearsing	practicing
Retrieving	getting back
Saliency	standing out
Seizure	physical attack
Startling	amazing
Thrusts	push suddenly or violently
Trivial	unimportant

Glossary of difficult words and expressions	Definition
Unravel	separate; figure out
Unsettling	troubled, anxious or uncertain
Vanished	disappeared
Wander	to move about without a definite purpose
What had become of	what happened to

CHAPTER 7
COGNITION AND INTELLIGENCE

OUTLINE: Develop a Study Plan

Use this outline to help you grasp the organizational structure of the chapter contents. The learning objectives (LOs) for each section are included. Use them as tools for developing your study plan. Space has been provided for you to write any notes or questions that come to mind as you begin your exploration into this material.

Heading:	Learning Objective:	Your Notes:
I. Thinking: Forming Concepts and Reasoning to Conclusions	**L.O. 7.1:** Discuss the two strategies that psychologists have adopted to investigate the nature of thought: Concepts and images.	
A. Basic Elements of Thought: Concepts and Images		
B. Reasoning: Transforming Information to Reach Conclusions	**L.O. 7.2:** Explain the difference between formal and everyday reasoning processes.	
	L.O. 7.3: Know the basic sources of bias in reasoning.	
C. Animal Cognition: Tails of Intelligence	**L.O. 7.4:** Discuss the research findings concerning animal cognition.	
II. Making Decisions: Choosing Among Alternatives		
A. Heuristics: Using Quick -- But Fallible -- Rules of Thumb to Make Decisions	**L.O. 7.5:** Describe the use of heuristics in decision making.	
B. Framing and Decision Strategy	**L.O. 7.6:** Describe the influences of framing on decision making.	
C. Escalation of Commitment: Getting Trapped in Bad Decisions	**L.O. 7.7:** Explain how we can become committed to bad decisions.	

Heading:	Learning Objective:	Your Notes:
III. Problem Solving and Creativity: Finding Paths to Desired Goals		
A. Techniques for Solving Problems: From Trial and Error to Heuristics	**L.O. 7.8:** Survey the different techniques that can be used for solving problems.	
B. Factors That Interfere with Effective Problem Solving	**L.O. 7.9:** Discuss factors that can interfere with effective problem solving.	
C. Creativity: Innovative Problem Solving	**L.O. 7.10:** Discuss what psychologists know about the nature of creativity.	
D. Artificial Intelligence: Can Machines Really Think?	**L.O. 7.11:** Discuss the important issues confronting the field of artificial intelligence.	
IV. Language: The Communication of Information		
A. Language: Its Basic Nature		
B. The Development of Language	**L.O. 7.12:** Compare and contrast the different views of language development and describe the basic milestones of language development.	
C. Language and Thought: Do We Think What We Say or Say What We Think?	**L.O. 7.13:** Describe the contrasting views on the relationship between language and thought.	
D. Language in Other Species	**L.O. 7.14:** Discuss the research on animal language and communication.	
V. Intelligence: Its Nature and Measurement		
A. Human Itelligence: Some Contrasting Views	**L.O. 7.15:** Comapre and contrast the different views on the nature of intelligence.	
	7.16: Discuss the findings as to whether there are differences between males and females in cognitive abilities.	

Heading:	Learning Objective:	Your Notes:
B. Measuring Human Intelligence	**L.O. 7.17:** Describe the different measures of human intelligence and discuss their positive and negative features.	
C. Reliability and Validity: Basic Requirements for All Psychological Tests	**L.O. 7.18:** Describe the concepts of test reliability and validity and the different types of reliability and validity.	
D. Intelligence Testing and Public Policy: Are Intelligence Tests Fair?	**7.19:** Describe the findings related to cultural bias in intelligence tests and efforts to design culture-fair tests to overcome this bias.	
VI. Human Intelligence: The Role of Heredity and the Role of Environment		
A. Evidence for the Influence of Heredity	**7.20:** Discuss the evidence for the roles of heredity and the environment in intelligence.	
B. Evidence for the Influence of Environmental Factors		
C. Environment, Heredity, and Intelligence: Summing Up		
VII. Making Psychology Part of Your Life: Making Better Decisions		

SURVEY AND QUESTION

This section presents the major topics and ideas from the chapter. Use it as a tool for seeing how the components of the chapter fit together. At the end of each major topic, we have asked you questions that relate to the major learning objectives. If you can answer these questions, you have taken a major step toward mastering this material.

I.   Thinking: Forming Concepts and Reasoning to Conclusions

Two strategies have been used to understand the nature of thought. One strategy is to focus on the basic elements of thought. A second strategy is to determine the way in which we reason. These strategies are discussed in the following sections.

A.   Basic Elements of Thought: Concepts, Propositions, Images

Our thought consists of 3 basic components: concepts, propositions, and images. Mental frameworks for categorizing diverse items as belonging together are concepts. Artificial concepts can be clearly defined by a set of rules or properties. Concepts that we use in everyday life and that have "fuzzy" boundaries are called natural concepts. These are based on the best examples of concepts or prototypes. The more similar a stimulus is to the prototype, the more likely it is placed in the category. This is a probabilistic strategy. Several possibilities exist concerning how concepts are represented. One possibility is that they may be represented in terms of the features or attributes they possess. A second possibility is that they're presented in terms of mental pictures or visual images of the external world. Concepts are closely related to schemas, which are cognitive frameworks that represent our knowledge of and assumptions about the world. Schemas are more complex than concepts.

Thinking involves the active manipulation of internal representations of the external world. Because we possess highly developed language skills, these cognitive actions often take the form of propositions or sentences that can stand as separate assertions. Propositions are useful for relating one concept to another, or for relating one feature to the entire concept. Controversy exists as to whether our use of visual images in thinking is precisely that of actual vision.

B.   Reasoning: Transforming Information to Reach Conclusions

Drawing accurate conclusions from available information is called reasoning. In formal reasoning, all the required information is supplied, the problem to be solved is straight-forward, and there is typically only one correct answer. Syllogistic reasoning is one example of this type of reasoning. It involves situations in which conclusions are based on two propositions. In contrast, everyday reasoning involves planning, making commitments, and evaluating arguments in our daily lives.

Reasoning is subject to error and can be influenced by cultural factors and beliefs. For example, in Western cultures, where formal rules of logic are taught, people can solve simple syllogisms quite successfully. This may not be the case in preliterate cultures, perhaps because the laws of formal logic are viewed as less trustworthy than one's own senses.

Reasoning also is also affected by emotions and beliefs. Further, we tend to be selective in overlooking flaws. This phenomenon is the oversight bias. We also tend to test conclusions for hypotheses by examining only evidence that we expect will confirm them. This is called confirmation bias. Learning that an event actually happened can cause individuals to assume that they knew it all along. This is the hindsight effect. This hindsight effect may be reduced if individuals are asked to explain a reported outcome along with other possible outcomes that did not occur.

C.   Animal Cognition: Tails of Intelligence

A growing body of researchers suggests that animals do possess cognitive abilities. First, many instances of animal learning cannot be explained through conditioning alone. Second, evidence suggests that animals form complex mental representations of their environment. Recent work on this question uses the ecological approach, which tests for cognitive processes appropriate to a particular species.

Research indicates that there are some similarities between the cognitive processes of animals and human beings. Some studies have indicated that animals can categorize stimuli that differ in physical similarity. This does not appear to be a product of simple conditioning; pigeons learned to categorize faster and more accurately when the stimuli were relevant categories (human categories) than when they were arbitrary. Additional evidence for animal cognition comes from research on baboons. Baboons appear to be able to mentally rotate visual forms.

Questions:

7-1.   What are the two strategies adopted for studying the nature of thought? _____

_____

_____

_____

7-2.   What are the basic characteristics of concepts? _____

_____

_____

_____

7-3.   How are propositions and concepts related? _____

_____

_____

_____

7-4.   How does formal reasoning differ from everyday reasoning? _____

_____

_____

_____

7-5.   What are the basic sources of bias in reasoning? _____

_____

_____

_____

7-6.   What are the research findings concerning animal cognition? _____

_____

_____

_____

II.   Making Decisions: Choosing Among Alternatives

Decision making is a process of choosing among various courses of action or alternatives. One description of a rational decision maker is expected utility -- the product of the probability and value of each possible outcome. Usually, we don't take the time to reason in such a systematic way. The following material describes more typical decision-making strategies.

A.   Heuristics: Using Quick -- But Fallible -- Rules of Thumb to Make Decisions

When we have to make decisions quickly, we may use guidelines from our past experience (heuristics). The more easily we can think of instances of something, the more frequent we judge it to be. This is the availability heuristic.

When we judge the likelihood of something based on how much an item resembles the prototype, we are using the representativeness heuristic. This heuristic may lead us to ignore the relative frequency of objects or events in the world (base rates).

Our tendency to make decisions by using a reference point as an initial starting point is the anchoring and adjustment heuristic. In this heuristic, the reference point is known as the anchor.

B.   Framing in Decisiong Making

Decisions can be affected by the way in which decisions are framed. Framing involves the presentation of information about potential outcomes in terms of gains or in terms of losses. Research indicates that when emphasis is on potential gains, people are risk averse -- they prefer to avoid unnecessary risks. When the emphasis is on potential losses, people are risk prone -- they prefer to take risks rather than accept certain losses.

C.   Escalation of Commitment: Getting Trapped in Bad Decisions

Entrapment occurs when decision-makers feel they must stay with their original decisions and they feel a need to justify their decisions. There can be several phases in the escalation of commitment process. In the initial phase, decisions are based on rational considerations. Later, psychological factors, such as the desire for self-justification comes into play when there are early losses. External factors, such as political pressure comes into play with continued losses.

Research suggests that escalation can be reduced if available resources to commit to further action are limited and the evidence of failure is overwhelming. If responsibility can be diffused for taking part in a bad decision, escalation can be prevented.

Questions:

7-7. How do people make decisions based on expected utility? _____

_____

_____

_____

7-8. How do we use heuristics in decision making? _____

_____

_____

_____

7-9. How can framing influence decision making? _____

_____

_____

_____

7-10. How do we become committed to bad decisions? _____

_____

_____

_____

III. Problem-Solving and Creativity: Finding Paths to Desired Goals

A. Methods For Solving Problems: From Trial and Error to Heuristics

Trial and error is the problem-solving technique that involves trying a variety of different responses. Rules for solving problems that eventually will lead to the solution are algorithms. Problem-solving strategies suggested by prior experience are heuristics.

Dividing a problem into a series of smaller subproblems is a means-end analysis. This involves deciding on the ends we want to attain and the means used to get there. Assuming that a problem is similar to a past one and applying solutions that worked on it is the analogy strategy.

B.   Factors that Interfere with Effective Problem Solving

Our tendency to think of using objects only in the way that they were used before is known as functional fixedness. This tendency has been shown to interfere with problem solving. Once we have solved a problem in a particular way, we tend to stay with it. We develop a mental set based on our past experience that interferes with our ability to see better alternatives.

C.   Creativity: Innovative Problem Solving

Creativity is cognitive activity that results in a new or novel way of viewing or solving a problem. There are several phases to this process. The first involves preparation -- individuals spend long periods of time in activities such as gathering knowledge. The second often involves a period of incubation during which people stop actively working on the problem. Third, individuals often report suddenly seeing the first glimmer of the solution known as insight. This is not, however, the end of the process. Rather, considerable refinement must follow in which the idea must be worked out, translated, and tested.

Research suggests that creativity results from divergent thinking that moves outward from conventional knowledge into unexplored paths. In contrast, convergent thinking does not appear to foster creativity.

There are several ways to foster creativity. One should develop a broad and rich knowledge base. Creative people take risks, so its important to foster independence. The use of analogies should be encouraged; this skill can be taught. Creative people often have a high level of curiosity. A growing body of evidence also suggests that enhanced positive affect may increase creativity.

D.   Artificial Intelligence: Can Machines Really Think?

The field of artificial intelligence studies the capacity of computers to demonstrate performance that, if produced by humans, would be described as intelligent. Computers carry out complex computations at a very fast pace. Computers can be efficient problem solvers and also have some language abilities.

Recently, computers have been designed with neural networks -- structures consisting of highly interconnected elementary computational units that work together in parallel. There are two major advantages to neural networks. First, the units can work together. Second, they have the capacity to learn from experience by adjusting output strength. However, most psychologists believe that the early predictions about the capacities of computers to show characteristics such as intention, understanding, and consciousness were greatly overstated.

Questions:

7-11.   What are the characteristics of problem solving? _____

_____

_____

_____

7-12.   What are the different methods of problem solving? _____

_____

_____

_____

7-13.   How can functional fixedness and mental set interfere with effective problem solving? _____

_____

_____

_____

7-14.   What are the phases of the creative process? _____

_____

_____

_____

7-15.   How can creativity be fostered? _____

_____

_____

_____

7-16.   In what ways do the capacities of computers resemble human intelligence; in what ways do they **not** resemble human intelligence? _____

_____

_____

_____

IV. Language: The Communication of Information

A.   Language: Its Basic Nature

Language uses symbols for communicating information. For a set of symbols to be a language, three criteria must be met. They must transmit information or carry meaning. It must be possible to combine the symbols into an infinite number of sentences.   And, the meaning of these sentences must be independent of the settings in which they are used.

B.   The Development of Language

Table 7.3 (p. 249 of your text) summarizes some major milestones of language development. We mention several of these here for you.

Vowel and consonant sounds are made while cooing at 20 weeks. Understanding of some words occurs around 12 months. At 18 months about fifty words can be produced. A 1000-word vocabulary may be reached at 36 months. At 48 months most aspects of language are well established.

There are several views of language development. The social learning view suggests that speech is acquired through operant conditioning and imitation. According to Chomsky and the innate mechanism view, we have a built-in neural system which provides an intuitive grasp of grammar. That is, humans are prepared to acquire language skills.

A third view is that both innate mechanisms and learning are important. This view assumes children have certain information-processing abilities that they use in acquiring language. These operating principles are assumed to be present, or develop, very early in life. Each view has some empirical support. It is safe to conclude that language development involves several complex processes.

There are three basic areas of language development. The development of the ability to pronounce the sounds and words of one or more languages is phonological development. Many children use phonological strategies to simplify the pronunciation of many words. The second area is semantic development -- learning to understand the meaning of words. Some psychologists believe that children are able to build a vocabulary of more than 14,000 words by age six because they engage in fast mapping -- a process of "mapping" a new word to an underlying concept in a single exposure. During semantic development, children learn the meaning of language. There are systematic errors in the development.

Children tend to attach a new word to an inappropriate concept (mismatching). In addition, they often apply a term to either a smaller or larger range of objects or events than its true meaning. Underextension is the label for applying a term to a smaller range and the overextension is the label for applying a term to a larger range.

The third area is grammatical development. Grammar refers to a set of rules dictating how words can be combined into sentences. Before the age of two, grammar poses little problems in that speech is holophrastic. In holophrastic speech, single words are used to express complex meanings. Around age two, speech is telegraphic in that less important words are omitted. Between two and three years of age, most children use simple sentences. Between three and six years of age, more complex grammatical forms appear, including the use of conjunctions. Complexity continues to develop and is not complete until early adolescence.

C.   Language and Thought: Do We Think What We Say or Say What We Think?

The idea that language shapes or determines our thought is the linguistic relativity hypothesis. The other view is that thought shapes language. The evidence best supports the second view. For example, evidence suggests that having more words for color does not affect one's recognition of differences in color.

D.   Language In Other Species

Primates (and other animals) lack the vocal control necessary to produce words. However, animals can learn to use some forms of language. For example, chimps are able to learn sign language.

Evidence suggests that language may not be a uniquely human skill -- it may be a part of a continuum of skills that different animals exhibit to varying degrees.

Questions:

7-17. What are the characteristics of language and speech? _____
_____
_____
_____

7-18. What are the different views of language development and what are the general findings concerning these views? _____
_____
_____
_____

7-19. What are the basic milestones of development? _____
_____
_____
_____

7-20. What are the contrasting views and research findings on the relationship between language and thought? _____
_____
_____
_____

7-21. What is the evidence concerning the use of language by animals? _____
_____
_____
_____

V. Intelligence: Its Nature and Measurement

A. Human Intelligence: Some Contrasting Views

Psychologists generally agree that intelligence involves the ability to think abstractly and to learn from experience. Some theorists feel that intelligence is a general, unified capacity. For example, researchers such as Spearman proposed that intelligence consists of a general ability to solve problems. Theorists who feel intelligence is composed of several distinct abilities believe intelligence is multifaceted. For example, Thurstone proposed that intelligence consists of seven distinct primary mental abilities. Among these were verbal meaning, number, and space.

Cattell took a more integrated approach. He proposed that intelligence consists of two major components. General intelligence is called fluid intelligence. It involves the ability to form concepts, reason, and identify similarities. Specific knowledge gained from experience is called crystallized intelligence. For example, vocabulary tests involve crystallized intelligence. Fluid intelligence reaches its peak in early adulthood. Crystallized intelligence increases across the lifespan.

Most psychologists believe that intelligence involves both general ability and specific abilities. Sternberg's triarchic theory proposes that there are three distinct types of intelligence. He takes an information-processing approach. Intelligence that is related to effectiveness in information processing is componential. This is associated with ability to think critically. The intelligence related to insight and the ability to develop new ideas is experiential. Individuals high on this are good at combining seemingly unrelated facts. People who have practical sense have contextual intelligence. They can quickly figure out what it takes to be successful at various tasks and how to accomplish various goals. Recently, Sternberg has considered the relationship between intelligence and personality in his mental self-government theory. This theory suggests we must consider intellectual styles.

According to a neuroscience approach, intelligence is related to rapid or efficient neural processing. There is research supporting this approach. First, in one study the speech of nerve impulses was correlated with scores on a written test of intelligence. Second, when asked to perform a complex cognitive task, persons scoring highest on written tests of intelligence expended less mental energy than those scoring lowest. Third, scores on a standard intelligence measure was related to the size of certain portions of the brain.

B.   Measuring Human Intelligence

The intelligence test was first developed by Binet and Simon. They selected items that children could answer without special training. Therefore, they used either new or unusual items or very familiar ones. In a later version, they grouped items by age. An item was placed at a particular level if about 75 percent of the children of that age could pass it correctly. It was adopted in the U.S. as the Stanford-Binet test and yielded a single score of intelligence or IQ.

IQ stands for intelligence quotient. An IQ is obtained by dividing an individual's mental age by the chronological age and multiplying by 100. Mental age is determined by adding the number of items passed correctly on the test. One problem with this type of test is that at some point, mental growth levels off or stops while chronological age continues to grow.

A major drawback of the Stanford-Binet is that it is predominantly verbal in content. To overcome this problem, Wechsler devised both verbal and nonverbal (or performance) items. Wechsler believed that differences between those two components reflected important diagnostic information. It was believed that differences between scores on the various subsets could be used to diagnose mental disorders. Research has yielded mixed results. Although not conclusive, individuals diagnosed as delinquent or as having an antisocial personality disorder have higher nonverbal than verbal IQs. Children with learning disabilities sometimes score higher on picture completion and object assembly but lower on tests such as arithmetic, vocabulary, and information.

Group tests of intelligence can be administered to many persons at once. However, such tests have been criticized. Critics believe they are unfair in several respects to children from disadvantaged backgrounds.

C.   Reliability and Validity: Basic Requirements for all Psychological Tests

To be useful, measuring devices must give the same result each time they are applied to the same person; that is, they must be reliable. To see if the items on the test are measuring the same thing, one can divide them in half to see if the scores are similar. This is split-half reliability and is a measure of internal consistency. A formula, termed coefficient alpha, considers all of the possible ways of splitting into halves the items on a test. Giving the test to the same group several times to determine the similarity of scores over time is test-retest reliability. Typically, the longer the time between testing intervals, the lower the reliability. To reduce practice effects, psychologists often use alternative forms of the same test.

The ability of a test to measure what it is supposed to is validity. The extent to which the items sample behaviors that are thought to be related to the characteristic in question is content validity. The type of validity related to whether differences in scores on the test are related to differences in behavior is criterion validity. The type of criterion validity in which scores on a test are used to predict later performance is predictive validity. The type of validity in which test scores are related to present behavior or performance is concurrent validity. Whether or not a test measures a concept or process in a theory is construct validity. Evidence for construct validity can be derived from convergent evidence. This evidence is obtained when, for example, scores on a particular health test are related to other accepted measures of health.

D.   Intelligence Testing and Public Policy: Are Intelligence Tests Fair?

On group tests of intelligence, African-Americans, Native Americans, and Hispanics score lower than those of European ancestry. This may reflect cultural bias for several reasons. First, children from minority or disadvantaged backgrounds may not have had the opportunity to acquire the knowledge necessary for a successful performance. Second, the tests may incorporate implicit European values about how to judge the correctness of answers. Therefore, they favor Europeans. This may reflect cultural bias in that these tests were developed for white middle-class children. The fact that recent immigrants from Asia do well on these tests may reflect the emphasis on education and a high degree of social support within families in these groups. The precise basis for such differences remains unknown.

Attempts have been made to develop culture-fair tests that use items to which all groups have been exposed. One of these is the Raven Progressive Matrices test. A related test is the Culture-Fair Intelligence Test. Another is the Kauffman Assessment Battery for Children, which is designed to measure ability to process information. It has tasks that involve sequential processing and that require simultaneous processing.

Differences between ethnic and racial groups are smaller on these tests than other tests. Culture-fair tests are less successful in predicting success in school or other contexts. Perhaps, physiological measures of intelligence may eventually eliminate, or reduce, the impact of cultural bias.

One major purpose of individual tests of intelligence is educational intervention -- they are used to identify those who are mentally retarded and intellectually gifted. Mental retardation is determined by at least two factors: IQ scores and success in carrying out daily activities normally expected of persons their age. Mental retardation seems to be influenced by environmental and genetic factors.

In one study, intellectually gifted children experienced more successful occupational success, better personal and social adjustment, and were healthier than the average adult. There is a growing concern that the intellectually gifted are not being exposed to the most advantageous academic environment because they are not being grouped with similar others.

Questions:

7-22. Why do many psychologists believe it is important to consider people's relative position on various measures of intelligence? _____

_____

_____

_____

7-23. What are the different views concerning the nature of intelligence? _____

_____

_____

_____

7-24. What are the different measures of human intelligence and what are their positive and negative features? _____

_____

_____

_____

7-25. What is test reliability and validity and what are the different types of reliability and validity?

_____

_____

_____

7-26. What are the sources of cultural bias in intelligence tests? _____

_____

_____

_____

7-27. How can intelligence tests be culturally fair? _____

_____

_____

_____

7-28. What are the practical applications of intelligence tests? _____

_____

_____

_____

VI. Human Intelligence: The Role of Heredity and the Role of Environment

A. Evidence for the Influence of Heredity

Human intelligence seems to be the result of both heredity and environmental factors. Evidence for heredity comes from the fact that the closer two people are related, the more similar their IQs. IQs of identical twins are more highly correlated than those of siblings. IQs of siblings are more highly correlated than those of cousins.

The IQs of adopted children correlate more highly with those of their biological parents than their adoptive parents. However, in some cases IQs become increasingly similar to those of their adoptive parents. The IQs of identical twins reared apart correlate almost as highly as those of twins reared together. Twins reared apart are also similar in appearance and personality. Additional evidence for a genetic basis for intelligence comes from the fact that those who score high on intelligence tests may also have efficient brains.

B. Evidence for the Influence of Environmental Factors

The worldwide gains in IQ studies of environmental deprivation and enrichment suggest the importance of environmental factors. Depriving children of certain forms of environmental stimulation early in life can reduce intelligence. Studies have shown that enrichment can improve intelligence. Removing children from sterile environments and placing them in a more favorable environment improved intelligence. Further, individuals raised in the same environment often have more similar IQs than those reared apart. And the longer students remain in school, the higher their IQs tend to be. Nutrition, family background, and the quality of education are other environmental factors influencing intelligence.

One account for why a child's environment contributes to intelligence suggests that the quality of the intellectual environment declines as more children are born because parents have to divide their attention over more children.

C. Environment, Heredity, and Intelligence: Summing Up

Heredity and environment are both important in shaping intelligence. Work in behavioral genetics has led some psychologists to suspect that genetic factors may be more important than environmental factors. Genes provides a range of possible responses to a given context. This is called malleability. Therefore, if genes do strongly influence intelligence, environment can still influence where a person's intelligence level will fall within the range of intelligence levels set by genetic factors.

Questions:

7-29. What is the evidence for the role of heredity in intelligence? _____

_____

_____

_____

7-30. What is the evidence for the role of environmental factors in intelligence? _____

_____

_____

_____

7-31. How do genetic and environmental factors interact to affect the development of intelligence?

_____

_____

_____

VII. Making Psychology Part of Your Life

A. Making Better Decisions

The information in this chapter can help you make better decisions. Here are a few guidelines. See page 291 for further details.

1)   Don't trust your own memory, or beware of availability heuristics.
2)   Don't take situations at face value, or question all anchors.
3)   Remain flexible, or don't fall in love with your own decisions.
4)   Consider all options, or is half an orange better than none?

Question:

7-32. How can you incorporate these guidelines into your decision-making strategies? _____

_____

_____

_____

MAKING PSYCHOLOGY PART OF YOUR LIFE: Key Terms and Concepts

Knowing the important concepts and key terms contained in this chapter is a very important part of mastering the material. We have presented a sample of these concepts below. Define each concept and check your definition with that presented in your textbook. It will also be beneficial for you to think of an example of each concept. Whenever possible, use your own personal experience to provide an example of each term below.

7-1. __Algorithms__: _____

  Example: _____

7-2. __Anchoring-and-Adjustment Heuristic__: _____

  Example: _____

7-3. __Artificial Concepts__: _____

  Example: _____

7-4. __Artificial Intelligence__: _____

  Example: _____

7-5. __Availability Heuristic__: _____

  Example: _____

7-6. __Babbling__: _____

7-7. __Cognition__: _____

  Example: _____

7-8. __Concepts__: _____

  Example: _____

7-9. __Confirmation Bias__: _____

  Example: _____

7-10. **Concurrent Validity**: _____

7-11. **Construct Validity**: _____

7-12. **Content Validity**: _____

7-13. **Contextual Intelligence**: _____

Example: _____

7-14. **Convergent Thinking**: _____

Example: _____

7-15. **Creativity**: _____

Example: _____

7-16. **Criterion-related Validity**: _____

7-17. **Cultural Bias**: _____

Example: _____

7-18. **Crystallized Intelligence**: _____

Example: _____

7-19. **Decision Making**: _____

Example: _____

7-20. **Divergent Thinking**: _____

Example: _____

7-21. **Down Syndrome**: _____

7-22. **Escalation of Commitment**: _____

Example: _____

7-23.   **Experiential Intelligence**: _____

        Example: _____

7-24.   **Fast Mapping**: _____

        Example: _____

7-25.   **Fluid Intelligence**: _____

        Example: _____

7-26.   **Framing**: _____

        Example: _____

7-27.   **Functional Fixedness**: _____

        Example: _____

7-28.   **Grammar**: _____

7-29.   **Heuristics**: _____

        Example: _____

7-30.   **Hindsight Effect**: _____

        Example: _____

7-31.   **Intelligence**: _____

        Example: _____

7-32.   **IQ**: _____

7-33.   **Language**: _____

        Example: _____

7-34.   **Linguistic Relativity Hypothesis**: _____

7-35.   **Means-End Analysis**: _____

        Example: _____

7-36.   **Mental Retardation**: _____

        Example: _____

7-37.   **Mental Set**: _____

        Example: _____

7-38.   **Natural Concepts**: _____

        Example: _____

7-39.   **Neural Networks**: _____

7-40.   **Oversight Bias**: _____

        Example: _____

7-41.   **Phonemes**: _____

        Example: _____

7-42.   **Phonological Development**: _____

7-43.   **Phonological Strategies**: _____

        Example: _____

7-44.   **Problem Solving**: _____

        Example: _____

7-45.   **Prototypes**: _____

        Example: _____

7-46. **Reasoning**: _____

   Example: _____

7-47. **Reliability**: _____

7-48. **Representativeness Heuristic**: _____

   Example: _____

7-49. **Semantic Development**: _____

7-50. **Split-half Reliability**: _____

7-51. **Stanford-Binet Test**: _____

   Example: _____

7-52. **Syllogistic Reasoning**: _____

   Example: _____

7-53. **Test-retest Reliability**: _____

7-54. **Triarchic Theory**: _____

CHALLENGE: Develop Your Critical Thinking Skills

Making Better Decisions

Decision-making is an important part of our day-to-day lives. We make decisions that vary in importance all the time -- from what to have for lunch to where to go to college. The material in this chapter can help you make better decisions. And it can help you become aware of the pitfalls that may interfere with effective decision-making. Complete the following exercises and provide an analysis of each. An analysis of these exercises can be found at the end of this section.

7-1.   Your cousin, Susan, just moved to New York City. You hear that she is in the hospital.

   A. What is the probability that she was mugged? _____ .

   B. What is the probability that she was in an automobile accident? _____

   Analysis: _____

   _____

   _____

   _____

   _____

   _____

7-2.   Prospect 1: Imagine that the U.S. is preparing for a disaster that could kill up to 600 people. Please decide which option you would choose:

   If Option A is taken, 200 lives will be saved
   If Option B is taken, there is a 1/3 probability that 600 people will be saved and a 2/3 probability that 600 people will die

   Which option would you choose? _____

   Analysis: _____

   _____

   _____

   _____

   _____

   [Note #2 and #3 based on: Kahneman, D., & Tversky, A. (1979). An analysis of decision under risk. Econometrica, 47, 263-291.]

7-3.   Prospect 2: Imagine that the U.S. is preparing for a disaster that could kill up to 600 people. Please decide which option you would choose:

If Option A is taken, 400 people will die
If Option B is taken, there is a 1/3 probability that no one will die and a 2/3 probability that 600 people will die

Which option would you choose? _____

Analysis: _____

_____

_____

_____

_____

_____

_____

Problem Analyses

Making Better Decisions

7-1.   If you chose Option A, your decision was probably influenced by the **availability heuristic** -- the tendency to make judgments about the likelihood of events in terms of how readily examples of them can be brought to mind. The extensive publicity about violent crimes in New York City leads us to bring this information to mind and overestimate the probability of our cousin being a victim.

7-2.   The prospects presented in these two problems are identical except that, in Prospect 1, the options are
&   framed in terms of lives saved, and in Prospect 2 this framing is in terms of lives lost. This framing
7-3.   significantly affects the choices people make between options. If you chose Option A with Prospect 1 and Option B with Prospect 2, you demonstrated the typical pattern of choices.

CHALLENGE: Making Psychology Part of Your Life

In this chapter, you've learned a great deal about how people can get caught=up in bad decisions. Try applying what you've learned to the following situation:

Situation

As her wedding day approached, Patsy felt increasingly depressed. Why had she agreed to marry Jeff when she knew it wouldn't work? At first it seemed the right thing to do, since they had been dating for years. Marriage seemed to be the logical next step. But now it seemed like a bad idea. "Well, what's done is done," she thought to herself. "I can't get out of this now. The invitations have been mailed, the dress is paid for; and the food and flowers have been ordered. And what will people think if I back out now?"

The only person she confided her feelings to was her best friend -- Carol. Carol suggested that she have a heart-to-heart talk with Jeff and her parents.

"Maybe Jeff feels the same way," Carol observed. "You know, your parents really pushed both of you into this step. But they're not the ones that have to live with this decision."

Application Questions

7- 1.   Do you think Patsy is caught up in an "escalation of commitment" spiral?

_____

_____

7- 2.   Can you describe the factors that may be affecting Patsy's decision to marry Jeff?

_____

_____

7- 3.   How might the unpleasant consequences of backing out of her engagement affect her decision to get married?

_____

_____

7- 4.   What role, if any, might external pressures from others play in her decision process?

_____

_____

7- 5.   Can you relate the various phases of her thoughts to the course of escalation processes (see Figure 7-5, p. 272, in your textbook)?

_____

_____

7- 6.   Can you relate Carol's advice to strategies that have been found to counter pressures to escalate their commitment?

_____

_____

7- 7.   What would you do in these circumstances?

_____

_____

YOUR NOTES:

CHALLENGE: Review Your Comprehensive Knowledge

SAMPLE TEST QUESTIONS

Once you have worked through the preceding sections, you should be ready for a comprehensive self-test. You can check your answers with those at the end of this section. An additional practice test is given in the supplementary section at the end of this study guide.

7-1.   Mental frameworks for categorizing diverse items as belonging together are:
   a. hypotheses.   c. prototypes.
   b. ideas.   d. concepts.

7-2.   Concepts that can be clearly defined by a set of rules are called:
   a. images.   c. natural concepts.
   b. prototypes.   d. artificial concepts.

7-3.   According to the availability heuristic, the more easily we think of something, the more:
   a. common we judge it to be.   c. we dislike it.
   b. we like it.   d. we understand it.

7-4.   The style of thinking most likely to produce creative outcomes is known as:
   a. expert thinking.   c. convergent thinking.
   b. novice thinking.   d. divergent thinking.

7-5.   The anchoring and adjustment heuristic is strongly influenced by:
   a. expected utility.   c. a reference point.
   b. base rates.   d. ambiguous information.

7-6.   Rules for solving problems that eventually will lead to solutions are:
   a. trial-and-error rules.   c. algorithms.
   b. heuristics.   d. inducers.

7-7.   Research on framing decisions indicates when the emphasis is on potential gains of outcomes, people are _____ and when the emphasis is on potential losses people are _____.
   a. risk averse, gain averse   c. gain prone, gain averse
   b. risk averse, risk prone   d. risk prone, risk averse

7-8.   Rules about how words can be combined into meaningful sentences are called:
   a. phonemes.   c. grammar.
   b. syntax.   d. semantics.

7-9.   The type of knowledge that involves understanding of the meaning of words is known as:
   a. semantic.   c. syntactical.
   b. phonological.   d. morphological.

7-10.   The social learning view of language development suggests that:
   a. language is innate.
   b. language is acquired through operant conditioning and imitation.
   c. language is acquired through the application of operating principles.
   d. language is based on deep structure.

7-11.   The view that language determines thought is known as:
    a. the linguistic relativity hypothesis.   c. Chomsky's hypothesis.
    b. the social learning approach.   d. the artificial intelligence approach.

7-12.   What are the three basic areas of language development?
    a. holophrastic, telegraphic, semantic   c. intuitive, semantic, phonological
    b. phonological, semantic, grammatical   d. deep structure, surface structure, fast mapping

7-13.   Psychological tests need to be:
    a. reliable and valid.   c. reliable and consistent.
    b. reliable and difficult.   d. valid and current.

7-14.   Assessment of simliarity of scores over time is called:
    a. split-half reliability.   c. split-half validity.
    b. test-retest reliability.   d. test-retest validity.

7-15.   The type of validity in which test scores are related to present behavior is:
    a. content.   c. concurrent.
    b. predictive.   d. construct.

7-16.   Spearman felt that intelligence consisted of:
    a. a general ability to reason, and solve problems. c. a compositive of seven primary mental abilities.
    b. multiple types of intelligence.   d. culturally determined skills.

7-17.   According to Sternberg's triarchic theory, people who have practical sense have _____ intelligence.
    a. componential   c. contextual
    b. experiential   d. intuitive

7-18.   Originally, IQ scores were obtained by dividing _____ age by _____ age and multiplying by 100.
    a. mental, chronological   c. general, specific
    b. chronological, mental   d. specific, general

7-19.   It seems likely that the worldwide increase in IQ scores is due to:
    a. environmental factors.   c. actual increase in intelligence.
    b. genetic factors.   d. the ozone layer.

7-20.   One major problem with the use of individual tests of intelligence is that they are:
    a. too difficult.   c. too easy.
    b. culturally biased.   d. not influenced by training.

Answers and Feedback for Sample Test Questions

7-1.   D   Concepts are mental frameworks for categorizing diverse items as belonging together. (p. 231)

7-2.   D   Artificial concepts are defined by sets of rules. (p. 231)

7-3.   A   The availability heuristic leads us to overestimate the frequency or base rates of events. (p. 237)

7-4.   D   Divergent thinking, which moves outward from conventional knowledge to unexplored paths, is most likely to lead to creative solutions. (p. 246)

7-5.   C   Our tendency to make decisions by using a reference point is known as the anchoring and adjustment heuristic. (p. 239)

7-6.   C   Algorithms are rules that, when followed, will eventually lead to a solution. (p. 242)

7-7.   B   Research indicates that when decisions are framed in terms of potential gains, people are risk averse -- they prefer to avoid unnecessary risks. When the emphasis is on potential losses, they are risk prone -- they prefer to take risks vs. accept certain losses. (p. 239)

7-8.   C   Grammar defines rules about how words can be combined into meaningful sentences. (p. 250)

7-9.   A   Semantic knowledge involves understanding the meaning of words. (p. 250)

7-10.   B   Social learning theory suggests that both operant conditioning and imitation contribute to language development. (p. 249)

7-11.   A   The idea that language shapes or determines our thought is the linguistic relativity hypothesis. (p. 251)

7-12.   B   The three milestones of language development are: phonological development (the ability to pronounce the sounds and words of language), semantic development (the ability to understand the meaning of words), and grammatical development (the ability to correctly combine words into sentences). (p. 250)

7-13.   A   Reliability measures the extent to which a measuring device gives the same result each time it is applied to the same person. Validity refers to the ability of a test to measure what it is suppose to measure. Both are essential for a good psychological test. (p. 264)

7-14.   B   Test-retest reliability refers to the similarity of scores over time. (p. 264)

7-15.   C   Concurrent validity refers to how test scores are related to present behavior on performance. (p. 266)

7-16.   A   Spearman felt that intelligence consisted of a general ability to reason and solve problems. (p. 254)

7-17.   C   Contextual intelligence refers to having practical sense. (p. 255)

7-18.   A   Intelligence quotients are obtained by dividing an individual's mental age by his/her chronological age and multiplying by 100. (p. 261)

7-19.   A   The worldwide gains in IQ suggest the importance of environmental factors. (p. 273)

7-20.   B   Cultural bias is a serious problem for IQ tests. (p. 268)

Glossary of difficult words and expressions	Definition
Agonized over	spent a lot of effort or worry about something
"All-or-nothing decision"	a choice that something is very important and excludes other possibilities
Aloof	distant, beyond approach
Arranged counterparts	put in a certain order persons that are matched on some dimensions such as age
Assessing	making a judgment
Assets	advantages
Bargain	good deal or fair price
Bewildered	puzzled; confused
Bogus	not real or truthful
Boundaries	limits
Concessions	giving in
Conjure	create as an image
Conversely	opposite to; in opposition to
Disparity	inequality; not equal
Enhance	add to; make better, improve
Feedback	a response to a previous event; for example, a grade on a test
Flawed	not perfect, having a defect
Fluttering	quick movements, going back and forth
Graded	to a greater or less degree; small increments
Grasp	understand
Hang-out	spend time socializing with; being around a place
Harsh	not easy or smooth; somewhat negative
Hunches	vague feeling or ideas
Infinite	having no end; going on forever
Kinship	family tie; being related to
Lasting gains	long-term gains; benefits that continue a long time
Mannerisms	behavior patterns; nonverbal behavior
Milestones	important marker
Neat	clean cut

Glossary of difficult words and expressions	Definition
Neglect	pay little or no attention to
Obstacle	something that blocks or stands in the way
Overt	done or shown openly; obvious
Pervasive	tending to spread through every part of; showing up everywhere
Plausible	seeming to be right or reasonable
Progress	moving forward; advancing
Prone to	have a tendency to
Purport	claim; suggest something in strong terms
Readily	very easily
Refrain	not to do something, stop from doing
Refuted	proved to be wrong or mistaken
Relentless	not giving up, continuing to act
Share the burden	share the responsibility or weight
Solely	only; the single element
Sought to	tried to, attempted
Steady	constant; on an even course
Subtle	not obvious
The launch of	to begin or propel
Tradeoffs	exchanges, one event balances another
Trustworthy	dependable
Vacillate	doubt or to see two sides
"Wandering about"	going from place to place without any special purpose or destination
Widespread	popular or common
Yield	to give in or produce
Zeroing	concentrating on; pinpointing

Chapter 8
HUMAN DEVELOPMENT: FROM CHILD TO ADULT

OUTLINE: Develop a Study Plan

Use this outline to help you grasp the organizational structure of the chapter contents. The learning objectives (LOs) for each section are included. Use them as tools for developing your study plan. Space has been provided for you to write any notes or questions that come to mind as you begin your exploration into this material.

Heading:	Learning Objective:	Your Notes:
I. Physical Growth and Development During Childhood	**L.O. 8.1:** Describe the scope of developmental psychology.	
A. The Prenatal Period	**L.O. 8.2:** List the main events of the prenatal period.	
B. Prenatal Influences on Development: When Trouble Starts Early		
C. Physical and Perceptual Development During Our Early Years	**L.O. 8.3:** Describe the course of infants' physical and perceptual development.	
II. Basic Methods for Studying Human Development	**L.O. 8.4:** Compare and contrast the basic methods for studying human development.	
III. Cognitive Development During Childhood: Changes in How We Know the External World...and Ourselves		
A. Piaget's Theory: An Overview	**L.O. 8.5:** Understand the assumptions underyling Piaget's theory of cognitive development and describe its stages.	
B. Piaget's Theory: A Modern Assessment		
C. Cognitive Development: An Information Processing Perspective	**L.O. 8.6:** Explain the assumptions of the information-processing perspective of cognitive development.	
	L.O. 8.7: Compare and contrast the attentional focus of younger and older children.	

Heading:	Learning Objective:	Your Notes:
	L.O. 8.8: Survey the various ways in which memory improves with age.	
	L.O. 8.9: Define "metacognition" and explain its importance for cognitive functioning.	
D. Moral Development: Reasoning About "Right" and "Wrong"	**L.O. 8.10:** Provide an overview of Kohlberg's stages of moral understanding and assess the evidence concerning Kohlberg's theory.	
IV. Social and Emotional Development During Childhood: Forming Relationships With Others		
A. Emotional Development and Temperament	**L.O. 8.11:** Describe the course of children's emotional development including temperament and attachment.	
B. Gender: The Development of Gender Identity and Gender-Stereotyped Behavior	**L.O. 8.12:** Compare and contrast the various views on the development of gender identity.	
V. Adolescence: Between Child and Adult		
A. Physical Development During Adolescence	**L.O. 8.13:** Describe the characteristics of physical development during adolescence.	
B. Cognitive Development During Adolescence	**L.O. 8.14:** Discuss the controversy concerning whether adolescents do or do not think like adults.	
C. Social and Emotional Development During Adolescence	**L.O. 8.15:** Characterize the emotional changes and social development of the adolescent.	
D. Erickson's Eight Stages of Life	**L.O. 8.16:** List the eight stages of life proposed by Erickson.	
E. Adolescence in the 1990s: A Generation at Risk	**L.O. 8.17:** Survey the potential problems that face an adolescent in the 1990s and the steps that can be taken to minimize some of the risks associated with high-risk environments.	

Heading:	Learning Objective:	Your Notes:
VI. Adulthood and Aging	**L.O. 8.18:** Compare and contrast the internal crisis vs. the external life-event models of adult development.	
A. Adult Development: Internal Crisis or External Life Events?		
B. Physical Change During Our Adult Years	**L.O. 8.19:** Describe the physical changes that occur during early adulthood, midlife, and later life.	
C. Cognitive Change During Adulthood	**L.O. 8.20:** Discuss the research on the influences of aging on cognitive performance.	
D. Social Change in Adulthood: Tasks and Stages of Adult Life	**L.O. 8.21:** Outline Levinson's stage theory concerning the social changes that occur during adulthood.	
E. Crises of Adult Life	**L.O. 8.22:** Summarize the major crises of adult life.	
F. Gender and the Adult Years: How Males and Females Differ	**L.O. 8.23:** Describe the similarities and differences in patterns of male and female adult development.	
VII. Aging and Death: The End of Life		
A. Theories of Aging: Contrasting Views about Why We Grow Old	**L.O. 8.24:** Discuss the contrasting views concerning why we grow old.	
B. Meeting Death: Facing the End of Life		
C. Bereavement: Mourning the Death of Loved Ones	**L.O. 8.25:** Provide a survey of stages in the dying and bereavement processes.	
VIII. Making Psychology Part of Your Life: Preparing for Tomorrow's Job Market Today		

SURVEY AND QUESTION

This section presents the major topics and ideas from the chapter. Use it as a tool for seeing how the components of the chapter fit together. At the end of each major topic, we have asked you a question that relates to the major learning objectives. If you can answer these questions, you have taken a major step toward mastering this material.

I.   Physical Growth and Development During Childhood

The area of psychology concerned with physical, social, and mental change during the lifespan is developmental psychology. Our survey begins with an exploration of physical growth and development.

A.   The Prenatal Period

Development begins when the sperm fertilizes the ovum. The ovum travels to the uterus. Ten to fourteen days after fertilization, the ovum becomes implanted in the uterus and is known as the embryo for the next six weeks. It develops rapidly, and by the third week, the heart begins to beat. By the eighth week the face, arms, and legs are developed. The major internal organs have begun to form, the sex glands begin to function, and the nervous system is developing rapidly.

During the next seven months, the developing child is now called a fetus. During this time the hair, nails, and eyes develop and physical growth is rapid. By the seventh or eighth month, the fetus appears to be virtually fully formed. However, if born prematurely, the baby may still experience difficulties. Tiny air sacs (alveoli) in the lungs are not fully formed.

There is evidence that cognitive abilities develop during the prenatal period. In one study, the fetus could distinguish familiar and unfamiliar stories. Familiar stories were associated with decreased heart rate, which is thought to indicate increased attention.

B.   Prenatal Influences on Development: When Trouble Starts Early

Many environmental factors can interfere with prenatal growth. Such factors are known as teratogens. Since the blood supply of the mother and fetus come close together in the placenta, disease from the mother's blood can infect the child.

C.   Physical and Perceptual Development During Our Early Years

Physical growth is rapid during infancy -- they increase in body length by one-third during the first year. Newborns also possess a variety of simple reflexes at birth. These include: tracking a light with their eyes, sucking, and turning their head in the direction of a touch on the cheek. Table 8-1 in your text (p. 284) summarizes the major milestones of motor development. Keep in mind that these ages represent averages, not exact ages.

Newborns can learn through classical conditioning. However, for young infants, conditioning occurs most readily for stimuli that have survival value. A considerable body of evidence indicates that newborns demonstrate operant conditioning. Evidence also suggests that infants are capable of imitating the facial gestures of adults.

Because infants can't talk, it is necessary to use indirect methods to study their perceptual abilities. These methods include observing changes in heart rate, sucking responses, or the amount of time they spend gazing at stimuli. The rationale of this method is that if infants can detect differences between two stimuli, we may observe changes in their responses to the stimuli. The use of these methods has demonstrated that infants can distinguish between different colors, odors, and auditory stimuli. Classic research by Fantz has shown that six-month-old babies prefer patterned stimuli. This research also suggested that babies prefer the human face as opposed to all other tested stimuli.

Studies using the visual cliff show that infants as young as six months perceive depth. This test is limited by infants' ability to crawl. Studies using tests without this limitation have shown that three-month-old infants can perceive depth.

Questions:

8-1. What is the scope of developmental psychology? _____

_____

_____

_____

8-2. What are the characteristics of the prenatal period? _____

_____

_____

_____

8-3. What are the influences of environmental factors on prenatal development? _____

_____

_____

_____

8-4. What is the course of physical development in infancy and childhood? _____

_____

_____

_____

8-5. What kind of learning abilities do newborns have? _____

_____

_____

_____

8-6. What is the course of infant's perceptual development? _____

_____

_____

_____

II.   Basic Methods for Studying Human Development

The method that involves testing individuals on several occasions over a period of time is longitudinal research. There are advantages to this method. First, individual variations can be studied. Second, because the same persons are tested, it may be possible to draw conclusions about how specific events influence development. However, there are also disadvantages. There may be a loss of participants and this research is subject to practice effects. The method that involves testing different age groups only once is called cross-sectional research. There are several advantages to this method. It can be conducted more quickly than longitudinal research and it minimizes practice effects in that participants are tested only once. However, this method has disadvantages. For example, it is subject to cohort effects. This refers to the fact that differences correlated to age could influence the results, such as being born at different times, different life experiences and different cultural conditions.

An approach that maximizes the advantages of both of the above while minimizing their disadvantages is known as the longitudinal-sequential design. It involves studying several samples of people of different ages for a number of years. It allows for both longitudinal and cross-sectional comparisons in that it tests for each participant across time and also tests different age groups. For example, it can test for cohort effects by comparing persons born in different years with one another when they reach the same age.

Question:

8-7.   What are the advantages and disadvantages of the three basic methods for studying human

development? _____

_____

_____

_____

III.   Cognitive Development During Childhood: Changes in How We Know the External World...and Ourselves

A.   Piaget's Theory: An Overview

Piaget believed that children begin life with limited cognitive skills. He believed that cognitive development occurs in a series of stages that represent different ways of thinking and reasoning. Stage theorists assume that all persons move through a set series of stages, that they do so at certain ages, and that the order of progress is fixed. Many psychologists question this assumption.

Piaget believed that the mechanism responsible for cognitive development is adaptation. This process results in the development of mental representations of the world through interaction. Interactions with the world have two consequences. First, our experiences can be fit into existing schemes; this tendency is called assimilation. Second, interactions with the world can alter existing schemes; this tendency is called accommodation. The interplay between these two components of adaptation fosters cognitive development. Cognitive development results in progress through ever-more complex conceptions of the world around us.

According to Piaget, young children do not think or reason like adults. He proposes that children go through an orderly sequence of four major stages toward cognitive maturity. The first stage is the sensorimotor stage. In this stage, the infant knows the world only through motor activities and sensory impressions. They acquire the basic concept of cause and effect. But they have not learned to use symbols to represent objects, so they will act as if an object hidden from view no longer exists. Understanding that such objects do exist is called object permanence.

Between the ages of 18 to 24 months, children acquire the ability to form mental images of the world around them and begin to think in verbal symbols. This marks the beginning of the preoperational stage. Their thought is still immature in many ways. They are egocentric in that they have difficulty understanding that others may see the world differently from them. [However, this effect depends on how the question is asked.] They can also be fooled by appearance and believe that a dog mask on a cat makes it a dog. Their thought is also animistic in that they often attribute human feelings to inanimate objects. They also lack understanding of relational terms (e.g., "larger") and cannot arrange objects in order along some dimension (serialization). They lack the principle of conservation, which is the knowledge that an underlying dimension remains unchanged by minor shifts in appearance.

By age seven, most children can solve the problems of the previous stage and enter the period of concrete operations. During this stage, they understand that many physical changes can be undone by reversing the original actions or reversibility. They begin to make greater use of conceptual categories and begin to engage in logical thought.

At about age 12, most children enter the final stage of cognitive development known as formal operations. In this stage, the major features of adult thought emerge. In contrast to the concrete operational child who can think logically, the formal operational child can think abstractly. The formal operational child is capable of hypothetic-deductive reasoning in which a general theory is formulated and tested in problem-solving. A person in this stage can also assess the logical validity of verbal assertions even when these refer to possibilities rather than to events in the real world (i.e., propositional reasoning). It should be noted that although individuals in this stage have the capacity or ability for logical thought, there is no guarantee that such systematic reasoning will occur. In addition, older children and adolescents often fall prey to formal operational egocentrism in which they cling rigidly to the validity of their own personal viewpoints. Thought is limited by the amount of experience the individual has had in the world.

B.   Piaget's Theory: A Modern Assessment

Research focusing on Piaget's theory suggest that Piaget's theory is incorrect or in need of revision for three reasons. First, it suggests that he underestimated the cognitive abilities of infants and young children. For example, infants of 4.5 months appear to possess a rudimentary understanding of object permanence and three year olds show some understanding of the concept of conservation. Second, research suggests that development may not proceed through discrete stages and that these stages may not be discontinuous in nature. Rather, cognitive changes may be gradual. Finally, research suggests that Piaget downplayed the importance of language and social interactions. For example, Piaget believed that private speech was egocentric. Research supports Vygotsky's contention that private speech is not egocentric but represents their efforts to engage in self-guidance. Further, research supports Vygotsky's belief that social communication and social interaction with caregivers plays a central role in cognitive development.

C.   Cognitive Development: An Information-Processing Perspective

During the past 20 years, an information-processing perspective to cognitive development has been developed by psychologists who seek to understand how, and in what ways, children's capacity to process, store, retrieve, and actively manipulate information increases with age. According to this approach, children show increasing ability to notice subtle features of the external world and develop increasingly sophisticated cognitive frameworks or schemas.

Children show an increasing ability to focus their attention and block out distractions. Three to five percent of all children suffer from attention-deficient hyperactivity disorder (ADHD). It is four to five times more likely in males than females. Children who suffer from this disorder have normal intelligence but find it difficult to ignore irrelevant information and are unable to concentrate their attention on any task for more than a few minutes. It can be effectively treated with medication and therapy.

With maturity, children's memory improves in many ways. Improvements occur with respect to short-term and long-term memory. A key change associated with short-term memory is the increasing use of strategies for retaining information. Rehearsal and organizational strategies both improve as children mature. Children as young as three years appear to engage in efforts to improve their memories; and by eight years of age, they engage in simple forms of rehearsal. One key change associated with long-term memory involves expression of knowledge that pertains to specific areas of life and activity. This knowledge is called domain-specific knowledge. Another key change involves the acquisition of increasingly sophisticated scripts. This change helps children improve their episodic memory -- memory for events in their own lives.

Metacognition refers to an awareness and understanding of our own cognitive processes. With maturity, children develop an increasing awareness and understanding of their cognitive processes, which allows them to become increasingly capable of self-regulation. They can develop more sophisticated strategies for maximizing their own efficiency and for enhancing attention and memory. Further, they can monitor their own progress toward goals as well as remember and evaluate their own understanding.

D.   Moral Development: Reasoning About "Right" and "Wrong"

The issue of whether children and adults reason about moral issues in similar ways is a key question addressed by research on moral development. The most influential theory in this area was proposed by Kohlberg. He proposed that human beings move through three distinct levels of moral reasoning. Each level is divided into two separate phases. The method he uses to assess moral reasoning involves asking subjects to imagine moral dilemmas in which competing causes of action are possible. The subjects' explanation is the critical key to their stage of moral development.

In the preconventional level of moral development, morality is judged in terms of the consequences of actions. For example, actions that lead to punishment are viewed as unacceptable. Within Stage 1 of this level, known as the punishment and obedience orientation, children cannot grasp the existence of two points of view in a moral dilemma. As a result, they unquestioningly accept an authority's perspective as their own. In Stage 2 of this level of moral development, known as the naive hedonistic orientation, children judge morality in terms of what satisfies their own or others needs.

The second level is known as the conventional level. At this level, children judge morality in terms of what supports and preserves the social order. Stage 3 of moral development occurs within this level, known as the good boy - good girl orientation, and reflects moral judgments based on a desire to seek approval from the people they know by adhering to social norms. In Stage 4, known as the social-order-maintaining orientation, children extend judgments of morality to include the perspective of people they do not know. Thus, they believe that the law applies to everyone.

In adolescence or early adulthood, some people enter the postconventional or principles level. At this level, morality is judged by abstract principles or values. Stage 5 represents a values orientation in which individuals realize that laws can be inconsistent with the rights of individuals and can envision alternative laws. This stage is termed the social contract, legalistic orientation stage. In Stage 6, known as the universal ethical principle orientation, individuals believe that certain obligations and values transcend the laws of society at points in time. Morality is judged in terms of self-chosen ethical principles.

Evidence supports the suggestion that moral reasoning increases in complexity with age and that individuals pass through these stages. Few individuals reach the highest stage in Kohlberg's theory. However, development is more variable and less universal than Kohlberg assumed. Research indicates that children from cultures having little contact with formalized systems of government and law rarely reach Stage 4. Therefore, it may be the case that having contact with systems of government and law may lead to a higher scores on moral development tests. Consistent with this reasoning, kibbutz-reared Israelis who participated in the cooperative institutions of their society scored higher in moral development than Americans of comparable age. This research does suggest that Kohlberg's theory seems to be applicable to cultures other than Western ones stages of moral development increased with age in both cultures. However, cultural factors influenced the participants' responses. One conclusion is that moral development requires a consideration of universal principles and culture-based factors as well.

Some early studies suggested that men scored higher than females in moral reasoning. Girls attained Stage 3 but then progressed no further whereas boys moved into Stage 4, 5, and 6. This led to the belief that women's morality was based on concerns for interpersonal approval and men's morality was based on abstract principles. In response to this work, Gilligan proposed that Kohlberg's theory was sex-biased. Kohlberg used only males in his original work and morality was judged only on abstract reasoning about moral dilemmas. According to Gilligan, Kohlberg overlooked concern for others as is a key factor for women. In Gilligan's analysis, women move from concrete commitments to universal obligation. Women are not less complex than males but emphasize different aspects of this process. Research suggests that males and females do not focus on different aspects of moral dilemmas as postulated by Gilligan. Further, females score as high as males in moral reasoning on both hypothetical dilemmas and everyday moral problems. If anything, females tend to score higher in moral reasoning than males. These findings are counter to the early studies that suggested that females lag behind males in moral reasoning. Thus, contrary to initial findings, there is no evidence that men and women attain different levels of moral development.

Questions:

8-8. What are the general assumptions of Piaget's theory of cognitive development? _____

_____

_____

_____

8-9. What are the characteristics of the sensorimotor stage? _____

_____

_____

_____

8-10. What is the nature of a child's thought during the preoperational stage? _____

_____

_____

_____

8-11. Why does the stage of concrete operations mark a major turning point in cognitive development?

_____

_____

_____

8-12. What are the competencies of adolescents during the formal operational stage? _____

_____

_____

_____

8-13. Why do many psychologists believe that Piaget's theory is inaccurate or in need of revision?

_____

_____

_____

8-14. What are the major assumptions and major goals of the information-processing perspective of cognitive development? _____

_____

_____

_____

8-15. Do infants form mental representations of the external world? _____

_____

_____

_____

8-16. How does the attentional focus of younger children compare to that of older children? _____

_____

_____

_____

8-17. What are the consequences, possible causes, and treatment of ADHD? _____

_____

_____

_____

8-18. What are the ways in which memory improves with age? _____

_____

_____

_____

8-19. What is metacognition and why is it important? _____

_____

_____

_____

8-20. What are the major characteristics of Kohlberg's stages of moral development? _____

_____

_____

_____

8-21. What is the evidence concerning Kohlberg's theory? _____

_____

_____

_____

8-22. What is the status of the controversy concerning whether Kohlberg's theory is gender-biased?

_____

_____

_____

IV. Social and Emotional Development During Childhood: Forming Relationships With Others

A.   Emotional Development and Temperament

A crucial question in the area of emotional development concerns when infants begin to experience and demonstrate discrete emotions. Because infants cannot describe their feelings, efforts to answer this question focus on discrete facial expressions. Infants as young as two months old demonstrate social smiling in response to human faces and show laughter by three or four months. Many other emotions such as sadness, surprise, and anger appear quite early and are readily recognized by adults. Research indicates that emotional development and cognitive development occur simultaneously. Children also acquire increasing abilities to determine the emotional expressions of others and to regulate their own emotional reactions.

Stable individual differences in the quality or intensity of emotional responding is known as temperament. Infants do differ in their emotional style at birth. These differences have a powerful influence on infants' interactions with caregivers and can influence the course of social development. Children can be divided into three categories: easy, difficult, and slow-to-warm-up. Some aspects of temperament, like attentiveness, activity level, and irritability, appear to be quite stable. In one study the reactivity of a population of infants remained relatively stable into middle childhood. However, other studies suggest that extended stability in various aspects of temperament may only occur for persons who have relatively extreme scores on these measures. Differences in temperament appear to be influenced by both biological and environmental factors.

By age of six or seven months most infants show a strong bond or attachment to their caregivers. This may be partly due to classical and operant conditioning. However, learning based on conditioning may not be the most important foundation for strong bonds between infants and caregivers. Once formed, strong bonds persist even when (due to physical separation) the caregivers cannot provide reinforcement. An alternative account of attachment follows from ethological theory. From this view, infants are born with a set of behaviors that elicit parental care and attention. This increases the infant's chances of survival and produces strong reciprocal attachment bonds between the caregivers and the infant.

The strange situation test is used to study attachment in young children. Children are placed in a distressing environment and their reactions when their mother leaves and returns are monitored. There are four patterns of attachment: (1) secure attachment -- discomfort when the mother leaves the room, not comforted by a stranger, and seeks contact with mother when she returns; (2) avoidant attachment -- don't cry when mother leaves room and don't seek contact with her when she returns; (3) resistant attachment -- reject mother angrily when she returns after separation; and (4) disorganized attachment -- contradictory reactions to mother after separation.

Close physical contact with soft objects is an additional factor that plays an important role in attachment. Studies with monkeys have shown that the satisfaction of physical needs is not a sufficient condition for attachment. Harlow found that the need for contact comfort seems to be the important factor. Provisions of milk by a mother does not increase attachment. In other studies, he found that the presence of soft cloth mothers, but not wire mothers, was able to reduce fear of monkeys in the presence of strange objects. Having cloth mothers reject the baby monkeys by presenting various noxious stimuli did not alter the degree of attachment. There is some evidence that human babies also have a need for contact comfort.

B.   Gender Identity and Gender-Stereotyped Behavior

The knowledge that a child belongs to a specific sex is called gender identity. Evidence exists that this process beings early in life. By the age of two years, many children use gender labels appropriately. Between three and 1/2 and four and 1/2 years, children begin to understand that gender is stable over time.

According to the social learning view, gender identity is acquired through operant conditioning and observational learning.   Through observational learning, children gradually come to match their behaviors to the behaviors of same-sex individuals. This imitation is actively reinforced by adults. The gender schema theory suggests that children develop cognitive frameworks reflecting their society's beliefs about gender. Once established, gender schemas influence the processing of social information. In addition, children's self-concepts become linked to other attitudes and beliefs so that their own attitudes and behaviors are only seen as acceptable to the extent that they are consistent with the schemas.

Beliefs about the supposed characteristics of males and females are called gender-role stereotypes or beliefs. Understanding how society expects males and females to behave is called gender stereotyped behaviors.   Gender-stereotyped beliefs and behaviors are influenced by environmental and genetic factors.   For example, Maccoby has proposed that hormonal differences between boys and girls influence their style of play; boys show a rough, noisy style and girls show a calm, gentle style. Because of these style differences, children spend much more time interacting with same-sex peers.

Questions:

8-23. What is the course of children's emotional development? _____

_____

_____

_____

8-24. What are the individual differences that exist in temperament? _____

_____

_____

_____

8-25. What are the learning and ethological approaches to attachment? _____

_____

_____

_____

8-26. How is attachment measured? _____

_____

_____

_____

8-27. What are the characteristics of the four different patterns of attachment? _____

_____

_____

_____

8-28. How does daycare influence social development? _____

_____

_____

_____

8-29. What did Harlow's research teach us about the role of contact comfort in attachment?

_____

_____

_____

8-30. What is the father's role in child development? _____

_____

_____

_____

8-31. What are the two different views on the development of gender identity? _____

_____

_____

_____

8-32. What is the nature of gender stereotyped beliefs and behavior? _____

_____

_____

_____

V.   Adolescence: Between Child and Adult

Adolescence traditionally is thought to begin with the onset of puberty and end when individuals assume the responsibilities of adulthood. Adolescence is not a clearly defined developmental period in that it is culturally defined. Social factors play an important role in determining when adolescence begins.

A.   Physical Development During Adolescence

The beginning of adolescence is signaled by a sudden growth spurt. This occurs sooner for females than males. During puberty, the gonads or sex glands produce increased levels of sex hormones and the external sex organs assume their adult form. Females begin to menstruate, and males begin to produce sperm. These changes are referred to as primary sexual characteristics.

B.   Cognitive Development During Adolescence

According to Piaget, adolescents are in the stage of formal operations. Therefore, they can assess the logical validity of verbal statements and test theories they have generated (reason deductivity). However, their theories may be naive because of lack of experience and they tend to be egocentric -- assume that no other view but their own is correct. In addition, they tend to feel they are the focus of others' attention -- the imaginary audience. At the same time, they often feel that their feelings and thoughts are totally unique. This is referred to as the personal fable.

Adolescents engage in many high risk behaviors, such as reckless driving. A common explanation for this is that they do not perceive risks the same way adults do. However, recent evidence indicates that adolescents and adults do not differ in their perceptions of their own vulnerability. Adolescents may engage in high-risk behaviors for a variety of reasons. For example, the high-risk behaviors may be pleasurable or the adolescents may be reacting to social norms.

C.   Social and Emotional Development During Adolescence

Research confirms the common folklore that adolescents experience frequent and large swings in mood. Other widely accepted views about adolescent emotionality are not supported. For example, it is often assumed that adolescents experience great stress and unhappiness; rather, most teenagers report feeling quite happy and self-confident. Teenagers also report that they have good relationships with their parents. Being part of a social group is essential to the self-esteem and self-confidence of most adolescents. Friendship plays an important role in the personal identity of adolescents.

In contrast to Piaget's stage theory, Erikson's theory is primarily concerned with social development across the life-span. He contends that each stage of life is marked by a specific conflict or crisis. The first four occur during childhood. One takes place during adolescence. The final three take place during adulthood.

The first phase in Erikson's theory determines the development of trust in one's environment. The second centers around the development of self-confidence and involves resolving a crisis between autonomy vs. shame and doubt. The third, occurring in preschool years, involves the crisis of initiative vs. guilt. The fourth involves the crisis of competence versus inferiority.

Adolescents must integrate various roles into a consistent self-identity. Failure to do so results in role confusion. The social conflict associated with young adulthood involves the development of a sense of intimacy versus isolation. During middle adulthood, individuals are faced with a conflict that leads to either generativity or self-absorption. In the closing years of life, individuals ask whether their lives have had meaning and develop either a sense of integrity or despair.

To summarize, Erikson's eight stages of psychosocial development are:

1)   trust vs. mistrust
2)   autonomy vs. shame and doubt
3)   initiative vs. guilt
4)   industry vs. inferiority
5)   identity vs. role confusion
6)   intimacy vs. isolation
7)   generativity vs. self-absorption
8)   integrity vs. despair

D.   Adolescence in the 1990s: A Generation at Risk

There are many risks that face an adolescent in the 1990s. For example, many adolescents will live in a one-parent family -- since more than half of all marriages end in divorce. Many children live in dysfunctional families -- families that do not meet the needs of children and may do them serious harm. They can, for example, be harmed by exposure to drugs or by sexual abuse. Some experts feel that children are at greater risk for sexual abuse than was true in the past.

Although teenagers and parents agree on many issues, they often hold strikingly different views on sex. The size of this "generation gap" may have peaked during the early 1980s. Surveys indicate adolescents and college students have become more conservative about sexual behavior while parents have become less conservative. Conservative adolescent attitudes may reflect justified concerns with sexually transmitted diseases. Research on the aspect of adolescent sexuality involving teenage pregnancy is less encouraging. Teenage pregnancy is on the rise.

To minimize the risks associated with high risk environments, several steps can be taken. For example, families can use protective strategies. They can negotiate with authorities when their children get in trouble, place their children in safer niches like parochial schools, provide support against negative behaviors such as drug use, and seek out resources from various organizations such as health-care facilities. In addition, parents can work with teachers to establish support in the classroom and ties between home and school.

Questions:

8-33.   Why is it difficult to define the dividing line between childhood and adolescence? _____

_____

_____

_____

8-34.   What are the characteristics of physical development during adolescence? _____

_____

_____

_____

8-35.   What are the different views concerning whether adolescents do or do not think like adults?

_____

_____

_____

8-36.   What are the emotional changes and social development of the adolescent?   _____

_____

_____

_____

8-37.   What are Erikson's eight stages?   _____

_____

_____

_____

8-38   What are the potential risks that face an adolescent in the 1990s and the steps that can be taken to minimize some of the risks associated with high-risk environments?   _____

_____

_____

_____

VI.   Adulthood and Aging

A.   Adult Development: Internal Crisis or External Life Events?

Assuming an average life length, you will spend more than 70 percent of your life as an adult. Recent research has focused on the changes that occur during adulthood. The driving mechanism behind such change is a source of debate. Erikson's theory is an example of the crisis approach. As individuals grow older, individuals are assumed to confront new combinations of biological drives and societal demands. The drives reflect growth and physical change, while the societal demands reflect the expectations and requirements of society for individuals at different stages of life. The three crises that face individuals during adulthood are: intimacy vs. isolation, generativity vs. self-absorption, integrity vs. despair. The way in which we deal with these crises determine the course of our adult lives. All human beings are assumed to pass through these sequences in a fixed manner.

In contrast to the internal crises approach, the life events model assumes that development does not occur in accordance with a built-in biological clock. Rather, development is tied to a social clock. This model divides the social events that shape development into two categories. Normative events are expected life events and include events such as graduation, marriage, and parenthood. Non-normative events are unexpected life events and include such events as divorce, accidents, and death. The timing of such events is important.

B.   Physical Change During Our Adult Years

Physical changes that occur during adulthood are a reflection of the lifestyles individuals adopt as well as genetically-determined biological clocks. Aging, like physical growth, is a continuous process that begins early in life. This process proceeds slowly at first, but then proceeds rapidly in later decades. Muscular strength, sensory acuity, heart action and output are at the peak during the mid-twenties. These biological systems decline very slowly through the mid-thirties.

Most people are aware of physical changes in the strength and vigor of several organ systems and changes in their body shape and skin by the time they are in their 40s. The climacteric is a period of several years during which the functioning of the reproductive system and aspects of sexual activity change greatly. Sexual activity tends to decrease for both sexes in their late 40s or early 50s. Women experience menopause, which involves hormonal changes, cessation of menstruation and infertility. In the past, this was considered to be a stressful period for women; now research suggests that many women feel better after menopause. Males do not experience a process that corresponds to menopause. However, levels of testosterone and sperm counts do decline with age.

While some physical decline is inevitable during middle adulthood, the rate and magnitude of decline is strongly influenced by individuals' lifestyles. Evidence suggests that factors such as exercise, nutrition, and stress management may be better predictors of health and vigor than age.

Carefully conducted interviews indicated that women from different cultures have different experiences during menopause. This research suggests that the effects of menopause are strongly influenced by cultural factors -- biology is only part of the picture.

It is important to distinguish between two kinds of aging. Changes produced by increasing age per se are part of primary aging. Changes that can be traced to disease, disuse, or abuse of our bodies are part of secondary aging. Our physical state during later life is more under our own control than many have thought. However, aging does produce important physical changes. Sensory abilities such as visual acuity decline with age. Although there are large individual differences, there is also a slowing in reflexes.

C.   Cognitive Change During Adulthood

There is reason to expect that cognitive abilities might increase with age. Practice and a greater knowledge base might be expected to enhance cognitive performance. Research suggests that the short-term memory of older adults is as good as that of younger adults, as long as the information does not need to be processed. For example, anagram-solving abilities appear to decline with age. Young adults seem to have better long-term memories, but not better recognition memory. The long-term memory advantage of younger adults appears to disappear when older adults are expert in the area under investigation.

With respect to meaningful information, older adults often perform as well as younger adults. For example, younger adults outperformed older adults in terms of incidental memory (memory for material that one does not intend to remember), but not with respect to intentional memory. Prospective memory -- remembering to perform various actions -- does decline with age. However, this does not appear to be true for adults with high verbal ability.

Research suggests that age-related declines in memory may stem, in part, from the impact of stereotypes and expectations. It is also the case that research should take into account the time of day testing is conducted. With age, adults tend to shift more and more toward being "morning" persons. Therefore, the memory of older adults may be better in the morning than afternoon.

Young persons in their twenties and thirties outperform middle-aged and older adults on problem-solving tasks for abstract problems unrelated to everyday life. This is not true for practical problems.

Psychologists believed that intelligence increases into early adulthood, remains stable through the 30s, and then begins to decline as early as the 40s. However, this belief was based on cross-sectional research. Recent longitudinal research on standardized intelligence tests indicate that many intellectual abilities seem to remain stable across the entire lifespan. However, these tests did not capture the difference between crystallized and fluid intelligence. Fluid intelligence appears to increase into the early twenties and then gradually decline whereas crystallized intelligence tends to increase across the lifespan. Fluid intelligence involves the ability to form concepts, reason, and identify similarities, whereas crystallized intelligence involves drawing from previously learned information.

Research using standard tasks indicates that creativity declines with age. The age at which peak creativity occurs in a career varies greatly from one field to another. In some fields, peak creativity tends to occur when persons are in their 40s or 50s.

D.   Social Change in Adulthood: Tasks and Stages of Adult Life

Levinson suggests that there are four major eras of life, each separated by a transition period. The first transition occurs between the preadult era and early adulthood. This transition involves establishing one's independence. Once this transition is complete, individuals enter early adulthood. The two key components of their life structure are the dream and mentor. At about age 30, Levinson suggests people experience the "age 30 transition." At this point, people realize they are nearing the time at which they will have too much invested in their present life course to change and they reappraise their initial choices. This is followed by a period in which individuals stick to their existing life structures.

After the closing years of early adulthood (around 40-45), individuals move into a potentially turbulent transitional period called the mid-life transition. At this time, individuals must come to terms with their mortality and come to view themselves as part of the older generation. This realization leads to a period of emotional turmoil and leads people to review their lives up to this point and reexamine their possibilities. A new life structure is formed which takes account of the individual's new position in life as a middle-aged person. Life structures are often modified again between the ages of 50 and 55. A more dramatic transition occurs between the ages of 60 and 65 -- at the close of the middle years and the start of late adulthood. During this late adult transition, individuals come to terms with their impending retirement and the leisure activities this will bring. All of these transitions involve a series of changes in the individual's life structure or cognitive framework concerning the nature and meaning of his/her life.

Critics of Levinson's theory argue that it was based on a small and restricted sample. There is also debate about whether it applies to women as well as men. Therefore, it should be viewed as an interesting but unverified theory.

E.   Crisis of Adult Life

In contrast to Levinson's stage model, other psychologists focus on the impact of major life events. For example, divorce and unemployment can be viewed as two major crises of adult life. This approach focuses on how major crises affect our development.

Divorced persons experience anger, depression, and disequilibrium. Research has identified many factors associated with couples who remain happily married. For example, happily married couples agree with their spouse on many important issues, are committed to the relationship, and engage in a high level of positive communication. In contrast, unhappy married couples often engage in a negative pattern of communication. Divorced couples are bored in the relationship and report that their spouse no longer satisfies their needs. Additional factors associated with divorce include low income, unrealistic expectations, a brief courtship, and pregnancy at the time of marriage. Recent work indicates that genetic factors may also play a role in divorce. This unexpected finding suggests that individuals from divorced families may inherit chracteristics that make it hard for them to maintain long-term relationships.

Unemployment is an increasingly common experience. Unemployed individuals reported lower self-esteem, greater depression, more negative affect and poorer personal health than those who are employed. This is a crisis in life that can threaten both physical and psychological health.

F.   Gender and the Adult Years: How Males and Females Differ

There are important differences between genders in adult development. For example, all of the men studied by Levinson possessed a dream -- a vision of future accomplishments. The majority of females formed a split dream, giving equal attention to careers and relationships. A study of women indicated that employed women evidenced mastery and pleasure which are aspects of well-being. Unemployed married women without children scored lowest on mastery and pleasure.

It seems clear that men and women do experience somewhat different patterns of change during adulthood. These differences should be taken into account in further studies of adult development.

Questions:

8-39.   What are the internal crisis and life-event models of adult development? _____

_____

_____

_____

8-40.   According to the crisis approach, what are the three major crises that are faced during adulthood? _____

_____

_____

_____

8-41.   What are the major life events that are thought to affect the course of adult development?

_____

_____

_____

8-42.   What are the physical changes that occur during early adulthood? _____

_____

_____

_____

8-43. What are the physical changes that occur during mid-life, and what are the cultural influences on menopause? _____

_____

_____

_____

8-44. What are the physical changes that occur in later life, and what are primary and secondary aging factors? _____

_____

_____

_____

8-45. What is the influence of aging on memory? _____

_____

_____

_____

8-46. How do problem-solving abilities change with age? _____

_____

_____

_____

8-47. How is intelligence influenced by age? _____

_____

_____

_____

8-48. How are wisdom and creativity influenced by age? _____

_____

_____

_____

8-49. How does Levinson's stage theory address adult change? _____

_____

_____

_____

8-50.   What are the similaritires and differences in male and female development? _____

_____

_____

_____

VII.   Aging and Death: The End of Life

A.   Theories of Aging: Contrasting Views About Why We Grow Old

One question concerning the end of life centers around the causes of aging. The wear-and-tear view suggests that we grow old because of the small highly charged atoms. These atoms are called free radicals and are very unstable. They react violently with other chemical compounds producing damage. When the damage affects DNA, they interfere with cell maintenance and repair. Indirect evidence for this view comes from persons who expose their bodies to harmful environmental conditions. These persons often show premature signs of aging.

According to genetic programming theories, built-in biological clocks regulate the aging process by regulating the number of times cells can reproduce. Once reached, no further cell divisions can occur. This produces biological decline. Another genetic theory, gene mutation theory, suggests that when genetic mutations reach high enough levels, death results. Support comes from evidence suggesting that certain cells only divide a certain number of times and environmental conditions seem unable to alter this number. It is also the case that members of all species do not live more than a specified period of time under optimal conditions.

The best conclusion concerning the aging process is that aging is the result of several different mechanisms and results from a complex interplay between environmental and genetic factors.

B.   Meeting Death: Facing the End of Life

Defining death is complex. There are several different kinds of death: physiological death, brain death, cerebral death, and social death. Physiological death occurs when all life sustaining physical processes cease. A total absence of brain activity for at least 10 minutes defines brain death. Cerebral death is defined by the lack of activity in the cerebral cortex. Social death refers to the process of giving-up our relationships with the deceased. There are a number of complex ethical issues that stem from the question of whether individuals have the right to die when they choose.

Kübler-Ross conducted detailed interviews with terminally ill persons and concluded that they pass through a series of five distinct stages in their reactions to impending death. The first is denial. The second is anger over being singled out. The third is bargaining followed by a stage of depression. Many persons move from this to a final reaction of acceptance in which they face death with calm and dignity. Evidence suggests that all people do not move through these stages.

C.   Bereavement: Mounrning the Death of Loved Ones

A bereaved person mourns the loss of a loved one. The results of research on bereavement indicate that most persons experience shock followed by protest and yearning. A third stage is disorganization and despair. For most persons this is followed by detachment, reorganization, and recovery. After a prolonged period of mourning, most people recover and are able to go on with their lives.

Questions:

8-51.   What are the contrasting views on why we grow old? _____

_____

_____

_____

8-52.   What are the stages in Kübler-Ross's stages in the dying process? _____

_____

_____

_____

8-53.   What are the stages that follow the loss of a loved one? _____

_____

_____

_____

VIII. Making Psychology Part of Your Life: Preparing for Tomorrow's Job Market Today

The job market is uncertain, and it is wise to take all the steps you can in order to prepare for your future. Baron offers several steps that may be helpful. These are:

1)   choose a field with a future
2)   focus on small and medium-sized companies
3)   be ready to work for a foreign company
4)   consider part-time or contract work as a way to get started

Question:

8-54.   Discuss the ways you can increase your chances for success in the job market. _____

_____

_____

_____

_____

_____

MAKING PSYCHOLOGY PART OF YOUR LIFE: Key Terms and Concepts

Knowing the important concepts and key terms contained in this chapter is a very important part of mastering the material. We have presented a sample of these concepts below. Define each concept and check your definition with that presented at the end of this chapter. It will also be beneficial for you to think of an example of each concept. Whenever possible, use your own personal experience to provide an example of each term below.

8-1.   **Accommodation**: _____

Example: _____

8-2.   **Adaptation**: _____

Example: _____

8-3.   **Adolescence**: _____

8-4.   **Adolescent Invulnerability**: _____

Example: _____

8-5.   **Assimilation**: _____

Example: _____

8-6.   **Attachment**: _____

Example: _____

8-7.   **Attention-Deficit Hyperactivity Disorder**: _____

8-8.   **Avoidant Attachment**: _____

Example: _____

8-9.   **Bereavement**: _____

Example: _____

8-10.   **Climacteric**: _____

8-11.   **Cognitive Development**: _____

8-12.   **Cohort Effects**: _____

   Example: _____

8-13.   **Concrete Operations**: _____

   Example: _____

8-14.   **Conservation**: _____

   Example: _____

8-15.   **Conventional Level (Morality)**: _____

   Example: _____

8-16.   **Developmental Psychology**: _____

8-17.   **Disorganized or Disoriented Attachment**: _____

   Example: _____

8-18.   **Dysfunctional Families**: _____

8-19.   **Egocentrism**: _____

   Example: _____

8-20.   **Embryo**: _____

8-21.   **Ethological Theory (of attachment)**: _____

8-22.   **Fetus**: _____

8-23.   **Formal Operations (Stage of)**: _____

   Example: _____

8-24.   **Gender**: _____

8-25.   **Gender Constancy**: _____

Example: _____

8-26.   **Gender Roles**: _____

Example: _____

8-27.   **Gender Schema Theory**: _____

8-28.   **Genetic Theories of Aging**: _____

8-29.   **Hypothetico-Deductive Reasoning**: _____

Example: _____

8-30.   **Information-Processing Perspective**: _____

8-31.   **Life Structure**: _____

Example: _____

8-32.   **Longitudinal Research**: _____

Example: _____

8-33.   **Longitudinal-Sequential Design**: _____

Example: _____

8-34.   **Make-Believe Play**: _____

Example: _____

8-35.   **Menopause**: _____

8-36.   **Metacognition**: _____

Example: _____

8-37.   **Moral Development**: _____

　　　　Example: _____

8-38.   **Physical Growth and Development**: _____

8-39.   **Postconventional Level**: _____

　　　　Example: _____

8-40.   **Preconventional Level**: _____

　　　　Example: _____

8-41.   **Preoperational Stage**: _____

　　　　Example: _____

8-42.   **Primary Aging**: _____

8-43.   **Private Speech**: _____

　　　　Example: _____

8-44.   **Resistant Attachment**: _____

　　　　Example: _____

8-45.   **Scripts**: _____

　　　　Example: _____

8-46.   **Secondary Aging**: _____

8-47.   **Secure Attachment**: _____

　　　　Example: _____

8-48.   **Sensorimotor Stage**: _____

　　　　Example: _____

8-49.   **Sexual Abuse**: _____

8-50.   **Social and Emotional Development**: _____

8-51.   **Stage Theory**: _____

Example: _____

8-52.   **Strange Situation**: _____

Example: _____

8-53.   **Teratogens**: _____

Example: _____

8-54.   **Wear-and-Tear Theories of Aging**: _____

CHALLENGE: Develop Your Critical Thinking Skills

<u>Going Beyond Definitions</u>

A critical thinker is able to go beyond definition terms and is able to recognize situations where a concept is applicable. The ability to extend basic definitions to more complex applications is a sign of true understanding. Stretch your skills in "going beyond definitions" in the following exercises. Check your answers with those that we suggested at the end of this section.

8-1.   Carrie is babysitting Johnny for the very first time. She is nervous because he is 4-months-old. He begins to cry and she attempts to distract him by playing a game. She holds a stuffed bunny in front of him and then hides it beneath a blanket. Johnny shows no interest in this game. According to Piaget, why would this be the case?

_____

_____

8-2.   Given the information that Sam has read about the amount of sugar children consume, he is trying to restrict the sugar in his 4-year-old's diet. But Gary is unhappy about this and insists on having two cookies. Given Sam's knowledge about Piaget's stages of development, he breaks a cookie in half and gives the two halves to Gary. Gary is now content. Why?

_____

_____

8-3.   Susie does poorly on her biology exam. Of course, she is disappointed, but thinks to herself, "Next time, I need to concentrate on examples of concepts." What cognitive skill has Susie acquired?

_____

_____

8-4.   Jessica is involved in the anti-nuclear power movement. She argues with her parents that blocking the entrance to a nuclear power plant is justified by saying, "I know it is against the law to trespass -- but it is justified. Doing this will help save our planet and life is more important than property." What stage of moral development is she in, according to Kohlberg?

_____

_____

Discussion of Critical Thinking Challenge

8-1.   Johnny shows no interest in this game because he is in the early part of the sensorimotor stage of development. In this stage, he lacks the concept of object permanence. When the bunny disappears…it is truly "out of sight - - out of mind."

8-2.   Gary is in the preoperational stage of development and lacks, according to Piaget, the ability to <u>conserve</u>. Changing the outward appearance of the cookie (from 1 cookie to 2) is interpreted as obtaining more cookies; he does not realize that the physical attributes of the cookie remains unchanged in spite of its outward appearance.

8-3.   Metacognition: Awareness and understanding of our own cognitive processes.

8-4.   The postconventional stage. In this stage, morality is judged in terms of abstract principles and values, rather than existing law or rules of society. Specifically, she would be at Stage 5 within this level, known as the social contract, legalistic orientation.

YOUR NOTES:

CHALLENGE: Making Psychology Part of Your Life

<u>Stages of Life</u>

Your text discusses one of the most famous theories of life span development -- that of Erik Erikson. As you recall, Erikson proposed that development proceeds through a series of distinct stages, each separated by a specific crisis. How does this view relate to your life experiences?

We have listed these stages below. For each stage that you have experienced, write a brief discussion of the societal demands and feelings you experienced during that time. Did you experience the type of crisis Erikson suggests? For those stages that you have not yet reached, speculate on your probable feelings and reactions. How will you respond to the challenges of this developmental period?

<u>Crisis/Phase</u>

Trust vs. Mistrust: _____

_____

_____

Autonomy vs. Shame and Doubt: _____

_____

_____

Initiative vs. Guilt: _____

_____

_____

Industry vs. Inferiority: _____

_____

_____

Identity vs. Role Confusion: _____

_____

_____

Intimacy vs. Isolation: _____

_____

_____

Generativity vs. Self-Absorption: _____

_____

_____

Integrity vs. Despair: _____

_____

_____

YOUR NOTES:

CHALLENGE: Review Your Comprehensive Knowledge

SAMPLE TEST QUESTIONS

Once you have worked through the preceding sections, you should be ready for a comprehensive self-test. You can check your answers with those at the end of this section. An additional practice test is given in the supplementary section at the end of this study guide.

8-1.   The face, arms, and legs are present by the _____ week of prenatal development.
   a.   third
   b.   fourth
   c.   sixth
   d.   eighth

8-2.   The method of studying development that provides the clearest picture of the course of human development is the:
   a.   cross-sectional approach.
   b.   longitudinal approach.
   c.   longitudinal-sequential design.
   d.   experimental design.

8-3.   According to Piaget, cognitive development involves interplay between _____ and _____.
   a.   sensation and cognition
   b.   the id and the ego
   c.   assimilation and accommodation
   d.   emotion and motivation

8-4.   The morality of behavior is judged in terms of consequences at the _____ level of morality.
   a.   preconventional
   b.   conventional
   c.   postconventional
   d.   abstract

8-5.   What are psychologists measuring when they use the strange situation test?
   a.   cognitive development
   b.   conservation
   c.   the appearance-reality distinction
   d.   attachment to the mother

8-6.   Fitting experience into existing schema is known as:
   a.   preoperation.
   b.   adaptation.
   c.   accommodation.
   d.   assimilation.

8-7.   Environmental factors that interfere with prenatal growth are called:
   a.   teratogens.
   b.   health hazards.
   c.   cohort effects.
   d.   poisons.

8-8.   The information-processing perspective of cognitive development _____:
   a.   seeks to map out the stages of development.
   b.   seeks to understand how, and in what ways, children's capacity to process, store, retrieve, and actively manipulate information changes with age.
   c.   proposes that private speech is egocentric.
   d.   proposes that private speech represents attempts in social communication.

8-9.   The proposal that changes in the ability of children to perform cognitive tasks result from changes in their ability to block out distractors and focus attention is most consistent with _____ view of development.
   a.   Piaget's
   b.   Vygotsky's
   c.   the psychodynamic
   d.   the information processing

8-10.   The proposal that changes in the ability of children to perform cognitive tasks represent different stages of cognitive development is most consistent with _____ view of development.
a.   Piaget's   c.   Kohlberg's
b.   Vygotsky's   d.   the information processing

8-11.   According to Erikson's theory, the most important internal crisis faced by adolescents concerns resolving:
a.   competence vs. inferiority.   c.   sexuality vs. sexual confusion.
b.   initiative vs. guilt.   d.   identity vs. role confusion.

8-12.   In the terminology of life events models of adult development, graduation from school would be an example of:
a.   an internal crisis.   c.   a non-normative event.
b.   a normative event.   d.   a social clock.

8-13.   Crisis theories view adult development as:
a.   the resolution of a series of internal conflicts.
b.   the responses of individuals to important life events.
c.   the influence of social clocks.
d.   all of the above

8-14.   Physical changes that are due to increased age per se are referred to as:
a.   primary aging.   c.   sensory aging.
b.   secondary aging.   d.   genetic aging.

8-15.   The importance of free radicals in aging is emphasized by which of the following theories of aging?
a.   wear-and-tear theories   c.   crisis theories
b.   genetic programming theories   d.   life events theories

8-16.   According to Kübler-Ross, the first stage of the dying process is:
a.   denial.   c.   depression.
b.   anger.   d.   bargaining.

8-17.   Research supports all but one of the following statements about social and emotional development during adolescence. Identify the incorrect statement.
a.   Adolescents generally experience large swings in mood.
b.   Adolescents generally report that they have poor relationships with their parents.
c.   Adolescents generally report feeling happy.
d.   Adolescents generally report feeling self-confident.

8-18.   Which of the following is not true of cognitive change during adulthood?
a.   Prospective memory declines with age.
b.   The memory of older adults was equal to that of younger adults in terms of incidental memory.
c.   With age, adults tend to shift more and more toward being morning persons.
d.   With respect to relatively meaningless information, older adults often perform better than younger adults.

8-19.   For Levinson, the two key components of a person's life in early adulthood are dream and:
a.   transition.   c.   crisis.
b.   mentor.   d.   trust.

8-20.   Research suggesting that intelligence declines with age was based on the _____ research model.
a.   cross-sectional   c.   longitudinal-sequential
b.   longitudinal   d.   experimental

Answers and Feedback for Sample Test Questions:

8-1.   D   By the 8th week of prenatal development, the face, arms, and legs are developed. (p. 282)

8-2.   C   The longitudinal-sequential research design provides the clearest view of development because it allows us to sample people of different ages and track their development over a number of years. (p. 287)

8-3.   C   Piaget believed that development results from the interplay between assimilation (fitting experience into existing schemas) and accommodation (altering existing schemas as a result of experience). These two processes are part of the adaptation mechanism. (p. 288)

8-4.   A   In Kohlberg's theory, the preconventional stage of moral development is characterized by judging the morality of a behavior in terms of its consequences. (p. 294)

8-5.   D   The strange situation test is used to study attachment. It involves placing children in a distressing environment and monitoring their reactions to their mother leaving and returning. (p. 301)

8-6.   D   Assimilation is the process in which we fit experience into existing schemas. (p. 288)

8-7.   A   Teratogens are environmental factors that interfere with prenatal development. (p. 283)

8-8.   B   The information processing view of development seeks to understand how children's information processing abilities change with age. (p. 292)

8-9.   D   Information processing views of development explain change by analyzing how cognitive processes, such as attention, vary as a function of age. See also 8-17 above. (p. 292)

8-10.   A   Piaget proposed a stage view of cognitive development. (p. 288)

8-11.   D   In Erikson's theory, adolescence involves a crisis in which we must resolve role confusion vs. identity. (p. 308)

8-12.   B   Normative events are expected life events. Graduation fits in this category. (p. 314)

8-13.   A   Internal crisis models propose that the way we resolve a series of internal conflicts determines the course of our adult lives. (p. 314)

8-14.   A   Primary aging refers to physical changes due to age per se. (p. 316)

8-15.   A   Free radicals are biological factors associated with aging in wear-and-tear theories. (p. 323)

8-16.   A   Denial is the first stage of dying in Kübler-Ross's theory. (p. 324)

8-17.   B   In contrast to our pre-conceptions, most adolescents report good relationships with their parents. (p. 307)

8-18.   B   Younger adults perform better than older adults on recall of relatively meaningless information. (p. 317)

8-19.   B   According to Levinson, mentors and dreams are key components of our early adulthood. (p. 319)

8-20.   A   Cross-sectional research suggested that intelligence declined with age. This conclusion is flawed by the fact that persons of different ages have different life experiences, which affects their measured IQs. (p. 317)

Glossary of difficult words and expressions	Definition
A backdrop for life	the background or context of one's life
Amicable	friendly; easy to get along with
Bitterly	in an intense or harsh way
Bleak	not good
Cessation of	termination of; end of
"Chasm"	wide difference of feelings or interests; a gap that separates
Chatted	informal talk
Countless	numerous; many
Cuddling	hugging tenderly
Deterred	held back; not allowed to; stopped
Disconcerting	upsetting
Distressed	suffering
Doomed	condemned
Drawback	disdvantage; negative part
Dutiful	showing respect and obedience
Fixated	to focus one's eyes or attention on
Fond farewell	be full of love; take pleasure in
Foster	encourage
Frail	weak; fragile; easily damaged
Frazzled	become exhausted physically or emotionally
Gazing	looking steadily, intently
Go astray	go out of, off the right path
Grasp of	having an understanding of
Harsh	rough and disagreeable
Hinge on	depend on
Hinder	prevent, make more difficult
"Hobgoblin of little minds"	something that should not be attended to
Hurdles	obstacles; things that block one's way
Indulge	give way to and satisfy
Intrusive	to put or force inappropriately

Glossary of difficult words and expressions	Definition
It merits...	it deserves
Milestones	important breakthrough
Mystified	puzzled mentally; bewildered
Naive	not sophisticated; unknowledgeable
Negative affect	negative feelings
Niches for...	suitable or fitting position
Novel	new; never thought of previously
Onset	start; the beginning
Outbursts	bursting out of steam, anger, laughter
Out-of-wedlock	outside marriage
Outside the realm	outside the limits; not applicable
Overt	shown openly
Painful bouts	painful period of something
Peak levels	highest point; the top
Perils	serious dangers
Prognosis	prediction of the probable cause and outcome of a disease
Protégé	person to whom another gives protection or help
Protrusions	sticking out
Preach	to proclaim or advocate
"Pulling the plug"	disconnecting; unplugging; stopping
Ranging in	varying in
Realm of	boundaries of; applies to
Reckless	not thinking or caring about the consequences
Rudimentary	elementary
Rut	a fixed and boring way of living so that it becomes difficult to change
Scraps of	pieces of
Scrutiny	a close, careful examination
Shallow	lacking physical depth; not deep
Siblings	brother or sister
Spurring	edging on; promoting
Struck by	impressed by

Glossary of difficult words and expressions	Definition
Sweeping theories	having wide-ranging influence or effects
Swings in mood	change sin mood that vary dramatically
Tiny speck	small spot or mark
Transcend	pass beyond the limits of
Unruly	not easily controlled; naughty
Upbeat	happy; cheerful
Wary	in the habit of being careful about possible danger or trouble
Wide array	wide variety; a lot of choices

CHAPTER 9
MOTIVATION AND EMOTION

OUTLINE: Develop a Study Plan

Use this outline to help you grasp the organizational structure of the chapter contents. The learning objectives (LOs) for each section are included. Use them as tools for developing your study plan. Space has been provided for you to write any notes or questions that come to mind as you begin your exploration into this material.

Heading:	Learning Objective:	Your Notes:
I. Motivation: The Activation and Persistence of Behavior	**L.O. 9.1:** Discuss how the concept of motivation is useful in explaining behavior.	
A. Theories of Motivation: Diverse Views of a Complex Process	**L.O. 9.2:** Describe the drive theory of motivation.	
	L.O. 9.3: Discuss how and why expectancy theory takes a cognitive approach to motivation.	
	L.O. 9.4: Survey Maslow's hierarchy of needs.	
B. Hunger: Regulating Our Caloric Intake	**L.O. 9.5:** Describe the factors involved in the regulation of eating, including the factors that may lead to anorexia nervosa and bulimia.	
C. Sexual Motivation: The Most Intimate Motive	**L.O. 9.6:** Describe the relationships between hormones and sexual behavior.	
	L.O. 9.7: Survey the basic phases of human sexual behavior and list the factors that are thought to stimulate sexual arousal.	
	L.O. 9.8: Be able to explain reasons why there may be gender differences in sexual jealousy.	
	L.O. 9.9: Be able to discuss the various views on what determines or influences sexual preferences.	
D. Aggressive Motivation: The Most Dangerous Motive	**L.O. 9.10:** Compare and contrast the views of the roots of aggression.	

Heading:	Learning Objective:	Your Notes:
E. Achievement and Power: Two Complex Human Motives	L.O. 9.11: Discuss individual differences in achievement motivation and how they are measured.	
F. Intrinsic Motivation: How (Sometimes) To Turn Play Into Work	L.O. 9.12: Discuss the research findings concerning intrinsic motivation.	
II. Emotions: Their Nature, Expression, and Impact		
A. The Nature of Emotions: Some Contrasting Views	L.O. 9.13: Compare and contrast the Cannon-Bard and James-Lange theories of emotion.	
	L.O. 9.14: Explain Schacter and Singer's two-factor theory.	
	L.O. 9.15: Discuss the assumptions of opponent-process theory.	
B. The Physiology of Emotion	L.O. 9.16: Provide a survey of the physiology of emotion and how emotion is communicated through external expressions.	
C. The External Expression of Emotion: Outward Signs of Inner Feelings		
D. Emotion and Cognition: How Feelings Shape Thoughts and Thoughts Shape Feelings	L.O. 9.17: Discus the relationships that exist between emotion and cognition.	
III. Making Psychology Part of Your Life -- Getting Motivated: Some Practical Techniques	L.O. 9.18: Be able to apply your knowledge of this material to your motivational levels.	

SURVEY AND QUESTION

This section presents the major topics and ideas from the chapter. Use it as a tool for seeing how the components of the chapter fit together. At the end of each major topic, we have asked you a question that relates to the major learning objectives. If you can answer these questions, you have taken a major step toward mastering this material.

I.   Motivation: The Activation and Persistence of Behavior

Motivation refers to internal processes. These serve to activate, guide, and maintain our behavior. In satisfying various motives, we often experience emotion. Emotion consists of physiological responses, subjective cognitive states, and expressive reactions. Emotions often influence motivation.

Motives are internal processes that cannot be readily observed. Motives are often assumed to be a cause for behavior, especially when the cause of a particular behavior cannot be readily discerned in the immediate context.

A.   Theories of Motivation

Before using motivation as an explanation for many kinds of behavior, psychologists used instincts as explanatory concepts. Instincts are innate patterns of behavior that are universal in a species. They are independent of experience and are elicited by specific stimuli. A problem with the use of instincts is that they are often used in a circular way. That is, they are inferred from observations of behavior and then used to explain the occurrence of the same behavior.

Drive theory is a motivational account of behavior. It assumes that when our biological needs are not satisfied, a state of deprivation exists. This state is unpleasant. People are pushed to restore a balanced state (homeostasis) and reduce unpleasant states of arousal. Actions that satisfy these drives tend to be repeated. Actions that do not satisfy drives tend not to be repeated. One problem with this theory is that people often tend to increase rather than decrease various drives.

Arousal theory suggests that people seek an optimal level of arousal -- a level that is best suited to personal characteristics and the activity being performed. Although there is at least indirect support for arousal theory, there are limitations associated with this view. It is difficult to determine in advance what level of arousal will be optimal for a given task and for a given individual.

Expectancy theory assumes that our expectation of obtaining important outcomes or goals is the major factor underlying our motivation. For this approach, people are not pushed by inner urges but are pulled by expectations of obtaining desired outcomes or incentives.

Maslow proposes that motives exist in a hierarchy. The ones at the bottom must be satisfied first. Deficiency needs include physiological, safety, and social needs. Growth needs include self-actualization and esteem needs. Research on this view is mixed. Some studies suggest that growth needs come into play only after deficiency needs have been satisfied. However, other studies indicate that people sometimes seek higher-order needs, even when deficiency needs have not been satisfied. Furthermore, several needs may be active at once. Maslow's needs hierarchy theory may be best viewed as an interesting, but largely unverified framework.

B.   Hunger: Regulating Our Caloric Intake

Hunger motivation is the urge to obtain and consume food. It tends to take precedence over all other things. Mechanisms that regulate body weight and hunger contain special detectors that respond to levels of glucose, protein, and liquids. Hunger is also influenced by the sight, smell, and taste of food. In addition, it is affected by the feedback produced by chewing and swallowing. Further, hunger is influenced by learning and experience, as well as cognitive factors.

Consumers spend huge sums of money on weight-loss programs and products. Two important motives for slimness are the desire to be attractive to others and the desire to protect our health. Obesity has been linked to high blood pressure, arthritis, and diabetes. Several factors have been proposed for why people are overweight. First, overweight persons may have become classically conditioned to eat. Second, overweight persons may eat more when under stress. Third, genetic factors may influence eating; overweight persons may have a low basal metabolic rate. This refers to the number of calories required at rest within a given period of time. Fourth, overweight persons may respond more strongly to external cues relating to food.

People who starve themselves until they loose dangerous amounts of weight have a condition known as anorexia nervosa. People who engage in repeated cycles of binge eating, followed by purging (through vomiting or laxatives) have a condition known as bulimia. These conditions occur primarily among females and seem to reflect a dissatisfaction with body image. Bulimics seem to be overly preoccupied with their body image and are low in social self-confidence.

C.   Sexual Motivation: The Most Intimate Motive

Sexual motivation is a strong force in human behavior. In most species (other than humans), sexual hormones exert activational effects; sexual behavior does not occur or takes place with a low frequency in the absence of sexual hormones. Although sexual hormones play a role with humans, other bodily factors may play a more direct role. When sexually attracted to another person, chemical substances related to amphetamines or stimulants are produced.

The Kinsey reports found that most men and the majority of women reported having premarital sex. There was also great individual variation in sexual behavior. There are problems with the surveys -- people may not report their experiences accurately, and many persons refuse to participate in surveys involving reports of sexual activity.

Based on the work of Masters and Johnson, it appears that we move through four phases during sexual behavior. In response to sexual stimuli, we may enter the excitement phase. At this time, the penis and clitoris are enlarged. During the following plateau phase, changes in sexual organs continue. In this phase there is increased muscle tension, respiration, heart rate, and blood pressure. During the orgasmic phase, there are contractions in the genital muscles and intense sensations of pleasure. The patterns of contractions and their timing is similar for males and females.

Following orgasm comes the resolution phase. With males, there is a reduction in sexual and physiological arousal. They also enter a refractory period during which they cannot be sexually aroused. Females may either return to an unaroused state or may experience additional orgasms if stimulation continues.

Sexual stimulation may be produced by direct contact or by naturally occurring odors. In one study, perfume containing vaginal secretions or copulins increased sexual activity in about 20% of the couples. Humans also respond to real or imagined erotic stimuli. In contrast to other species, humans can generate their own sexual arousal on the basis of erotic fantasies. In this and other ways, cognitive abilities play a major role in sexual motivation for humans. Most persons respond with physiological arousal to erotic materials. After repeated exposures to X-rated films, individuals may overestimate the frequency of unusual sexual practices. They may also view some societally disapproved sexual behaviors as less inappropriate. A decrease of satisfaction in one's own sex life can also be a consequence of exposure to x-rated films.

There may be gender differences in sexual jealousy. Men may experience more intense jealousy in response to sexual infidelity; whereas, women may experience more intense jealousy in response to emotional jealousy. According to sociobiology, the strong reaction of men to sexual infidelity occurs because they can never be perfectly certain that they are the fathers of their children. Therefore, they may be investing resources in another man's family. The strong reaction of women to emotional jealousy occurs because they need the assistance of the male to raise their children. These conclusions are not definite.

About two percent of all adults are exclusively homosexual. About two or three percent of each sex are bisexual. There do not appear to be clear-cut answers about the basis of sexual orientation. Male homosexuals do not have lower levels of male sex hormones than other persons. Injections of male sex hormones do not reduce homosexual tendencies. They do not have different relationships with their family or different experiences during childhood. However, genetic factors may play a role. Homosexual preferences may be inherited and linked to the X chromosome.

D.   Aggressive Motivation

The desire to inflict harm on others is termed aggressive motivation. It often results in aggressive behavior. Most psychologists do not accept the view that aggression is an inherited and unavoidable human tendency. This is not to say it has no biological roots. Most psychologists believe that aggression is often elicited by external events. One hypothesis states that people experience a desire to harm others when these individuals have prevented them from obtaining what they want. This is termed the frustration-aggression hypothesis. Frustration, however, does not appear to be the only cause of aggression. For example, aggression is often caused by direct provocation from others and the consumption of alcohol. Further, frustration often produces depression or resignation rather than aggression. Cultures with different self-perceptions have been shown to differ in their rates of aggression. Culture has also been shown to influence reactions to frustration.

E.   Achievement and Power: Two Complex Human Motives

Achievement motivation is the motive concerned with meeting standards of excellence and accomplishing difficult tasks. These motives are not directly derived from biological factors. Power motivation is the desire to be in charge and have status. One technique for measuring these motives involves responding to ambiguous stories -- the Thematic Apperception Test. Individuals high in achievement orientation tend to get higher grades. They also earn more rapid promotions, and are better at running their own businesses. High achievement oriented individuals prefer tasks of moderate risk or difficulty. Low achievement individuals prefer situations with either very low or high risk.

Some early studies have found evidence for what was called fear of success in females. Recent research has not replicated these findings. Further, recent work suggests that the women in the early studies may not have feared success, but rather feared social rejection.

F.   Intrinsic Motivation: How (Sometimes) to Turn Play Into Work

Activities that we perform mostly for pleasure are based on intrinsic motivation. When individuals are paid or rewarded for such intrinsic activities, their motivation or interest may be lowered. However, if the rewards are offered as a sign of recognition, or are large and satisfying, motivation may be maintained or enhanced.

Questions:

9-1.   What are emotion and motivation? _____

_____

_____

_____

9-2.   Why is the concept of motivation useful in explaining behavior? _____

_____

_____

_____

9-3.   Why has the concept of motivation replaced instinct in psychology? _____

_____

_____

_____

9-4.   What is the drive theory of motivation? _____

_____

_____

_____

9-5.   What is the arousal theory of motivation? _____

_____

_____

_____

9-6.   Why does expectancy theory take a cognitive perspective? _____

_____

_____

_____

9-7.   What is Maslow's hierarchy of needs, and what are the findings surrounding this view?

_____

_____

_____

9-8.   What are the factors involved in the regulation of caloric intake? _____

_____

_____

_____

9-9.   Why do some persons experience difficulty in regulating their caloric intake and body weight?

_____

_____

_____

9-10.   What are the factors that may lead to anorexia nervosa and bulimia? _____

_____

_____

_____

9-11.   What is the relationship between hormones and sexual behavior? _____

_____

_____

_____

9-12.   What are the basic facts about human sexual behavior? _____

_____

_____

_____

9-13.   What are the factors that are thought to stimulate sexual arousal? _____

_____

_____

_____

9-14.   According to sociobiology, why may there be gender differences in sexual jealousy? _____

_____

_____

_____

9-15.   What are the various views on the determinates of sexual preferences? _____

_____

_____

_____

9-16.   What are the different views concerning the roots of aggression? _____

_____

_____

_____

9-17.   What are the differences associated with achievement motivation, and how is it measured?

_____

_____

_____

9-18.   What are the research findings concerning intrinsic motivation? _____

_____

_____

_____

II.   Emotions: Their Nature, Expression, and Impact

A.   The Nature of Emotions: Some Contrasting Views

Emotions are thought to involve three components. They include: (1) subjective cognitive states, (2) physiological changes within the body; and (3) outward signs of these internal states or behaviors.

According to the Cannon-Bard theory, exposure to emotion related stimuli produces both the subjective experience of emotion and the accompanying physiological changes. The James-Lange theory of emotion proposes that subjective emotions are the result of changes within our bodies; recognition of these changes are responsible for emotional experience.

Destruction of the sympathetic nervous system does not eliminate emotional reactions. It also appears that many emotional states are associated with similar patterns of physiological activity. This research is contrary to the James-Lange theory. However, it is now evident that different emotions are accompanied by different patterns of physiological activity and outward expressions. In addition, support for the James-Lange theory comes from the facial feedback hypothesis. Studies have shown that changes in our facial expressions sometimes produce changes in our emotions.

In sum, consistent with the Cannon-Bard theory, emotional experiences often do occur in response to specific stimuli. However, consistent with James-Lange theory, they can be affected by changes in our bodily state.

The third important theory of emotion is the Schacter-Singer theory. According to this theory, emotional events produce internal arousal. We look to the environment for its base. From observed stimuli, we select a label for the arousal. This is known as the two-factor theory.

Support for the two-factor theory is seen in a study finding that males who met a female on a shaky suspension bridge rated her more sexually attractive than those who met her on a solid bridge. They interpreted their arousal in terms of the female instead of the bridge.

Opponent process theory assumes that emotional reactions to stimuli are automatically followed by an opposite reaction. In addition, repeated exposure to a stimulus causes the initial reaction to weaken and the opponent process to strengthen. Thus, emotional reactions occur in action-reaction cycles.

B.   The Physiology of Emotion

The physiological reactions that accompany emotions are regulated by the autonomic nervous system. The sympathetic nervous system readies the body for action. The parasympathetic nervous system is related to restoration of bodily resources.

Evidence indicates that different emotions are associated with different patterns of physiological reactions. Recently, evidence indicates that, although there are large individual differences associated with these patterns, positive feelings are associated with greater activation of the left hemisphere; whereas negative feelings are associated with greater activation of the right hemisphere.

C.   The External Expression of Emotion: Outward Signs of Inner Feelings

Lie detectors or polygraphs are used to determine if people are lying or telling the truth about an issue. These devices record several physiological reactions at once. They determine if a person's arousal level changes as a function of the type of question he/she is asked. Lie detectors yield uncertain results about whether a person is lying. First, lie detector tests measure only arousal. Second, a person's arousal can be influenced by many factors.

Nonverbal cues are external and observable signs of internal emotional states. Persons reveal these states through several basic channels including facial expressions, eye contact, body movements, posture, and touching. People have similar facial expressions when experiencing basic emotions such as anger, fear, surprise, happiness, sadness, and disgust. Generally, a high level of eye contact is seen as a sign of positive feelings or attraction. Avoidance of eye contact is a sign of negative feelings. Continuous gazing or staring is seen as a sign of hostility.

Nonverbal cues related to our posture and movements are called body language. A high level of body movement indicates arousal or anxiety. Different body orientations are associated with different emotional states. Body movements that provide specific information about emotions are called gestures.

Depending upon the context, touch can suggest such things as affection, sexual interest, caring, dominance, or even aggression. Interestingly, although context influences the meaning of touch, research indicates that touching someone in a manner that is considered acceptable for the current context generally produces positive reactions. There are also gender differences in touching.

Research findings suggests that our current feelings can influence our cognitions. Our cognitions can also influence our current feelings. Affect can influence cognitions in several ways. First our current mood can influence how we evaluate ambiguous stimuli. Second, affect can influence memory. When we are in a positive mood it is generally easier to remember positive information. When we are in a negative mood it is generally easier to remember negative information. Third, people in a good mood are sometimes more creative. Fourth, affect can influence risk-taking. Recent findings indicate that being in a good mood can sometimes make it easier for others to persuade us. This may occur because we are cognitively unable or because we are unwilling to engage in careful processing.

Questions:

9-19.   How does the Cannon-Bard theory differ from the James-Lange theory? _____

_____

_____

_____

9-20.   What are the components of the Schacter-Singer theory, and what are some of the research findings surrounding this view? _____

_____

_____

_____

9-21.   What are the assumptions of opponent-process theory? _____

_____

_____

_____

9-22.   What are the physiological characteristics of emotion? _____

_____

_____

_____

9-23.   How is emotion communicated through external expressions? _____

_____

_____

_____

9-24.   What relationships exist between emotion and cognition? _____

_____

_____

_____

III.   Making Psychology Part of Your Life -- Getting Motivated: Some Practical Techniques

Baron provides several techniques that can help us overcome behavioral inertia. These include: (1) set specific goals; (2) set challenging goals; (3) set attainable goals; (4) reward yourself for reaching each goal; (5) become committed to your goals; and (6) build feedback into the process.

Question:

9-25.   How can you apply what you've learned about motivation to motivational problems?

_____

_____

_____

MAKING PSYCHOLOGY PART OF YOUR LIFE: Key Terms and Concepts

Knowing the important concepts and key terms contained in this chapter is a very important part of mastering the material. We have presented a sample of these concepts below. Define each concept and check your definition with that presented in this chapter. It will also be beneficial for you to think of an example of each concept. Whenever possible, use your own personal experience to provide an example of each term below.

9-1.   **Achievement Movitation**: _____

      Example: _____

9-2.   **Affect**: _____

      Example: _____

9-3.   **Aggression**: _____

      Example: _____

9-4.   **Aggressive Motivation**: _____

      Example: _____

9-5.   **Anorexia Nervosa**: _____

      Example: _____

9-6.   **Arousal Theory**: _____

      Example: _____

9-7.   **Bisexual (Sexual Orientation)**: _____

      Example: _____

9-8.   **Body Language**: _____

      Example: _____

9-9.   **Body-Mass Index**: _____

      Example: _____

9-10.   **Bulimia:** _____

Example: _____

9-11.   **Cannon-Bard Theory:** _____

9-12.   **Discrepancy-Evaluation Theory:** _____

9-13.   **Drive Theory:** _____

9-14.   **Emotions:** _____

Example: _____

9-15.   **Expectancy Theory:** _____

9-16.   **Facial Feedback Hypothesis:** _____

Example: _____

9-17.   **Frustration:** _____

Example: _____

9-18.   **Gestures:** _____

Example: _____

9-19.   **Gonads:** _____

Example: _____

9-20.   **Heterosexual (Sexual Orientation):** _____

Example: _____

9-21.   **Homeostasis:** _____

Example: _____

9-22.   **Hierarchy of Needs:** _____

9-23.   **Homosexual (Sexual Orientation):** _____

       Example: _____

9-24.   **Hunger Motivation:** _____

       Example: _____

9-25.   **Incentives:** _____

       Example: _____

9-26.   **Instincts:** _____

       Example: _____

9-27.   **Instinct Theory:** _____

9-28.   **Intrinsic Motivation:** _____

9-29.   **James-Lange Theory:** _____

9-30.   **Motivation:** _____

       Example: _____

9-31.   **Nonverbal Cues:** _____

       Example: _____

9-32.   **Obesity:** _____

       Example: _____

9-33.   **Opponent-Process Theory:** _____

9-34.   **Power Motivation:** _____

       Example: _____

9-35.   **Schachter-Singer Theory (two-factor theory)**: _____

9-36.   **Sexual Jealousy**: _____

Example: _____

9-37.   **Sexual Motivation**: _____

Example: _____

9-38.   **Thematic Apperception Test**: _____

9-39.   **Work Motivation**: _____

Example: _____

CHALLENGE: Develop Your Critical Thinking Skills

Recognizing Relationships Between Thoughts and Feelings: "Sad But Smart or Happy But Dumb?"

As discussed in your text (see pp. 362-363), research suggests that moods significantly affect our information processing. Specifically, research suggests that we are less critical of information when we're in positive vs. negative moods. Thus, we seem to be "sad but smart -- happy but dumb." A critical thinker is aware of the influences of emotion on his/her thoughts. As an exercise toward recognizing these influences, chart your emotions for a few days and note your thoughts and behavior.

	Primary Mood	Your Thoughts	Your Behavior	Your Physiological Reactions
Day 1				
Day 2				
Day 3				
Day 4				
Day 5				

Assessment:

9-1.   Do you see any relationships among your mood, thoughts, and behavior?

9-2.   Were there any instances in which you made decisions that on second thought seemed less than perfect? If so, what was your mood state?

9-3.   Were there decisions that you made that were especially "good?" If so, what was your mood state?

Alternative Exercise

If you did not choose to track your moods for a week, retrospect on some of the decisions -- good and bad -- that you have made over the years. Use these "retrospections" to answer questions 1-4 above.

CHALLENGE: Making Psychology Part of Your Life

<u>Effective Goal Setting</u>

Your text provides you with some very practical guidelines for increasing your motivation (see p. 364-365). Take this opportunity to use these guidelines in preparing for your next major class assignment (a paper or an exam). If you follow these guidelines, you will see their utility and will, hopefully, make them a part of your life!

9-1.   <u>Set specific goals</u>.

Indicate precisely what will be defined as adequate performance (e.g., how many pages a day you should read to be ready for the test).

9-2.   <u>Set challenging but attainable goals</u>.

Assess the difficulty level of your goals. Are they high enough that they stretch your ability, but not so high that you can't possibly reach them?

9-3.   <u>Reward yourself for reaching each goal</u>.

Identify the rewards you will give to yourself for reaching each goal.

9-4.   <u>Become committed to your goals</u>.

Assess your level of commitment to each goal. Adopt only those goals you are committed to reaching.

9-5.   <u>Build feedback into the process</u>.

How will you know when you've reached each goal?

CHALLENGE: Review Your Comprehensive Knowledge

SAMPLE TEST QUESTIONS

Once you have worked through the preceding sections, you should be ready for a comprehensive self-test. You can check your answers with those at the end of this section. An additional practice test is given in the supplementary section at the end of this study guide.

9-1.   One major problem with instinct theory of motivation is that the existence of the instinct is inferred from:
    a.   physiological measures.   c.   the behavior it was designed to explain.
    b.   observations.   d.   experimental analyses.

9-2.   Basal metabolic rate refers to:
    a.   the number of calories a person consumes a day.
    b.   the number of calories a person uses during activity.
    c.   the number of calories the body requires at rest within a given period of time.
    d.   the number of calories the body requires to maintain a stable weight.

9-3.   According to drive theory, behaviors will be repeated if they tend to:
    a.   increase drives.   c.   decrease drives.
    b.   have no effect on drives.   d.   initiate drives.

9-4.   The Kinsey reports found that:
    a.   females were more sexually active than males.
    b.   there was great individual variation in sexual behavior.
    c.   only a minority of men and women have premarital sex.
    d.   rates of homosexuality were higher than expected.

9-5.   Which of the following is **not** true of high achievement oriented individuals?
    a.   high grades in school   c.   succeed in running their own business
    b.   prefer difficult tasks   d.   rapid promotions

9-6.   If we are going to reward people for intrinsically motivated activities, it is best if these rewards:
    a.   are a sign of recognition.   c.   are unsatisfying.
    b.   are small.   d.   are external.

9-7.   The theory that holds that emotional stimuli produce both the experience of emotion and accompanying physiological changes is:
    a.   James-Lange.   c.   Schachter-Singer.
    b.   Cannon-Bard.   d.   Watson-Levin.

9-8.   The theory of emotion that asserts that different patterns of emotional activity are associated with different emotions is the:
    a.   Cannon-Bard theory.   c.   Schachter-Singer theory.
    b.   James-Lange theory.   d.   facial feedback theory.

9-9.   Research on the facial feedback hypothesis supports the _____ theory.
    a.   James-Lange   c.   Schachter-Singer
    b.   Cannon-Bard   d.   Watson-Levin

9-10. What are the two factors that determine a person's emotional experience according to Schachter and Singer's two-factor theory?
  a. intensity of affect and behavior being performed
  b. intensity of affect and whether situation is positive or negative
  c. body gestures and transfer of excitation
  d. internal arousal and choice of label for this arousal based on external stimuli

9-11. Research on emotions comparing Cannon-Bard and James-Lange theories have found support for:
  a. neither.   c. only James-Lange.
  b. only Cannon-Bard.   d. both.

9-12. According to the opponent-process theory of emotion, the day following my graduation (a happy event), I may feel:
  a. sad.   c. afraid.
  b. free.   d. elated.

9-13. At times, people experience a desire to harm others when they have been prevented by these people from obtaining what they want. This is called the _____ hypothesis.
  a. frustration-aggression   c. frustration-catharsis
  b. leaning-catharsis   d. catharsis-frustration

9-14. One technique of measuring achievement and power motives is the _____ test.
  a. Briggs-Storm test   c. Strong-Davis test
  b. Thematic Apperception test   d. Thematic Illusion test

9-15. Opponent process theory assumes that repeated exposure to a stimulus causes the initial reaction to _____ and the opponent process to _____.
  a. strengthen, weaken   c. weaken, weaken
  b. weaken, strengthen   d. strengthen, strengthen

9-16. Which of the following is **not** a correct statement about Maslow's theory?
  a. Motives exist in a hierarchy.
  b. Motives at the bottom must be satisfied before those at the top.
  c. Deficiency needs include esteem needs.
  d. Self-actualization is a growth need.

9-17. Which of the following is **not** a correct statement about why people may have a desire to overeat.
  a. It is learned.   c. It is influenced by reactions to stress.
  b. It is influenced by basal metabolic rate. d. It is influenced by opioid barbiturates.

9-18. Individuals in positive moods:
  a. are less susceptible to persuasion.
  b. are more susceptible to persuasion.
  c. are likely to engage in critical thought.
  d. are motivated to engage in careful information processing.

9-19. Which of the following theories of motivation include the role of incentives in producing motivation?
  a. expectancy theory   c. drive theory
  b. arousal theory   d. instinct theory

9-20.   Contrary to past research that suggested that females fear success, recent research has suggested that women in the early studies may have:

a. feared social rejection.
b. been low need achievers.
c. not told the truth.
d. lacked motivation.

Answers and Feedback for Sample Test Questions:

9-1.   C   Using "instincts" as an explanation for behavior can be a circular form of explanation. For example, saying that a person was aggressive because he has an aggressive instinct is a problem because we are inferring the existence of this instinct from his behavior and then using it to explain his behavior. (p. 335)

9-2.   C   Basal metabolic rate refers to the number of calories the body requires at rest within a given period of time. Individuals differ in this rate. (p. 340)

9-3.   C   Behaviors tend to be repeated when they decrease aversive drive states. (p. 335)

9-4.   B   The Kinsey data show a basic theme: individual differences in sexual behavior are enormous. (p. 343)

9-5.   B   High achievement oriented individuals prefer tasks that are moderately difficult. (p. 351)

9-6.   A   Rewards that are seen as signs of recognition do not decrease intrinsic motivation for the activity. (p. 353)

9-7.   B   The Cannon-Bard theory of emotion suggests that emotion-provoking stimuli simultaneously elicit physiological arousal and the cognitive states we label as emotions. (p. 354)

9-8.   B   The James-Lange theory contends that emotion-provoking stimuli induce physiological reactions and that these form the basis for labeling emotions. (p. 354)

9-9.   A   This hypothesis states that facial expressions can influence our emotional states -- a view that is consistent with the theory that physiological reactions form the basis of labeling emotions (the James-Lange theory). (p. 355)

9-10.   D   According to Schachter-Singer theory, subjects emotional states are determined by both our internal state of arousal and the label we place on this feeling. (p. 355)

9-11.   D   There has been support for both of these theories of emotion. (pp. 354-355)

9-12   A   I may feel sad according to this view, because emotional reactions are followed automatically by an opposite reaction. Thus, feelings of happiness may be followed by feelings of sadness. (p. 355)

9-13.   A   According to the frustration-aggression hypothesis, aggression is caused by feelings of frustration that can be invoked, for example, by someone blocking my goals. (p. 348)

9-14.   B   The Thematic Apperception Test (TAT) is used to measure achievement and power motivation. (p. 351)

9-15.   B   This is the second assumption of opponent process theory. (p. 355)

9-16.   C   Esteem needs are **growth** needs. (p. 338)

9-17.   D   Opioid barbiturates are not implicated in obesity. (p. 340)

9-18.   B   Individuals in positive moods are more susceptible to persuasion because the mood state seems to reduce their motives to engage in careful information processing. (p. 362)

9-19.   A   Expectancy theory assumes positive incentives "pull" (motivate) behavior. (p. 337)

9-20.   A   Recent research suggests women in Horner's original research may have feared social rejection, not success. (p. 352)

Glossary of difficult words and expressions	Definition
A bout of	a period of
Ambiguous	uncertain; not clear
Banned	prohibited; prevented; not allowed
Bribe	something given, offered or promised in order to influence or persuade a person
Compel	force (a person or thing to do something)
Congruent	suitable; agreeing (with); consistent with
Distress	(case of) great pain, discomfort or sorrow
Elation	great happiness
Frowning	draw the eyebrows together forming lines on the forehead
Gorge	narrow opening
Mundane	dull; everyday; not special
Out on a limb	put oneself in a vulnerable position; taking a chance
Override	refuse to agree with, accept (a person's opinons, wishes, decisions, claims, etc.)
Overt	obvious; seen
Overwhelm	confuse; too much for a person to take
Paragon	model of a perfect person
Peak	highest point
Pendulum	weighed rod hung from a fixed point so that it swings freely
Pen poised	pen ready; being to write
Plunging	jumping into with force; getting involved in
Quest	dedicated effort; a special goal
Relish	have; enjoy something; with pleasure
Rubbing	move one thing backwards and forward on the surface of another
Skepticism	doubts about something
Soothing	making a person feel quiet or calm
Sorrow	cause of grief or sadness
Strenuous	using or needing a great effort; hard task
Striving for	trying to accomplish something; working toward a goal

Glossary of difficult words and expressions	Definition
Swaying	moving, first to one side and then to the other
Thwarting	obstruct; frustrate; keep from obtaining
Traits	characteristics; properties
Trivial	of small value or importance
Wane	become weaker; going away

CHAPTER 10
INDIVIDUAL DIFFERENCES:
PERSONALITY-CONSISTENCY IN THE
BEHAVIOR OF INDIVIDUALS

OUTLINE: Develop a Study Plan

Use this outline to help you grasp the organizational structure of the chapter contents. The learning objectives (LOs) for each section are included. Use them as tools for developing your study plan. Space has been provided for you to write any notes or questions that come to mind as you begin your exploration into this material.

Heading:	Learning Objective:	Your Notes:
I. The Psychoanalytic Approach: Messages From The Unconscious	**L.O. 10.1:** Survey the difference levels of consciousness and the three personality structures proposed by Freudian theory.	
A. Freud The Person: A Capsule Memoir		
B. Freud's Theory of Personality	**L.O. 10.2:** List the psychosexual stages of development proposed by Freud and discuss the consequences of fixation at each stage of development.	
C. Research Evidence Concerning Freud's Theory: Freudian Slips		
D. Freud's Theory: An Overall Evaluation	**L.O. 10.3:** Provide an evaluation of Freudian theory.	
II. Other Psychoanalytic Views: Freud's Disciples...and Dissenters		
A. Jung: The Collective Unconscious	**L.O. 10.4:** Describe Jung's views on the collectives unconscious.	
B. Horney: The Importance of Social and Cultural Factors	**L.O. 10.5:** Compare and contrast the views of Horney and Freud on the role of social and cultural factors in the personality development of males and females.	

Heading:	Learning Objective:	Your Notes:
C. Adler: Striving For Superiority	L.O. 10.6: Describe Adler's view on the roles of social factors and feelings of inferiority in shaping adult personality.	
D. The Neo-Freudians: An Evaluation		
III. Humanistic Theories: Emphasis On Growth		
A. Rogers' Self-Theory: Becoming a Fully Functioning Person	L.O. 10.7: Survey the central assumptions of Roger's theory.	
B. Maslow and The Study of Self-Actualizing People	L.O. 10.8: Describe Maslow's concept of the self-actualizing person.	
C. Humanistic Theories: An Evaluation	L.O. 10.9: Evaluate the humanistic perspective on personality development.	
D. Self-disclosure: The Potential Benefits of Revealing Ourselves to Others		
IV. Trait Theories: Seeking The Key Dimensions of Personality		
A. Allport's Central, Secondary, and Cardinal Traits	L.O. 10.10: Discuss the trait approach to personality and outline the trait theories of Allport and Cattell.	
B. Cattell's Surface and Source Traits		
C. Five Robust Factors: A Modern Framework	L.O. 10.11: List and define the "big five" robust factors of personality.	
D. Trait Theories: An Evaluation	L.O. 10.12: Evaluate the trait approach to the study of personality.	

Heading:	Learning Objective:	Your Notes:
V. Learning Approaches To Personality	**L.O. 10.13:** Discuss how the learning approaches can account for the consistency and uniqueness of human behavior.	
A. Social Cognitive Theory: Reciprocal Causality In Human Behavior	**L.O. 10.14:** Describe and evaluate the social learning approaches of Bandura and Rotter.	
B. Evaluation of The Learning Approach	**L.O. 10.15:** Evaluate the learning approach to personality.	
VI. Key Aspects of Personality: A Sample of Recent Research		
A. Two Aspects of The Self: Self-Esteem and Self-Monitoring	**L.O. 10.16:** Discuss the research on self-esteem and self-monitoring and discuss their impact on behavior.	
B. Sensation-Seeking: The Desire For Stimulation	**L.O. 10.17:** Describe the characteristics of high and low sensation-seekers.	
VII. Making Psychology Part of Your Life: How Accurate is Your Self-concept?	**L.O. 10.18:** Be able to describe how accurate your self-concept is and relate its accuracy to your everyday behavior.	

SURVEY AND QUESTION

This section presents the major topics and ideas from the chapter. Use it as a tool for seeing how the components of the chapter fit together. At the end of each major topic, we have asked you a question that relates to the major learning objectives. If you can answer these questions, you have taken a major step toward mastering this material.

I. The Psychoanalytic Approach: Messages From the Unconscious

Before discussing the psychoanalytic approach, lets first explore some basic definitions. Personality is generally defined as the unique, but stable, set of characteristics that set people apart from others. A question exists about whether people do behave consistently across situations. We generally assume that people have traits that make them behave in similar ways across situations. One group of scientists has held that people do not have traits. Rather, behavior is the result of external factors. This view predicts that individuals behave inconsistently across different situations. Others believe that stable traits exist and that individuals behave consistently across time and settings. Many psychologists believe that both traits and situations are important. It is clear that behavior is influenced by both situational factors and personal dispositions. Such dispositions do appear to be relatively stable over time and across situations.

A.   Freud the Person: A Capsule Memoir

Freud had a close relationship with his mother and a distant relationship with his father. Several persons have speculated on how these relationships may have affected his theories. As a young man, Freud was highly ambitious and wanted to be a medical researcher. He became discouraged in this field and entered private practice. During this time, he developed his theories. Freud was a powerful personality and attracted many followers -- some of whom later became dissenters.

B.   Freud's Theory of Personality

According to Freud, the human mind has three levels of consciousness. The part that holds our current and available thoughts is the conscious. Memories that can be brought to mind are part of the preconscious. The part that contains the thoughts, impulses, and desires of which we are not aware is the unconscious. This is the largest part of the mind. Freud believed that much of the unconscious contained thoughts or ideas that had been repressed because they were too anxiety provoking. These repressed thoughts were seen as responsible for some patient symptoms. One major goal of psychoanalysis is to bring repressed material to consciousness.

Freud proposed that personality has three parts. The id consists of our primitive innate urges. This part is unconscious and operates on the basis of the pleasure principle. The "reason" part of the personality or ego is concerned with holding the id in check until the impulses can be satisfied appropriately. It functions in accord with the reality principle. The third part of personality is our conscience or superego. It permits gratification of the id only when it is morally appropriate. The ego has to mediate between the conflicting aims of the id and superego.

Anxiety is experienced when unacceptable impulses get close to consciousness and close to the control limits of the ego. At this point, the ego may utilize one of several different defense mechanisms. All defense mechanisms serve to reduce anxiety. One defense mechanism channels unacceptable impulses into a socially acceptable action. This is called sublimation. A second defense mechanism in which a person behaves in a way that is directly counter to the threatening impulse is called reaction formation. Regression, rationalization, displacement, projection, and regression are other defense mechanisms.

According to Freud, there is an innate sequence of stages through which all human beings pass. These are known as the psychosexual stages of development. At each stage, pleasure is focused on a different body region. The concepts of libido and fixation are keys to understanding these psychosexual stages.

The instinctual life force that energizes the id is the libido. Fixation occurs if an excessive amount of energy is left at one stage of development. Fixation can result in psychological disorders.

Freud believed that events in the first few years of life determine adult personality. We supposedly pass through a series of psychosexual stages that reflect the id's focus on a part of the body to satisfy pleasure. During the oral stage, pleasure is sought through the mouth. During the anal stage, the id focuses on elimination. About age of four, we enter the phallic stage during which the genitals are the primary source of pleasure.

During the phallic stage, we presumably fantasize about relations with the opposite-sex parent. Freud called this the Oedipal complex for males. Boys fear castration; girls fear loss of love. For both genders, these fears are resolved by identifying with the same-sex parent. The male conflict was presumed to be resolved easier, resulting in stronger superego development in males. The idea that females experience penis envy is rejected by nearly all psychologists.

After resolution of the Oedipal conflict, sexual desires are repressed. We then enter the latency period. At puberty, we enter the genital stage when lust and affection are blended. Too much or too little gratification at one of these stages may lead to fixation and failure to develop normal adult personality.

C.   Research Evidence Concerning Freud's Theory: Freudian Slips

Slips of the tongue that reveal aspects of the unconsciousness are called Freudian slips. In the presence of an attractive female, male subjects made more slips of a sexual connotation than in the presence of a male experimenter. These findings seem to support Freud's theory, but other interpretations are possible.

D.   Freud's Theory: An Overall Evaluation

There have been many criticisms of Freudian theory. One criticism is that the theory is difficult to test. A second one is that several of his proposals are not consistent with present research findings. A third revolves around the way he collected his data through case studies. A fourth involves the fact that it can explain virtually all patterns of data after the fact. For these reasons, Freud's theory is not currently accepted, although it has influenced psychology.

Several of Freud's ideas have contributed to our understanding of people. One important idea is that behavior is affected by unconscious thoughts, motives, and memories. A second important idea is that early childhood experiences can influence our adult behavior. A third important idea is that anxiety does play an important role in many psychological problems.

Some researchers have argued against Freud's idea that we pass through fixed stages of development because there are cultural differences in ideas and the expression of love and intimacy.

Questions:

10-1.   What are the factors that are thought to influence the consistency of an individual's behavior across time and situations? _____

_____

_____

_____

10-2.   What factors influence the consistency of an individual's behavior across time and situations?

_____

_____

_____

10-3.   What are the different levels of consciousness proposed by Freudian theory? _____

_____

_____

_____

10-4.   What are the three personality structures proposed by Freud's theory? _____

_____

_____

_____

10-5.   How does the ego defend against unacceptable id impulses? _____

_____

_____

_____

10-6.   What are Freud's psychosexual stages of development? _____

_____

_____

_____

10-7.   What is the existing evidence concerning Freud's theory of personality? _____

_____

_____

_____

10-8. What are the strengths and weaknesses of Freud's theory? _____

_____

_____

_____

II. Other Psychoanalytic Views: Freud's Disciples...And Dissenters

Students of Freud who accepted many of his ideas are known as neo-Freudians. Most began by accepting his ideas, but later disagreed with some of his major assumptions. For example, although they accepted the importance of the unconscious, they rejected his emphasis on instinctual influences and early childhood development. Neo-Freudians placed greater emphasis on social experience.

A.   Jung: The Collective Unconscious

Jung proposed a unique aspect of the unconscious. He proposed that the material in the collective unconscious is shared by all humans: it is part of our biological heritage. Images that predispose us to perceive the external world in certain ways are called archetypes. The animus is the masculine side of females. The anima is the feminine side of males. Jung also believed that people are born with innate tendencies to be introverts or extroverts.

B.   Horney: The Importance of Social and Cultural Factors

Karen Horney rejected Freud's idea of penis envy. She countered with her own concept of womb envy to emphasize the fact that each gender has attributes that are admired by the other. For Horney, psychological disorders are not the result of fixation, but rather involve disturbed interpersonal relationships. One ineffective interaction style is called "moving toward people." Persons with this style compulsively seek affection and acceptance from others. Another pattern is "moving against and away from people." Persons with the moving against style assume others are hostile, while those with the moving away style have few friends and prefer isolation and privacy. She contended that psychological disorders stem largely from social factors rather than fixation.

C.   Adler: Striving for Superiority

Adler was a pampered and sickly child whose early experiences may have led to his theory that people are motivated by feelings of inferiority. According to Adler, as a reaction to these feelings, we develop an opposite superiority drive which compensates for these feelings of inferiority. Overcompensation can also occur. When this occurs, persons conceal their inferiority feelings from themselves. In contrast to Freud, Adler emphasized the importance of social factors, and believed that birth order and family constellation are important factors influencing a person's style of life.

D.   The Neo-Freudians: An Evaluation

The theories of the neo-Freudians are subject to some of the same criticisms applied to Freud's view. For example, they are not based on the kinds of hard data science requires. But, importantly, they have been a bridge between the psychoanalytic approach and modern theories of personality. Several of their ideas have been incorporated into humanistic theories.

Question:

10-9.   Summarize and evaluate the positions of the neo-Freudians. _____

_____

_____

_____

_____

_____

III. Humanistic Theories: Emphasis on Growth

Humanistic psychologists feel that human beings are basically good. Humanistic theories emphasize the importance of personal responsibility. They also emphasize the importance of the present and the importance of personal growth. Only when obstacles interfere or block these positive tendencies do problems occur.

A.   Rogers' Self Theory: Becoming a Fully Functioning Person

Carl Rogers emphasized the positive traits of human beings. He proposed that, if left to their own devices, people (over the course of their lives) move toward becoming fully functioning persons. Their actions become increasingly dominated by constructive impulses. However, anxiety produced by a discrepancy between a person's self-concept and reality can block personal growth. To reduce anxiety, people develop defenses like distortion and denial. Distorted self-concepts develop because people feel that they must behave in certain ways in order to gain the approval of other people, such as parents. In this setting, gaining the positive regard of other people is conditional. To repair a distorted self-concept, Rogers proposes establishing a setting where positive regard is unconditional. This is client-centered therapy.

B.   Maslow and the Study of Self-Actualizing People

Maslow proposed that there is a hierarchy of needs, with satisfaction of the lower-order needs being necessary before higher-order ones develop. These needs are, in order: physiological, safety, belongingness, esteem, and self-actualization. The last is similar to the esteem functioning person described by Rogers. Self-actualized people sometimes describe powerful feelings of unity with the universe and tremendous waves of power and wonder. These experiences are called peak experiences. According to Maslow, only a few people become self-actualized.

C.   Humanistic Theories: An Evaluation

Many of the ideas of humanistic psychology have entered the mainstream of psychology. Interest in the self and a positive view of people are two contributions of humanistic psychology. Criticisms of humanistic psychology center around their use of free will concepts, their loosely defined concepts and their overly optimistic assumptions about human nature. Despite these criticisms, this approach has been valuable in generating research on, for example, self-disclosure.

D.   Self-disclosure: The Potential Benefits of Revealing Ourselves to Others

Self-disclosure is the process of revealing information about oneself to another person. Although it tends to be a gradual process, it can occur with strangers. Self-disclosure among strangers probably occurs because this type of disclosure has few, if any, negative consequences. There are also slight gender differences in self-disclosure, probably due to differences in sex roles or norms. Women tend to engage in self-disclosure to a slightly greater extent than males. Self-disclosure is influenced by social anxiety. In one study, low socially anxious persons reciprocated while high socially anxious persons did not. Finally, self-disclosure appears to have positive effects on adjustment and health.

Questions:

10-10. What are the basic assumptions about human nature which underlie all humanistic theories?

_____

_____

_____

10-11. Describe Rogers' humanistic theory. _____

_____

_____

_____

10-12. Describe Maslow's theory. _____

_____

_____

_____

10-13. Why has humanism been praised and why has it been criticized? _____

_____

_____

_____

10-14. What are the potential benefits of self-disclosure? _____

_____

_____

_____

IV. Trait Theories: Seeking the Key Dimensions of Personality

A.   Allport's Central, Secondary, and Cardinal Traits

Trait theories of personality focus on identifying the key dimensions of personality. One approach for reducing the number of traits to a reasonable number is to look for clusters. Allport divided traits into secondary traits, central traits, and cardinal traits. Central traits are the 5-10 traits that best describe an individual; cardinal traits dominate a person's personality; secondary traits exert weak effects on behavior. At times a pattern of behavior that was acquired to satisfy one set of motives may be performed for a very different set of motives. This is called functional autonomy.

B.   Cattell's Surface and Source Traits

Using factor analysis techniques, Cattell identified 16 personality dimensions. He called these source traits and presumed that they underlie many other less important traits (surface traits).

C.   Five Robust Factors

Recent findings suggest that there may be five key dimensions of personality. These dimensions are: extraversion, agreeableness, emotional stability, conscientiousness, and openness to experience. These dimensions are often used by persons in describing themselves and are apparent to total strangers. They are useful in making judgments about others' personality.

D.   Trait Theories: An Evaluation

Most research in personality in recent years is based on the trait approach. However, the approach is not perfect. Several criticisms exist. First, it is descriptive in nature but doesn't explain how the traits develop or influence behavior. Second, although the five robust factor approach has come close to this goal, there is no universal agreement about what traits make up the basic parts of personality. However, we can conclude that the trait approach to personality is valuable.

Questions:

10-15. Compare and contrast the trait theories of Allport and Cattell. _____

_____

_____

_____

10-16. What are the five robust factors of personality? _____

_____

_____

_____

10-17. What are the strengths and weaknesses of the trait approach to the study of personality?

_____

_____

_____

V.   Learning Approaches to Personality

To answer the question "what accounts for the consistency and uniqueness of behavior?" Freud focused primarily on internal factors. The behavioral or social learning approach focuses on the role of learning and experience. Skinner took a radical position and denied the importance of virtually any internal cause of behavior. Most psychologists now believe that internal factors are important. The social cognitive learning theory discussed reflects this view.

A.   Social Cognitive Theory: Reciprocal Causality in Human Behavior

Bandura's social cognitive theory proposes that, in addition to operant and classical conditioning, observational learning is also important. Individuals do not respond automatically to external conditions. Rather, they plan, form expectancies, and so forth. In addition, humans also have the ability to self-regulate their own behavior and to strive for goals that are self-determined. Further, a person's thoughts and feelings, like self-efficacy can influence performance. Rotter's view shares similarities with Bandura in that he proposes that in addition to external factors, internal cognitive factors, like expectancies, must also be considered. He distinguished persons who believe they shape their own destinies (internals) and those that feel their outcomes are due to forces outside their control (externals).

B.   Evaluation of the Learning Approach

A key strength of the behavioral and social learning approach is that it is based on widely-accepted psychological principles. It has also had practical implications. A criticism of early forms of this general approach is that they ignored cognitive factors. This criticism does not apply to reciprocal determinism framework or to approaches like that of Rotter.

Questions:

10-18. How does the learning approach account for the consistency and uniqueness of human behavior?

_____

_____

_____

10-19. Compare and contrast Bandura's and Rotter's social learning theories. _____

_____

_____

_____

10-20. Evaluate the social learning approaches to understanding psychology. _____

_____

_____

_____

VI. Key Aspects of Personality: A Sample of Recent Research

A.   Two Aspects of the Self: Self-Esteem and Self-Monitoring

In recent years, psychologists have shifted their attention from "grand theories" to key aspects of personality. Research on self-esteem and self-monitoring reflects this trend.

The extent to which our self-evaluations are favorable or unfavorable defines our self-esteem. When these evaluations are favorable, people report fewer negative emotions, are less depressed, are better able to handle stress, and experience fewer negative health effects than those who are low in self-esteem.

In one study, the gap between anxious or depressed subjects' ideal and actual selves was greater than controls (nonanxious or nondepressed subjects). Further, anxious or depressed subjects showed signs of reduced immune system efficiency when they thought about themselves. This was not the case for control subjects.

Other findings indicate that high self-esteem persons (in contrast to low self-esteem persons), are less susceptible to influence, more confident in achieving their goals, more socially effective, more confident in their self-judgments, and are more consistent in their self-evaluations. It appears that high self-esteem persons have clearer self-concepts than low self-esteem persons. Persons with clear-cut self-concepts appear to be less vulnerable to stress. Although there are many benefits associated with high self-esteem, recent findings have indicated that there can also be costs, like overconfidence associated with high self-esteem. Self-monitoring is a personality trait involving sensitivity to social situations. Persons high in self-monitoring are sensitive to social settings and can adapt their behavior to the setting. These individuals are very good at reading others and make favorable impressions on others. In contrast, low self-monitors do not seem to be as sensitive to social demands; their behavior is more inner-directed. Low self-monitors show a higher degree of consistency in their behavior across situations.

B.   Sensation-Seeking: The Desire for Stimulation

Sensation-seekers desire new and exciting experiences. Differences in this desire may have biological origins. High sensation-seekers, in contrast to low sensation-seekers, pay more attention to unfamiliar stimuli, are better able to ignore irrelevant information, have lower levels of endorphins, and may be better able to handle stress.

Questions:

10-21. Compare and contrast the characteristics of persons with high and low self-esteem. _____

_____

_____

_____

10-22. Compare and contrast the characteristics of high and low self-monitors. _____

_____

_____

_____

10-23. What are the characteristics of high sensation seekers? _____

_____

_____

_____

VII.   Making Psychology Part of Your Life: How Accurate Is Your Self-Concept?

Baron provides you with a self-test assessing the accuracy of your self-concept. Self-knowledge is useful; it helps us make better choices and become better adjusted. This exercise should help you develop your self-knowledge. Take the test (see page 400 in your text) and discuss what you learned below.

Question:

10-24. What did you learn about your self-concept through this exercise? _____

_____

_____

_____

YOUR NOTES:

MAKING PSYCHOLOGY PART OF YOUR LIFE: Key Terms and Concepts

Knowing the important concepts and key terms contained in this chapter is a very important part of mastering the material. We have presented a sample of these concepts below. Define each concept and check your definition with that presented in the chapter. It will also be beneficial for you to think of an example of each concept. Whenever possible, use your own personal experience to provide an example of each term below.

10-1.   **Agreeableness**: _____

Example: _____

10-2.   **Anal Stage**: _____

10-3.   **Anima**: _____

Example: _____

10-4.   **Animus**: _____

Example: _____

10-5.   **Anxiety**: _____

Example: _____

10-6.   **Archetypes**: _____

Example: _____

10-7.   **Cardinal Trait**: _____

Example: _____

10-8.   **Central Traits**: _____

Example: _____

10-9.   **Collective Unconscious**: _____

10-10.   **Conscientiousness**: _____

Example: _____

10-11.   **Defense Mechanisms:** _____

       Example: _____

10-12.   **Ego:** _____

10-13.   **Emotional Stability:** _____

       Example: _____

10-14.   **Externals:** _____

       Example: _____

10-15.   **Extroverts:** _____

       Example: _____

10-16.   **Extraversion:** _____

       Example: _____

10-17.   **Fixation:** _____

       Example: _____

10-18.   **Freudian Slips:** _____

       Example: _____

10-19.   **Fully-Functioning Persons:** _____

       Example: _____

10-20.   **Functional Autonomy:** _____

       Example: _____

10-21.   **Genital Stage:** _____

10-22.   **Humanistic Theories:** _____

  Example: _____

10-23.   **Id:** _____

10-24.   **Internals:** _____

  Example: _____

10-25.   **Introverts:** _____

  Example: _____

10-26.   **Latency Stage:** _____

  Example: _____

10-27.   **Libido:** _____

10-28.   **Neo-Freudians:** _____

  Example: _____

10-29.   **Observational Learning:** _____

  Example: _____

10-30.   **Oedipus Complex:** _____

  Example: _____

10-31.   **Openness to Experience:** _____

  Example: _____

10-32.   **Oral Stage:** _____

  Example: _____

10-33. **Peak Experience:** _____

       Example: _____

10-34. **Personality:** _____

       Example: _____

10-35. **Personality Traits:** _____

       Example: _____

10-36. **Phallic Stage:** _____

       Example: _____

10-37. **Pleasure Principle:** _____

       Example: _____

10-38. **Psychoanalysis:** _____

10-39. **Psychosexual Stages of Development:** _____

10-40. **Reaction Formation:** _____

       Example: _____

10-41. **Reality Principle:** _____

       Example: _____

10-42. **Reciprocal Determinism:** _____

       Example: _____

10-43. **Secondary Traits:** _____

       Example: _____

10-44.   **Self-Actualization**: _____

Example: _____

10-45.   **Self-Concept**: _____

Example: _____

10-46.   **Self-Disclosure**: _____

Example: _____

10-47.   **Self-Efficacy**: _____

Example: _____

10-48.   **Self-Esteem**: _____

Example: _____

10-49.   **Self-Monitoring**: _____

Example: _____

10-50.   **Self-reinforcement**: _____

Example: _____

10-51.   **Sensation-Seeking**: _____

Example: _____

10-52.   **Social Cognitive Theory**: _____

10-53.   **Source Traits**: _____

Example: _____

10-54.   **Striving for Superiority**: _____

Example: _____

10-55. **<u>Sublimation</u>:** _____

   Example: _____

10-56. **<u>Superego</u>:** _____

10-57. **<u>Trait Theories</u>:** _____

   Example: _____

10-58. **<u>Unconditional Positive Regard</u>:** _____

   Example: _____

CHALLENGE: Develop Your Critical Thinking Skills

Explaining Personality: Developing Alternative Accounts

The critical thinker is able to recognize and formulate alternative explanations for the same event. By seeing "more than one side," he/she is in a position to take a more objective approach to problem-solving. Below, we provide you with a description of a person's behavior. As an exercise in developing your ability to "stretch your perspective," formulate an explanation for this person's behavior in terms of the theories of personality you have learned.

Situation:

Karen has never been married and has a hard time maintaining relationships with other persons. For example, she has been fired from her last two jobs because she got into arguments with her supervisors. Her parents were divorced when Karen was three and she lived with her grandmother until her grandmother died, when Karen was twenty. Since that time, she has lived alone. Although she desperately wants to have an active social life, she spends most of her time alone in her garden. Her garden is beautiful -- neat and colorful! She says she feels more comfortable with flowers than people. In her words, "I've never been rejected by a flower yet."

10-1.   How would Freud analyze Karen?

_____

_____

_____

_____

10-2.   In what stage of psychosexual development would Freud say Karen is fixated?

_____

_____

10-3.   Compare a Freudian account with that of a) Horney; b) Jung; c) Adler.

_____

_____

_____

_____

_____

_____

10-4.   Formulate an explanation of Karen's behavior based on a humanistic theory.

_____

_____

_____

_____

10-5.   How would a trait approach account for Karen's behavior?

_____

_____

_____

_____

_____

_____

10-6.   How could learning approaches to personality be applied to this case?

_____

_____

_____

_____

_____

_____

10-7.   What would you say about Karen's level of self-esteem?

_____

_____

YOUR NOTES:

CHALLENGE: Making Psychology Part of Your Life

<u>Understanding Your Own Personality</u>

A clear benefit that you can obtain from your psychology course is a gain in self-understanding. In fact, this is a common reason that students take this course! Take this opportunity to explore what each of the major personality theorists would suggest about your personality. Answer the questions below:

10-1.   Can you relate Freudian theory to your personality development?

_____

_____

_____

_____

_____

_____

10-2.   Have you ever made "Freudian slips?"

_____

_____

_____

_____

_____

_____

10-3.   How would Jung, Horney, and Adler explain aspects of your personality?

_____

_____

_____

_____

_____

_____

10-4.   What would the Humanistic approach suggest about your personality development?

_____

_____

_____

_____

_____

_____

10-5.   What do you identify as your personality traits? Relate these traits to those suggested by the trait theorists.

_____

_____

_____

_____

_____

_____

10-6.   Can you explain how learning approaches would account for aspects of your personality development?

_____

_____

_____

_____

_____

_____

YOUR NOTES:

CHALLENGE: Review Your Comprehensive Knowledge

SAMPLE TEST QUESTIONS

Once you have worked through the preceding sections, you should be ready for a comprehensive self-test. You can check your answers with those provided at the end of this section. An additional practice test is given in the supplementary section at the end of this study guide.

10-1. The part of the mind that contains the impulses which we are not aware of, according to Freud is the:
a. conscious.
b. preconscious.
c. unconscious.
d. subconscious.

10-2. According to Freud, the part of our personality that functions on the basis of the reality principle is:
a. the id.
b. the ego.
c. the superego.
d. the conscious.

10-3. According to Freud, adult personality is determined by what happens during:
a. adulthood.
b. the prenatal period.
c. infancy.
d. the psychosexual stages.

10-4. For males, the conflict whose resolution is supposedly related to moral development is the _____ conflict.
a. Oedipus
b. oral
c. anal
d. genital

10-5. The neo-Freudian who proposed the existence of the collective unconscious was:
a. Adler.
b. Jung.
c. Horney.
d. Fromm.

10-6. The humanistic theorists emphasize:
a. early development.
b. personal responsibility.
c. the unconscious.
d. learning.

10-7. Cattell used clustering techniques to identify _____ basic personality dimensions.
a. 4
b. 8
c. 16
d. 32

10-8. Which neo-Freudian emphasized the importance of social factors, such as birth order and family constellation, on personality development?
a. Adler
b. Jung
c. Horney
d. Fromm

10-9. According to Rogers, healthy development of the self-concept requires:
a. conditional regard.
b. environmental blocking.
c. control of emotions.
d. unconditional positive regard.

10-10. Which of the following is **not** one of the five key dimensions of personality identified by recent research?
a. Extroversion
b. Agreeableness
c. Intelligence
d. Conscientiousness

10-11. In Bandura's theory, our perceived ability to carry out a desired action is called:
a. self-reinforcement.
b. self-efficacy.
c. self-regulation.
d. self-esteem.

10-12. A defense mechanism that channels unacceptable impulses into a socially acceptable action is called:
    a. reaction formation.
    b. repression.
    c. regression.
    d. sublimation.

10-13. One potentially negative consequence of high self-esteem is that it may produce:
    a. a sense of overconfidence.
    b. vulnerability to stress.
    c. vulnerability to jealousy.
    d. a less clear self-concept.

10-14. Which of the following statements is not a typical criticism of Freudian theory?
    a. the theory is difficult to test
    b. several of his proposals are inconsistent with research
    c. behavior is not affected by unconscious thoughts
    d. his data collection methods were not appropriate

10-15. According to Jung, images that predispose us to perceive the external world in certain ways are:
    a. archetypes.
    b. conscious images.
    c. perceptual sets.
    d. defense mechanisms.

10-16. According to Maslow, the basic needs are:
    a. physiological, safety, belongingness, esteem, and self-actualization.
    b. physiological, safety, and self-actualization.
    c. physiological, safety, esteem, and self-actualization.
    d. physiological, belongingness, and self-actualization.

10-17. What concept best describes the example? A child first learned to play the piano because his parents make him do so but later plays because he enjoys it.
    a. functional autonomy
    b. self-efficacy
    c. reaction formation
    d. self-efficacy

10-18. Which of the following is **not** a characteristic of high sensation-seekers?
    a. more likely to engage in high risk sports
    b. more likely to engage in substance abuse
    c. less likely to withstand stress
    d. operate best at high levels of arousal

10-19. Which theory emphasizes the importance of generalized expectancies concerning internal or external control of outcomes?
    a. Rotter's social learning theory
    b. Cattell's source trait theory
    c. Roger's self-theory
    d. Maslow's need theory

10-20. Which of the following is not a characteristic of high self-monitors?
    a. They are better at reading others.
    b. They are better at regulating their own behavior.
    c. They are better at making favorable impressions on others.
    d. They show more consistent behaviors across situations.

Answers and Feedback for Sample Test Questions

10- 1.   C   In Freud's theory, hidden impulses are in the unconscious. (p. 372)

10- 2.   B   The ego operates according to the reality principle. (p. 374)

10- 3.   D   The psychosexual stages essentially shape the adult personality. (p. 376)

10- 4.   A   For males, the resolution of the Oedipus complex results in the development of a conscience. (p. 466)

10- 5.   B   Jung proposed the collective unconscious. (p. 381)

10- 6.   B   Humanistic theories emphasize personal responsibility and free will. (p. 383)

10- 7.   C   Cattell identified 16 basic personality dimensions. (p. 388)

10- 8.   A   In contrast to Freud, Adler emphasized social factors in personality development. (p. 382)

10- 9.   D   Unconditional positive regard is essential for healthy personality development, according to Rogers. (p. 384)

10-10.   C   Intelligence is not one of the five key dimensions of personality. The "Big 5" are: extroversion, agreeableness, conscientiousness, emotional stability, and openness to experience. (p. 389)

10-11.   B   Self-efficacy is our perception of our ability to carry out a desired action. The higher such feelings, the better persons tend to do on a wide range of tasks. (p. 392)

10-12.   D   Sublimation is the defense mechanism that channels unacceptable impulses into acceptable actions. (p. 374)

10-13.   A   Research indicates that persons high in self-esteem may sometimes have unrealistically optimistic expectations. (p. 395)

10-14.   C   In contrast to the other statements, Freud's theory is not subject to criticisms on the basis of this assumption. (p. 379)

10-15.   A   Archetypes are images that predispose us to perceive the world in a certain way. (p. 381)

10-16.   A   These are the five basic needs in Maslow's theory. (p. 385)

10-17.   A   Allport's concept of functional autonomy best describes this example. This refers to the idea that patterns of behavior can initially be acquired under one set of circumstances (the parents encouragement to play the piano) but may later be performed for different reasons (the person later plays for enjoyment). (p. 388)

10-18.   C   High sensation-seekers are more likely to withstand stress. (p. 399)

10-19.   A   Rotter's social learning theory emphasizes this factor. (p. 392)

10-20.   D   High self-monitors show **less** consistent behavior across situations. (p. 398)

Glossary of difficult words and expressions	Definition
Attuned	in touch with
Awkward	uncomfortable
Be neat	be clean cut; good grooming
Broker	person who buys and sells for others
Dam	barrier built to keep back water and raise its level
Dangling	hanging; on the edge
Flee	escape; run away from
Gloat	selfish delight
Innately good	naturally good; inherently positive
Jagged rocks	rough uneven edges
Lose their temper	upset; angry
Mainstream	current
Maladaptive	not good for; against one's best interests
Once-cherished	once cared for
Overly dependent	too dependent; relies too much on others
Pampered	treated very well
Poised	self-confident
Sip	taking a very small quantity at a time
Slimy	covered with slime
Strive	try; reach for
Swig (beer)	a deep swallow; gulp
Trivial	of small value of importance
Toppled	caused it to fall
"Wing it"	trying to accomplish something without really being prepared for it

CHAPTER 11
HEALTH, STRESS, AND COPING

OUTLINE: Develop a Study Plan

Use this outline to help you grasp the organizational structure of the chapter contents. The learning objectives (LOs) for each section are included. Use them as tools for developing your study plan. Space has been provided for you to write any notes or questions that come to mind as you begin your exploration into this material.

Heading:	Learning Objective:	Your Notes:
I. Health Psychology: An Overview	**L.O. 11.1:** Know the aim of health psychology and the findings surrounding the rapid development of this field.	
II. Stress: Its Causes, Effects, and Control		
A. Stress: Its Basic Nature	**L.O. 11.2:** Understand the basic nature of stress, including the general adaptation syndrome and the cognitive appraisal process.	
B. Stress: Some Major Causes	**L.O. 11.3:** Describe how stress can affect health and task performance and cause burnout.	
C. Stress: Some Major Effects	**L.O. 11.4:** Identify the individual characteristics that are related to resistance of stress.	
III. Understanding and Communicating Our Health Needs		
A. Symptom Perception: How Do We Know When We're Ill?	**L.O. 11.5:** Describe the factors that influence reporting and the interpretation of symptoms, including the health belief model of seeking medical advice.	
B. Health Beliefs: When Do We Seek Medical Advice?		
C. Doctor-Patient Interactions: Why Can't We Talk To Our Doctors?	**L.O. 11.6:** Discuss the nature of the communication process between doctors and patients.	

Heading:	Learning Objective:	Your Notes:
IV. Behavioral and Psychological Correlates of Illness: The Effects of Thoughts and Actions on Health	**L.O. 11.7:** Know the biological nature of cancer and the role of physical and psychological variables in its progression.	
A. Smoking: Risky For You and Everyone Around You	**L.O. 11.8:** Describe the reasons for smoking and the effects of smoking, including those associated with passive smoking.	
B. Diet and Nutrition: What You Eat May Save Your Life	**L.O. 11.9:** Describe the relationships of diet and nutrition to health and disease.	
C. Alcohol Consumption: Here's To Your Health	**L.O. 11.10:** Know the effects of excessive alcohol consumption.	
D. Emotions: Mood and Health	**L.O. 11.11:** Outline the influence of emotions and personality type on health.	
E. AIDS: The New Assault On Public Health	**L.O. 11.12:** Understand the nature and causes of AIDS.	
V. Promoting Wellness: Developing A Healthier Lifestyle		
A. Primary Prevention: Decreasing The Risks of Illness and Injury	**L.O. 11.13:** Discuss the use and effectiveness of primary prevention strategies such as health promotion in the mass media, control of alcohol consumption, and exercise.	
B. Secondary Prevention: The Role of Early Detection in Disease and Illness	**L.O. 11.14:** Understand the role of early detection in disease and illness.	
VI. Making Psychology Part of Your Life: Managing Stress: Some Useful Tactics	**L.O. 11.15:** Know how to apply this material to stress management.	

SURVEY AND QUESTION

This section presents the major topics and ideas from the chapter. Use it as a tool for seeing how the components of the chapter fit together. At the end of each major topic, we have asked you questions that relate to the major learning objectives. If you can answer these questions, you have taken a major step toward mastering this material.

I.   Health Psychology: An Overview

The area of study that regards both body and mind as important determinants of health and illness is health psychology. The field that combines behavioral and biomedical knowledge for the prevention and treatment of medical disorders is behavioral medicine. These fields have experienced rapid development over the past 20 years. This is probably due to the fact that many leading causes of death can be attributed to lifestyle.

Questions:

11-1.   What is the aim of health psychology and why has it developed rapidly over the past 20 years?

_____

_____

_____

II.   Stress: Its Causes, Effects, and Control

A.   Stress: Its Basic Nature

Events that are stressful have three characteristics. They are so intense that they produce overload. They produce incompatible tendencies to approach and avoid the same object or activity. They are beyond our limits of control or uncontrollable.

The sequence of responses to stress was termed the general adaptation syndrome by Selye. During the adaptation stage the body prepares itself for action. In the resistance stage arousal is lower as the body continues to cope with the stressor. Continued exposure to the stressor may lead to the stage of exhaustion.

Cognitive processes are also important in stress. Among these are the individual evaluations or cognitive appraisals. Individuals experience stress to the extent that they perceive the situation as threatening to important goals (primarily appraisals) or that they are unable to cope with their demands or dangers (secondary appraisals).

B.   Stress: Some Major Causes

The list of factors that contribute to stress is a long one. In general, individuals who have experienced stressful life events tend to have a high incidence of illness. The more stress individuals experience as a result of many minor problems or daily hassles, the poorer their psychological and physical health.

Natural and human-produced disasters can be a source of stress. Psychological problems suffered by survivors are termed post-traumatic stress disorder. Human-produced disasters can be more dramatic than natural disasters for several reasons. After human-produced disasters, our expectations may be violated, whereas, after a natural disaster, they may not. Therefore, we can experience a more intense sense of loss of control after human-produced disasters. Second, the consequences or negative outcomes associated with human-produced disasters can be larger than those associated with natural disasters in that human-produced disasters can exert their effects for years.

Work overload is being asked to do too much. Work underload is being asked to do too little. Role conflict is having to deal with conflicting demands or expectations. Procedures for evaluating employees' performance are known as performance appraisal. All of these can be stressors at work.

C.   Stress: Some Major Effects

The health effects of a variety of stressors (including disruptions in interpersonal relations, loneliness, academic pressure, daily hassles, and lack of social support) appear to be due to their interfering effects on the immune system. Optimism, regular exercise, and feelings of control may reduce the negative effects of stress.

People worn down by repeated exposures to stress at work are suffering from burnout. They often experience physical, emotional, and mental exhaustion. Feelings of low personal accomplishment are also common. These may come from feeling useless or unappreciated. Inflexible procedures and poor promotion opportunities are additional causes of burnout.

Optimists are more resistant to stress than pessimists. Optimists use problem-focused coping and seek social support. Pessimists may give up the goal or deny the occurrence of stressful events.

Individuals who are hardy are also stress resistant. They have a high level of commitment to their work. They see change as a challenge. They have a sense of control over events in their lives.

Questions:

11-2.   What is the basic nature of stress and what is the general adaptation syndrome and the cognitive process? _____

_____

_____

_____

11-3.   What are the characteristics and effects of the major causes of stress? _____

_____

_____

_____

11-4.   How does stress influence health? _____

_____

_____

_____

11-5.   How can stress influence burnout? _____

_____

_____

_____

11-6.   What are the individual characteristics that are related to the resistance from the effects of stress? _____

_____

_____

_____

III.   Understanding and Communicating Our Health Needs

A.   Symptom Perception: How Do We Know When We're Ill?

Sensations that reflect underlying medical conditions are symptoms. Persons who have few distractions in their lives are more likely to notice symptoms. Persons in a good mood report less symptoms than those in a bad mood. Our interpretations of symptoms are influenced by comparisons with others and our expectations.

B.   Health Beliefs: When Do We Seek Medical Advice?

The health belief model suggests that our willingness to seek medical help depends on the extent to which we perceive a threat to our health and believe that a particular behavior will reduce that threat. Perception of threat depends on our health values and our beliefs concerning susceptibility to illness and its seriousness. Perceived effectiveness depends on whether we believe actions will be effective or are worth the effort.

C.   Doctor-Patient Interactions: Why Can't We Talk To Our Doctors?

The most frequently observed communication skills of doctors are those dealing with mechanics of the illness. They infrequently display skills in the psychosocial aspect of the illness such as patient knowledge and emotional response. Good doctor-patient communication is related to successful treatment. Satisfaction, compliance, and recall of information is increased with amount of information given by the doctor.

Questions:

11-7.   What factors influence the reporting and interpretation of symptoms? _____

_____

_____

_____

11-8.   What is the health belief model of seeking medical advice? _____

_____

_____

_____

11-9.   What is the nature of the communication process between doctors and patients? _____

_____

_____

_____

IV.   Behavioral and Psychological Correlates of Illness: The Effects of Thoughts and Actions on Health

Families with high cancer rates have a diminished efficiency of the natural killer cells. Lifestyle features that affect our chances of becoming ill are risk factors. Cancer producing agents in our environment are carcinogens. Cancer is an illness in which rapidly growing abnormal cells overwhelm normal cells.

A.   Smoking: Risky for You and Everyone Around You

The largest preventable cause of illness and death in the U.S. is smoking. Smoking seems to be influenced by genetic, psychosocial and cognitive factors. Some people appear to be biologically predisposed to nicotine. Nicotine alters the availability of certain neurotransmitter substances. These substances produce temporary improvements in concentration, recall, alertness, arousal, and psychomotor performance. Psychosocial factors include peer pressure and exposure to role models. Cognitive beliefs may also play a role. Smokers may hold false beliefs that exempt them from the harmful consequences of smoking.

It is anticipated that over the next few years the percentage of deaths due to smoking among U.S. men and women will become increasingly similar. Smoke from others or passive smoke can increase the risk of developing lung cancer, brain tumors, and may cause more frequent and severe attacks of asthma in children with this disease. It can also decrease test performance in adolescents.

B.   Diet and Nutrition: What You Eat May Save Your Life

Eating vegetables may reduce the risk of cancer. Vitamin A inhibits the destruction of cells by carcinogens and dietary fiber may inhibit colorectal cancer.

Cross-cultural differences in breast cancer rates appear to be related to the amount of fat in the diet. Cardiovascular disease is affected by the amount of cholesterol in our blood or serum cholesterol.

C.   Alcohol Consumption: Here's to Your Health

Although a glass of red wine may be associated with health benefits, consumption of alcohol is also related to many disorders such as cancer, cirrhosis of the liver, and impaired cognitive and sexual functioning.

D.   Emotions: Mood and Health

Inhibiting the expression of negative feelings can have detrimental effects on health. The expression of both distress and positive feelings can aid recovery or survival of illness. Unexpressed anger has been related to high blood pressure or hypertension.

People who are competitive, hostile, aggressive, and important, show Type A behavior pattern. Those who are relaxed and easygoing are called Type B. Type A individuals appear to be more likely to suffer heart attacks. This is especially the case for those who do not express emotions such as anger, hostility, or cynicism. The most detrimental emotion appears to be cynical hostility.

The emotional responses of Type A individuals may lead to construction of peripheral blood flow, higher blood pressure, and increased pulse rate. It may also produce increased hormonal levels which may lead to heart disease. Type As are more likely to survive heart attacks than Type Bs.

E.   AIDS: The Assault on Public Health

A reduction in the immune system's ability to defend the body against disease is called AIDS. The cause of AIDS is human immunodeficiency virus or HIV. The two ways AIDS is spread is by unprotected sexual intercourse and infected blood or blood products. Worldwide, AIDS is transmitted primarily through heterosexual intercourse. At present, the only effective means of combating AIDS are primary prevention programs. These programs attempt to reduce risky behavior. Social norms and beliefs are two factors that play a role in determining why some groups engage in risky behavior.

Questions:

11-10.   What is the potentially important role of physical and psychological variables in the progression of cancer? _____

_____

_____

_____

11-11.   What are the effects of smoking? _____

_____

_____

_____

11-12. What are the effects of passive smoke? _____

_____

_____

_____

11-13. What are the effects of diet and nutrition on health? _____

_____

_____

_____

11-14. What are the effects of alcohol consumption? _____

_____

_____

_____

11-15. What is the influence of emotions and personality type on health? _____

_____

_____

_____

11-16. What are the nature and causes of AIDS? _____

_____

_____

_____

11-17. What factors influence the transmission and prevention of HIV? _____

_____

_____

_____

V. Promoting Wellness: Developing a Healthier Lifestyle

Communities in which a large number of persons live to be more than 100 years old tend to eat a high fiber diet and low to moderate amounts of meat and animal fat. They maintain low to moderate levels of daily caloric intake and consume only moderate amounts of alcohol each day. Physical activity is a very important factor contributing to longevity and good health. Additional factors may be continued sexual activity and continued social involvement.

Techniques designed to reduce or eliminate illness are called primary prevention strategies. Techniques attempting to decrease the severity of illness by early detection are called secondary prevention strategies.

A.   Primary Prevention: Decreasing the Risks of Illness and Injury

Limited success of mass media campaigns on health behavior may be due to the fact that most commercials promote unhealthy habits. A campaign on heart disease that combined the media and behavior therapy was quite effective. Beliefs may also influence our response to advertisements. Those who have a high fear of AIDS rate advertisements about AIDS as more effective than those with low fear.

Psychologists are studying the factors that tend to increase or decrease actual drinking behavior and the outcome of drinking in hopes of decreasing alcohol consumption. Private social gatherings and fraternity parties are two environments in which drinking takes place.

Exercise can reduce coronary heart disease. It can also improve our self-concept, alleviate feelings of depression and reduce anxiety. Exercise can also improve one's mood. An increase in mood may occur when companionship is associated with exercise or when it increases feelings of self-efficacy -- perceived confidence in one's ability to perform a behavior.

If starting and maintaining regular exercise, it is important to arrange the environment so that it supports the behavior and weakens competing behaviors. Supporting factors include cues that are a signal to exercise, rewards that maintain exercise and a strong social support network.

B.   Secondary Prevention: The Role of Early Detection in Disease and Illness

Use of available screening techniques could decrease the incidence of disease and the number of deaths due to disease. Early detection can decrease the incidence of cardiovascular disease and could significantly reduce the number of deaths due to cervical, colon, prostate, testicular, and breast cancer.

Questions:

11-18. What are the factors that appear to influence longevity and health? _____

_____

_____

_____

11-19. Why are psychologists in favor of preventive strategies? _____

_____

_____

_____

11-20. What is the use and effectiveness of primary prevention strategies such as health promotion in the mass media, control of alcohol consumption, and exercise? _____

_____

_____

_____

11-21. What is the role of early detection in disease and illness? _____

_____

_____

_____

VI. Making Psychology Part of Your Life: Managing Stress: Some Useful Tactics

One effective physiological technique of coping with stress is to reduce muscle tension by progressive relaxation. Another is exercise. A behavioral coping technique that involves efficient use of time is time management. One effective cognitive coping technique is replacing negative appraisals with positive ones. This is called cognitive restructuring.

Question:

11-22. What are the characteristics of the three major stress reduction techniques? _____

_____

_____

_____

MAKING PSYCHOLOGY PART OF YOUR LIFE: Key Terms and Concepts

Knowing the important concepts and key terms contained in this chapter is a very important part of mastering the material. We have presented a sample of these concepts below. Define each concept and check your definition with that presented in the chapter. It will also be beneficial for you to think of an example of each concept. Whenever possible, use your own personal experience to provide an example of each term below.

11-1.   **Acquired Immune Deficiency Syndrome (AIDS):** _____

11-2.   **Cancer:** _____

11-3.   **Carcinogens:** _____

Example: _____

11-4.   **Cardiovascular Disease:** _____

Example: _____

11-5.   **General Adaptation Syndrome:** _____

Example: _____

11-6.   **Hardiness:** _____

Example: _____

11-7.   **Health Belief Model:** _____

Example: _____

11-8.   **Health Psychology:** _____

Example: _____

11-9.   **Hypertension:** _____

Example: _____

11-10. **Lifestyle:** _____

Example: _____

11-11.   **Nicotine:** _____

      Example: _____

11-12.   **Passive Smoking:** _____

      Example: _____

11-13.   **Person-Environment (P-E) Fit:** _____

      Example: _____

11-14.   **Post Traumatic Stress Disorder:** _____

      Example: _____

11-15.   **Prevention Strategies:** _____

      Example: _____

11-16.   **Risk Factors:** _____

      Example: _____

11-17.   **Serum Cholesterol:** _____

      Example: _____

11-18.   **Social Norms:** _____

      Example: _____

11-19.   **Stress:** _____

      Example: _____

11-20.   **Stressors:** _____

      Example: _____

11-21.   **Type A Behavior Pattern:** _____

      Example: _____

CHALLENGE: Develop Your Critical Thinking Skills

Thinking Critically about Health

The critical thinker is able to "stand back" and access how habits that may have developed over the years may have adverse effects on his/her health. As an exercise in this skill, take a look at your health habits. then, think of ways you can do away with bad habits and substitute more healthy patterns of behavior.

11-1.   How often do you exercise? _____

_____

11-2.   Do you smoke? If so, what is maintaining this habit? _____

_____

_____

_____

11-3.   How often do you drink alcohol? _____

_____

11-4.   What problems do you see, if any, with your eating patterns? _____

_____

_____

_____

11-5.   Do you have a plan to handle the stress in your life? [See the application exercise.] _____

_____

_____

_____

11-6.   How can you improve your health habits? _____

_____

_____

_____

CHALLENGE: Making Psychology Part of Your Life

<u>Finding Ways to Reduce Stress</u>

Your textbook author provides you with examples of ways to cope with stress (see pp. 439-440). Below, we provide the major categories of coping techniques. For each category, list the techniques you presently use (and could use) to reduce the stress level in your life.

<u>Physiological Coping Techniques</u>

_____

_____

_____

_____

<u>Behavioral Coping Techniques</u>

_____

_____

_____

_____

<u>Cognitive Coping Techniques</u>

_____

_____

_____

_____

CHALLENGE: Review Your Comprehensive Knowledge

SAMPLE TEST QUESTIONS

Once you have worked through the preceding sections, you should be ready for a comprehensive self-test. You can check your answers with those at the end of this section. An additional practice test is given in the supplementary section at the end of this study guide.

11-1.   The field that combines behavioral and biomedical knowledge for the prevention and treatment of medical disorders is:
a. physiological psychology.
b. behavioral medicine.
c. bio-behaviorism.
d. neuroscience.

11-2.   The stage of the general adaptation syndrome when arousal is lowered as the body copes with the stressor is the:
a. coping stage.
b. resistance stage.
c. alarm stage.
d. exhaustion stage.

11-3.   According to the cognitive appraisal perspective, stress occurs when people:
a. are in the coping stage.
b. are goal oriented.
c. are in the resistance stage.
d. feel unable to cope with demands.

11-4.   According to research on stressful life events, it appears that people who have experienced a large number of serious events in a prior 12 month period will show:
a. a high incidence of illness.
b. a high level of stress resistance.
c. hardiness.
d. strong alarm reactions.

11-5.   Being asked to do too many things in a short period of time is called work:
a. conflict.
b. overload.
c. underload.
d. incompatibility.

11-6.   The negative effects of stress on health appears to result from its interference in the operation of our _____ system.
a. nervous
b. endocrine
c. cardiovascular
d. immune

11-7.   Which of the following factors is **not** one of those likely to be a cause of burnout?
a. being unappreciated
b. feelings of control
c. inflexible rules
d. poor opportunities for promotion

11-8.   Optimists tend to be more stress-resistant than pessimists. This may be due to optimists using _____ coping.
a. problem-focused
b. emotional
c. denial
d. psychological

11-9.   The model which explains why people do not use medical screening devices is the _____ model.
a. hardiness
b. optimism
c. health belief
d. cognitive appraisal

11-10.   If a doctor wants to enhance patient satisfaction and compliance, the doctor should do **all but one** of the following in communicating with the patient.
    a.   focus exclusively on the mechanics of the illness
    b.   give much information
    c.   make positive talk
    d.   engage in social conversation

11-11.   What is presently the second leading cause of death among American men between the ages of 18 and 44?
    a.   heart disease.   c.   AIDS.
    b.   car accidents.   d.   homocide.

11-12.   Which of the following is false?
    a.   Individuals who have experienced stressful life events tend to have a high incidence of illness.
    b.   Procedures for evaluating employees' performance are called performance appraisal.
    c.   Persons who have few distractions in their lives are more likely to notice symptoms than those who have many distractions.
    d.   Smoking does not appear to be influenced by psychosocial factors.

11-13.   At times, individuals experience stress because they perceive the situation as threatening to important goals. This is termed:
    a.   secondary appraisal.   c.   the general adaptation syndrome.
    b.   primary appraisal.   d.   post-traumatic stress syndrome.

11-14.   Which **is true** of hardy individuals?
    a.   They are not stress resistant.   c.   They do not have a sense of control.
    b.   They see change as a challenge.   d.   They have a low level of commitment.

11-15.   Lifestyle features that affect our chances of becoming ill are termed _____ factors.
    a.   risk   c.   punishment
    b.   carcinogen   d.   individual

11-16.   Which is false?
    a.   The percentage of deaths among U.S. men and women appears to be becoming increasingly dissimilar.
    b.   Passive smoke has been associated with an increased risk of asthma attacks.
    c.   Smoking can produce a temporary improvement in recall.
    d.   Dietary fiber may inhibit colorectal cancer.

11-17.   Which is **false** about Type As?
    a.   They are competitive and impatient.
    b.   They are more likely to suffer a heart attack than Type Bs.
    c.   They are aggressive.
    d.   They are less likely to survive heart attacks than Type Bs.

11-18.   The limited success of mass media campaigns on health behavior may be due to the fact that commercials:
    a.   promote unhealthy habits.   c.   are not interesting.
    b.   are too short.   d.   are not clear.

11-19.   An effective physiological technique of coping with stress is to reduce _____ by progressive relaxation.
    a.   cognitive tension   c.   muscle tension
    b.   cognitive appraisals   d.   time pressures

11-20.   Prevention strategies that are designed to increase early detection are called:
    a.   preliminary   c.   primary
    b.   tertiary   d.   secondary

Answers and Feedback for Sample Test Questions:

11-1. B   Behavioral medicine is the field that combines behavioral and biomedical knowledge. (p. 407)

11-2. B   The resistance stage is characterized by lowered arousal during coping. (p. 409)

11-3. D   The cognitive appraisal view suggests that people feel stressed when they believe that they can't cope with demands. (p. 410)

11-4. A   A high incidence of illness is expected when people have experienced a large number of serious events in a 12 month period. (p. 413)

11-5. B   Overload is a source of stress and is characterized by being asked to do too many things during a short period of time. (p. 416)

11-6. D   Stress appears to have a negative effect on our immune system, causing illness. (p. 419)

11-7. B   Feelings of control, in fact, prevent burnout. (p. 422)

11-8. A   Optimists appear to use problem-focused coping strategies, which increases their resistance to stress. (p. 422)

11-9. C   Health belief models suggest that people don't use screening devices. (p. 424)

11-10. A   A doctor should consider the individual, rather than focusing exclusively on illness mechanics. (p. 426)

11-11. C   AIDS is the second leading cause of death among males in the age group. (p. 433)

11-12. D   Smoking is influenced by psychosocial factors. (p. 428)

11-13. B   Primary appraisals involve the perception that a situation threatens important goals. (p. 410)

11-14. B   Hardy individuals are stress resistant, have a sense of control, and have high levels of commitment. Therefore, options A, C, and D are false. Option B states that hardy individuals see change as a challenge: the only true statement. (p. 422)

11-15. A   Risk factors are lifestyle features that affect our chances of becoming ill. (p. 427)

11-16. A   The percentage of deaths among U.S. men and women are becoming more **similar**. (p. 429)

11-17. D   Type As are more likely to survive heart attacks. (p. 423)

11-18. A   Many commercials promote unhealthy health habits. (p. 436)

11-19. C   Decreasing muscle tension is an effective stress reduction technique. (p. 439)

11-20. D   Secondary prevention strategies are designed to increase early illness detection. (p. 438)

Glossary of difficult words and expressions	Definition
Aches	dull, continuous pain
Blatant	obvious and intentional
Boosting	increasing; raising up; supporting
Buffering	lessening; protecting; preventing from harm
Cope	manage; deal with effectively
Cueing	giving ideas on the behavior that is expected
Culprits	the ones to blame; the guilty ones
Depiction	describe in words; show in some way
Depleted	empty until little or nothing remains
Detrimental	harmful; having a bad effect
Disaster strikes	disaster hits; something very bad happens
Disseminating	distributing; giving out
Domain	area of topic or thought
Engulfing	swallow up; taking in
Hardy	strong; can handle lots of stuff
Hassles	things that bother you
Hectic	always busy
"Kick the habit"	quit the habit; stop doing something
Mutates	changes in form
Plight	difficulty; dilemma; small problem
Prompted	led; invoked; started
Queasiness	feeling of sickness; uneasy feeling
Rapport	a relationship; able to speak with very easily
Refrain	not do something; prevent
Remission	lessening or weakening of; going away
Resilience	being able to recover quickly
Scribbles	writes something quickly
Soar	quickly rise to the top
Sterling	exceptional
Take it in stride	not to be bothered by; deal with very easily

Glossary of difficult words and expressions	Definition
Tickle	to touch someone in a way that makes them laugh
Transient	temporary; not permanent
Trapped	unable to escape
Withstand	resist; cope with; deal with

CHAPTER 12
PSYCHOLOGICAL DISORDERS: THEIR NATURE AND CAUSES

OUTLINE: Develop a Study Plan

Use this outline to help you grasp the organizational structure of the chapter contents. The learning objectives (LOs) for each section are included. Use them as tools for developing your study plan. Space has been provided for you to write any notes or questions that come to mind as you begin your exploration into this material.

Heading:	Learning Objective:	Your Notes:
I. Changing Conceptions of Psychological Disorders: A Brief Historical Perspective	**L.O. 12.1:** Know the definition and general characteristics of psychological disorders and describe how the concept of "abnormal" behavior has changed over time.	
A. From Demons to Disease: Changing Concepts of Abnormal Behavior		
B. The Biological/Medical Perspective: Psychological Disorders as Disease	**L.O. 12.2:** Discuss the biological/medical perspective, the psychodynamic perspective, and the modern psychological approach to psychological disorders.	
C. The Psychodynamic Perspective: Desires, Anxieties, and Defenses		
D. The Modern Psychological Approach: Recognizing The Multiple Roots of Abnormal Behavior		
II. Identifying Psychological Disorders: The DSM-IV	**L.O. 12.3:** Describe the features of the DSM-IV and discuss how it differs from previous versions.	
A. Describing Psychological Disorders: An Explanatory Note		
III. Mood Disorders: The Downs and Ups Of Life		
A. Depressive Disorders: Probing The Depths of Despair	**L.O. 12.4:** List the symptoms associated with depression and bipolar disorders.	

Heading:	Learning Objective:	Your Notes:
B. Bipolar Disorders: Riding The Emotional Roller Coaster		
C. The Causes of Depression: Its Biological and Psychological Roots	**L.O. 12.5:** Discuss the biological and psychological differences between depressed and nondepressed persons.	
D. Suicide: When Life Becomes Unbearable	**L.O. 12.6:** Know the findings concerning suicide rates, how suicide may be predicted, and the causes of suicide.	
IV. Anxiety Disorders: When Dread Debilitates		
A. Panic Attack: The Body Signals "Danger!" But Is It Real?	**L.O. 12.7:** Know the characteristics and potential causes of panic attacks and phobias.	
B. Phobias: Fear That Is Focused		
C. Obsessive-Compulsive Disorder: Behaviors And Thoughts Outside One's Control	**L.O. 12.8:** Describe the obsessive-compulsive disorder and the posttraumatic stress disorder.	
D. Posttraumatic Stress Disorder		
E. Anxiety: The Role of Subliminal Processing	**L.O. 12.9:** Discuss the research concerning how anxious persons may differ in how they use their information processing capacity.	
V. Somatoform Disorders: Physical Symptoms Without Physical Causes	**L.O. 12.10:** Describe the different somatoform disorders as well as their possible origins.	
VI. Dissociative Disorders: When Memory Fails	**L.O. 12.11:** Know the meaning of "dissociative disorder" and the different types of this disorder.	

Heading:	Learning Objective:	Your Notes:
VII. Sexual And Gender Identity Disorders		
A. Sexual Dysfunctions: Disturbances In Desire and Arousal	**L.O. 12.12:** Survey the different types of sexual disorders and gender identity disorders.	
B. Paraphilias: Disturbances In Sexual Object Or Behavior		
C. Gender Identity Disorders		
VIII. Eating Disorders	**L.O. 12.13:** Compare and contrast the characteristics of the two most common types of eating disorders.	
IX. Personality Disorders: Traits That Prove Costly		
A. Paranoid and Schizoid Personality Disorders: Cut Off From Human Contact	**L.O. 12.14:** Know the characteristics of the paranoid, schizoid, and antisocial personality disorders.	
B. The Antisocial Personality Disorder		
X. Schizophrenia: Out Of Touch With Reality		
A. The Basic Nature Of Schizohprenia	**L.O. 12.15:** Know the general nature and subtypes of schizophrenia as well as the major symptoms and origins of this disorder.	
B. Subtypes Of Schizophrenia		
C. The Origins of Schizophrenia		

Heading:	Learning Objective:	Your Notes:
D. Chronic Mental Illness And The Homeless		
XI. Making Psychology Part of Your Life: Preventing Suicide: Some Basic Steps	**L.O. 12.16:** Be able to use what you've learned to help prevent suicide.	

SURVEY AND QUESTION

This section presents the major topics and ideas from the chapter. Use it as a tool for seeing how the components of the chapter fit together. At the end of each major topic, we have asked you a question that relates to the major learning objectives. If you can answer these questions, you have taken a major step toward mastering this material.

I. Changing Conceptions of Psychological Disorders: A Brief Historical Perspective

Psychological disorders are maladaptive patterns of behavior and thought that cause the persons who experience them considerable distress. Although there is no single way of distinguishing between normal and abnormal behavior, most psychologists agree that all psychological disorders share four major features in common. First, these disorders cause distress in the people that experience them. They involve patterns of behavior or thought that are relatively atypical. Third, they are maladaptive in that they make it difficult for a person to meet the demands of their lives. Finally, psychological disorders are associated with behavior that is evaluated negatively by members of society. Recent surveys indicate that as many as 50 percent of all human beings have a psychological disorder at some point during their life.

A. From Demons to Disease: Changing Concepts of Abnormal Behavior

At different imes over the centures, psychological disorders have been perceived as stemming primarily from supernatural causes or primarily from natural causes.

B. The Biological/Medical Perspective: Psychological Disorders as Disease

The biological/medical approach views psychological disorders as disease. Prior to this conceptualization, patients were often shackled to walls and treated inhumanly. Phillipe Pinel, the director of a major hospital for the insane in Paris, treated patients as sick people and produced improvements in their conditions. Similar actions by other physicians produced encouraging results and strengthened the view that abnormal behavior is the result of mental illness. This view is influential today and is the basis for the field of psychiatry.

C. The Psychodynamic Perspective: Desires, Anxieties, and Defenses

Freud proposed a psychodynamic perspective of psychological disorders. He proposed that anxiety occurs when the ego feels overwhelmed by the demands of the id. To protect itself, the ego uses defense mechanisms. The id is the repository of our primitive desires and demands instant gratification. The superego represents our conscience. The ego strives to maintain a balance between the impulses of the id and superego. The importance of Freud's theory is in his suggestion that unconscious thoughts or impulses play a role in abnormal behavior.

D. The Modern Psychological Approach: Recognizing the Multiple Roots of Abnormal Behavior

The psychological perspective suggests that psychological disorders are better understood through studying processes such as learning, perception, and cognition. It further suggests that psychological disorders should be understood as resulting from the complex interplay between environmental influences and heredity that affect all forms of behavior.

Questions:

12-1.   What is the definition and what are the general characteristics of psychological disorders?

_____

_____

_____

12-2.   What are the biological/medical, psychodynamic, and modern perspectives of psychological disorders? _____

_____

_____

_____

II.   Identifying Psychological Disorders: The DSM-IV

The DSM-IV is a widely accepted classification system for identifying psychological disorders. In this manual, hundreds of disorders are described. These descriptions include information on diagnostic features or symptoms, associated features, and disorders and associated laboratory findings and physical examination signs. In addition, the DSM-IV classifies disorders along five axes. One relates to major disorders themselves, another to personality disorders, a third to general medical conditions relevant to each disorder, a fourth considers psychosocial and environmental problems and a fifth relates to global assessment of current functioning.

This version of the DSM differs from past versions in several respects. In this version, psychologists had major input. In addition, this version is more firmly based on empirical evidence and takes greater efforts to consider the role of cultural factors. One major drawback of this manual is that it is primarily descriptive in nature. It does not provide an explanation of abnormal behavior.

The DSM-IV attempts to address the important implications of cultural diversity. First, culturally-specific symptoms are described. Second, disorders like kitsunetsuki -- the belief among villagers in rural areas of Japan that they are possessed by foxes -- are described where they are relevant. Third, a special Appendix describes culture-bound disorders.

A.   Describing Psychological Disorders: An Explanatory Note

There are literally hundreds of different psychological disorders. All cannot be covered in this text. Your author focuses on the most common disorders.

Questions:

12-3.   What are the basic features of the DSM-IV and how does it differ from previous versions?

_____

_____

_____

12-4.   How have cultural influences been incorporated into the DSM-IV? _____

_____

_____

_____

III. Mood Disorders: The Downs and Ups of Life

Swings in mood are normal. But for some persons, disturbances in mood are both extreme and prolonged. Extreme and prolonged disturbances in mood are called mood disorders. There are two major categories of this disorder: depressive disorder and bipolar disorders.

A. Depressive Disorders: Probing the Depths of Despair

The criteria for the existence of depression include long periods of intense unhappiness, lack of interest in the usual pleasures of life, loss of energy, loss of appetite, disturbances of sleep and difficulties in thinking. If individuals experience five or more symptoms at once, they are classified as showing a major depressive episode. This is the most common psychological disorder and is more common among women.

B. Bipolar Disorders: Riding the Emotional Roller Coaster

Bipolar depression includes wide swings in emotion. Individuals suffering from this disorder move between deep depression and mania -- a state in which they are extremely excited.

C. The Causes of Depression: Its Biological and Psychological Roots

Depression tends to run in families, suggesting that there is a genetic component. The presence of low levels of the neurotransmitters serotonin and norepinephrine in depressed persons suggests a biochemical basis of depression.

Some research suggests that depression is related to feelings of lack of control or helplessness. Depressed persons attribute bad events to internal and stable causes. Others have proposed that depression is caused by negative beliefs about self, others, and faulty cognitive sets. Depressed people tend to overgeneralize and magnify the importance of negative events.

D. Suicide: When Life Becomes Unbearable

In the U.S., almost 2 million persons have attempted suicide. People who are depressed are more likely to commit suicide than others. The highest suicide rates occur among older people, but suicide has been on the rise among young persons for several decades. More attempts are made by women while more men actually succeed. Freud contended that suicide stems from the death instinct. Another view suggests that suicide is the result of individuals' efforts to escape self-awareness when they view themselves as inadequate and intolerable.

Questions:

12-5.   What are the symptoms associated with depression? _____

_____

_____

_____

12-6.   What are the characteristics of bipolar disorders? _____

_____

_____

_____

12-7.   What are the biological and psychological differences between depressed and nondepressed persons?

_____

_____

_____

12-8.   What are the findings concerning suicide rates and the research concerning how it may be predicted?

_____

_____

_____

IV.   Anxiety Disorders: When Dread Debilitates

When feelings of intense anxiety persist for long periods of time, one may be experiencing an anxiety disorder.

A.   Panic Attack: The Body Signals "Danger" But Is It Real?

Anxiety disorders take several different forms. Panic attacks are defined as brief periods of panic that have no specific cause. The symptoms include chest pains, nausea, feeling dizzy, shaking, fear of losing control, chills, hot flashes or numbness. For some persons, panic attacks are linked with specific situations. Agoraphobia is intense fear of specific situations in which individuals fear that they will experience panic attacks. These include fear of being in a crowd, car, being on a bridge, standing in line or merely leaving home. Biological factors and conditioning appear to play a role in these disorders.

B.   Phobias: Fear That is Focused

When people experience intense anxiety in the presence of an object or while thinking about it, they are said to have a phobia. These may be acquired by classical conditioning or we may be prepared biologically for certain phobias.

C. Obsessive-Compulsive Disorder: Behaviors and Thoughts Outside One's Control

Anxieties may sometimes lead to repetitive behaviors or compulsions. Recurrent thoughts or obsessions can also occur. This is known as the obsessive-compulsive disorder. Persons with this disorder cannot distract themselves from disturbing thoughts. Only by performing specific actions can they ensure their safety and reduce this anxiety.

D. Posttraumatic Stress Disorder

Posttraumatic stress disorder describes an anxiety disorder in which a person persistently reexperiences a traumatic event in thoughts or dreams, persistently avoids stimuli linked with the trauma, and experiences persistent symptoms of increased arousal. This disorder can stem from various traumatic events including rape, and accidents.

E. Anxiety: The Role of Subliminal Processing

Persons suffering from anxiety disorders are more likely to notice and process information relating to their anxieties. This tendency may interfere with the effectiveness of therapy focused on conscious thoughts and reactions.

Questions:

12-9. What are the characteristics and potential causes of panic attacks? _____

_____

_____

_____

12-10. What are the nature and potential causes of the various phobias? _____

_____

_____

_____

12-11. What is the obsessive-compulsive disorder? _____

_____

_____

_____

12-12. What are the characteristics of the post-traumatic stress disorder? _____

_____

_____

_____

12-13. What are the research findings concerning how anxious persons may differ in how they use their information processing capacity? _____

_____

_____

_____

V.   Somatoform Disorders: Physical Symptoms Without Physical Causes

People who exhibit physical symptoms that have no underlying physical cause have somatoform disorders. A common type of this disorder involves an excessive fear of disease -- hypochondriasis. Another type involves reports of physical complaints -- somatization disorder. Another somatoform disorder is conversion disorder. People suffering from this disorder may experience blindness, deafness, and paralysis even though there is no underlying medical condition that would produce these symptoms.

There are three interpretations for somatoform disorders. Freud believed that unacceptable conflicts are converted into various impulses. From a behavioral interpretation, persons with this disorder are being rewarded for adopting a sick person role. From a cognitive interpretation, individuals with this disorder tend to focus excessively on normal bodily sensations, to misinterpret these, and to attribute them to various serious conditions.

Question:

12-14. What are the different somatoform disorders as well as their possible origins? _____

_____

_____

_____

VI.   Dissociative Disorders: When Memory Fails

When people have lengthy losses of memory or identity, they are said to experience dissociative disorders. They can take several different forms. Sudden disruptions of memory that occur without any clear-cut physical cause are called dissociative amnesia and seem to be caused by an active motivation to forget. This type of amnesia can be localized -- involves all events in a particular period, or selective -- involves some events in a particular period or generalized.

Persons suffering from dissociative fugue have a sudden disturbance of memory and are unable to recall their past. These individuals often adopt a new identity.

When a person appears to have two or more distinct personalities, they are said to have dissociative identity disorder (multiple personality disorder in earlier versions of the DSM). This disorder is nine times more common in women than men. Although the origins of this disorder have proven difficult to determine, some persons speculate that individuals with this disorder generated alternative personalities to deal with the traumatic events experienced during childhood. Although there is still controversy, there is some evidence that this disorder is genuine. Individuals with this disorder sometimes have different brain waves and often score differently on standardized personality tests in each personality state.

Question:

12-15. What is the meaning of "dissociative disorder" and what are the different types of this disorder?

_____

_____

_____

VII.   Sexual and Gender Identity Disorders

A.   Sexual Dysfunctions: Disturbances in Desire and Arousal

Sexual dysfunctions involve disturbances in sexual desire, arousal, or the ability to attain orgasm. These problems are classified according to when in the normal pattern of sexual activity they occur. Sexual desire disorders involve a lack of interest or aversion to sexual activities. Sexual arousal disorders involve erectile disorders in males and the absence of vaginal swelling and lubrication in females. Orgasm disorders involve the delay or absence of orgasm in both sexes, and may also involve premature ejaculation in males.

B.   Paraphilias

Paraphilias exist when unusual images, acts, or objects are required for sexual arousal and performance. When individuals are aroused by inanimate objects, they have a fetish. Frotterism exists when individuals have fantasies and urges involving touching a nonconsenting person. Preference for sexual activity with children is pedophilia. Those who are aroused by hurting others are sexual sadists. Those who are aroused by such treatment are sexual masochists.

C.   Gender Identity Disorders

Gender identity disorders exist when individuals desire to alter their primary and secondary sex characteristics. Individuals suffering from these disorders feel they were born with the wrong gender identity and seek a change. About two thirds of individuals who undergo a sex-change operation report increased happiness.

Questions:

12-16. What are the different types of sexual disorders? _____

_____

_____

_____

12-17. What are the different types of sexual disorders that involve disturbances in sexual objects or behavior? _____

_____

_____

_____

12-18. What are gender identity disorders? _____

_____

_____

_____

VIII. Eating Disorders

When individuals are very fearful of gaining weight and fail to maintain a normal body weight, they are said to have anorexia nervosa. Bulimia nervosa involves alternating between binge eating and purging. Purging involves various forms of compensatory behaviors designed to avoid weight gain. Bulimics may be able to withstand the cycles of binge-purge due to reduced taste sensitivity making purging less unpleasant. Therefore, although social pressures may contribute to the onset of this disorder, sensory factors (reduced sensitivity) may strengthen and maintain these disorders.

Question:

12-19. What are the characteristics of the two most common types of eating disorders? _____

_____

_____

IX. Personality Disorders: Traits that Prove Costly

A. Paranoid and Schizoid Personality

Personality disorders are collections of long-standing, maladaptive and inflexible traits that cause distress and adjustment problems. A paranoid personality disorder involves strong feelings that others can't be trusted and delusions of persecution.

A schizoid personality disorder is characterized by social detachment and emotional coldness. Contact with other persons is of little interest to persons with this disorder.

B. The Antisocial Personality Disorder

Individuals who have the antisocial personality disorder show an almost total disregard for the rights and welfare of others and seem incapable of forming strong emotional ties. They do not adhere to rules and regulations. Therefore, they often have a history of antisocial behavior. They are often irritable and aggressive, highly impulsive, seemingly fearless in the face of danger, very deceitful and often perform hurtful actions without remorse. This disorder may stem from behavioral, cognitive or biological factors.

Questions:

12-20. What are the characteristics of the paranoid and schizoid personality disorder? _____

_____

_____

_____

12-21. What are the characteristics and potential causes of the antisocial personality disorder? _____

_____

_____

_____

X. Schizophrenia: Out of Touch With Reality

Schizophrenia is a very serious disorder involving profound distortions of thought, perceptions, and affect (mood). Persons with this disorder usually cannot live ordinary lives.

A. The Basic Nature of Schizophrenia

Schizophrenia involves a disruption in almost all aspects of psychological functioning. Reasoning is so strange that it is interpreted by others as incoherent. There are various symptoms of this disorder. First, they have disturbances of thought and language. They do not think or speak like others. Their ideas often seem totally unconnected and they often create words of their own (neologisms). In some cases their words are completely jumbled into what is called a "word salad." This may result from the failure of schizophrenics to use selective attention. Schizophrenics often have delusions -- firmly held beliefs that have no basis in reality. False beliefs that one is extremely important are delusions of grandeur. Delusions of control are beliefs that one is under control of outside forces. Beliefs that others are out to get one are delusions of persecution.

Schizophrenics also show many signs of disturbed perceptions. Many report intense and vivid experiences with no basis in reality (hallucinations). The most common type of hallucination is auditory. In addition, schizophrenics often experience deficits in social perception -- their ability to recognize the emotions of others. A third symptom involves disturbances of emotion. A fourth is unusual motor actions -- such as staring at the floor for hours. Schizophrenia can also involve seriously impaired social behavior.

Schizophrenia has been divided into positive symptoms (or Type I schizophrenia) and negative symptoms (or Type II schizophrenia). Positive symptoms involve the presence of something that is normally absent like hallucinations and delusions. Negative symptoms involve the absence of something that is normally present like emotion.

B. Subtypes of Schizophrenia

Schizophrenia is divided into several subtypes. The disorganized schizophrenia is characterized by silliness and incoherence. Paranoid schizophrenia involves delusions of persecution and grandeur. The type of schizophrenia in which people vary from a frozen posture to an excitable state is catatonic schizophrenia.

C. The Origins of Schizophrenia

It appears that genetic factors play a role in schizophrenia -- the closer the family relationship between people, the greater the odds of a person developing schizophrenia if one of the persons has the disorder. Biochemical factors may also be involved in schizophrenia. It may be the case that schizophrenia stems from an excess of dopamine in the brain. Growing evidence suggests that schizophrenia may also result from subtle differences in brain structure. Family or social factors aalso ppear to contribute to this disorder. Deficits in cognitive functioning may also be factors in this disorder. Type I schizophrenics demonstrate difficulty in ignoring irrelevant or distracting information. Type II schizophrenics appear to be underattentive to external stimuli.

D. Chronic Mental Illness and the Homeless

Many homeless persons suffer from psychological disorders. As many as one third have received care in hospitals, but were released after drug therapy reduced their symptoms.

Questions:

12-22. What is the general nature of schizophrenia as well as the major symptoms and subtypes of this disorder? _____

_____

_____

_____

12-23. What are the findings concerning the origin of schizophrenia? _____

_____

_____

_____

XI. Making Psychology Part of Your Life

Baron outlines some basic steps for preventing suicide. These include:

1. Take all suicide threats seriously.
2. If someone mentions suicide, don't be afraid to discuss it.
3. Recognize the danger signs.
4. Discourage others from blaming themselves for failure to attain unrealistic standards.
5. If a friend or family member shows the danger signs described above, don't leave him or her alone.
6. Most important of all: Get Help!

Question:

12-24. How can you help prevent suicide? _____

_____

_____

_____

MAKING PSYCHOLOGY PART OF YOUR LIFE: Key Terms and Concepts

Knowing the important concepts and key terms contained in this chapter is a very important part of mastering the material. We have presented a sample of these concepts below. Define each concept and check your definition with that presented in the chapter. It will also be beneficial for you to think of an example of each concept. Whenever possible, use your own personal experience to provide an example of each term below.

12-1.   **Agoraphobia:** _____

        Example: _____

12-2.   **Antisocial Personality Disorder:** _____

        Example: _____

12-3.   **Anxiety:** _____

        Example: _____

12-4.   **Anxiety Disorders:** _____

        Example: _____

12-5.   **Avoidant Personality Disorder:** _____

        Example: _____

12-6.   **Bipolar Disorder:** _____

        Example: _____

12-7.   **Bulimia Nervosa:** _____

        Example: _____

12-8.   **Conversion Disorder:** _____

        Example: _____

12-9.   **Delusions:** _____

        Example: _____

12-10.   **Dependent Personality Disorder:** _____

        Example: _____

12-11.   **Depression:** _____

        Example: _____

12-12.   **Diagnostic and Statistical Manual of Mental Disorders - IV:** _____

12-13.   **Diathesis-Stress Model:** _____

12-14.   **Dopamine Hypothesis:** _____

12-15.   **Double-Bind Communication:** _____

        Example: _____

12-16.   **Defense Mechanisms:** _____

        Example: _____

12-17.   **Eating Disorders:** _____

        Example: _____

12-18.   **Hallucinations:** _____

        Example: _____

12-19.   **Helplessness-Hopelessness Syndrome:** _____

        Example: _____

12-20.   **Hypochondriasis:** _____

        Example: _____

12-21.   **Learned Helplessness:** _____

        Example: _____

12-22.   **Medical Perspective:** _____

Example: _____

12-23.   **Modeling:** _____

Example: _____

12-24.   **Mood Disorders:** _____

Example: _____

12-25.   **Obsessive-Compulsive Disorder:** _____

Example: _____

12-26.   **Panic Attack Disorder:** _____

Example: _____

12-27.   **Paraphilias:** _____

Example: _____

12-28.   **Personality Disorders:** _____

Example: _____

12-29.   **Phobias:** _____

Example: _____

12-30.   **Posttraumatic Stress Disorder:** _____

Example: _____

12-31.   **Psychiatry:** _____

12-32.   **Psychodynamic Perspective:** _____

12-33.   **Psychogenic Fugue:** _____

Example: _____

12-34.   **Psychological Disorders:** _____

Example: _____

12-35.   **Schizoid Personality Disorder:** _____

Example: _____

12-36.   **Schizophrenia:** _____

Example: _____

12-37.   **Self-Schemas:** _____

Example: _____

12-38.   **Sexual Arousal Disorders:** _____

Example: _____

12-39.   **Sexual Desire Disorders:** _____

Example: _____

12-40.   **Somatization Disorder:** _____

Example: _____

12-41.   **Suicide:** _____

12-42.   **Trephining:** _____

CHALLENGE: Develop Your Critical Thinking Skills

Societal Implications: Genetic bases of schizophrenia

The critical thinker is able to recognize the implications of psychological research for society. Advances in our understanding of the causes of psychological research have increased our ability to treat psychological disorders, but they also create social and ethical issues that we must deal with. Stretch your ability to see the implications of psychological research by answering the following questions:

12-1.   As your text points out, there is strong evidence that genetic factors play a role in the occurrence of schizophrenia. Suppose that research confirms that this is the case. Further suppose that we are unable to treat this disorder. Should society pass laws prohibiting schizophrenics from having children?

12-2.   Baron points out that one important factor in homelessness is that many homeless persons suffer from psychological disorders, which interfere with their ability to function. It is estimated that as many as one-third previously received in-patient care, but were released when drug therapy reduced their symptoms. How might society better deal with this problem? Given that research suggests that effective treatments do exist for many of the disorders that some of the homeless suffer from, how can we get those in need of help into settings where they can receive it?

12-3.   Persons who have had psychological problems are often the targets of prejudice. For example, you may recall that the presidential campaign of Michael Dukakis was hurt by rumors that he had sought treatment for depression. Given what you have learned about psychological disorders, do you think that it is correct to use evidence that a person has had a psychological disorder as a basis for evaluating his/her suitability for positions of power? Why or why not? Would your answer change depending upon the nature of the psychological disorder? [Keep in mind that 50% of all persons have had a psychological disorder at some point during their lives.]

CHALLENGE: Making Psychology Part of Your Life

<u>Taking Steps to Prevent Suicide</u>

Baron provides you with some steps that can help prevent suicide. Although we don't like to think about it, there may be situations in which those we care about may contemplate such an act. We can help prevent this drastic act by following these simple steps. As an exercise in applying what you've learned, please think about (and write down) how you might use each of these steps.

Step 1. Take all suicide threats seriously.

What factors might lead us to ignore a person's threat? What can we do to minimize this possibility?

Step 2. Don't be afraid to discuss suicide with someone who mentions it.

Why do you think we hesitate to discuss this topic?

Step 3. Recognize the danger signs.

List and give examples of these danger signs.

Step 4. Discourage others from blaming themselves for failure to attain unrealistic standards.

Why is this important? Can you think of examples of when you or others are prone to this tendency?

Step 5. Don't leave a person alone who shows the danger signs of suicide.

In some cases, a person might insist that you do leave him/her alone. How would you handle this situation?

Step 6. Get help!

What resources do you have in your local community for getting help?

CHALLENGE: Review Your Comprehensive Knowledge

SAMPLE TEST QUESTIONS

Once you have worked through the preceding sections, you should be ready for a comprehensive self-test. You can check your answers with those at the end of this section. An additional practice test is given in the supplementary section at the end of this study guide.

12-1.   The percent of all humans who have a psychological disorder at some point during their life is:
a. 10.
b. 15.
c. 50.
d. 25.

12-2.   The Greeks' view of abnormal behavior provided the basis of today's:
a. psychodynamic perspective.
b. biological/medical model.
c. the psychological perspective.
d. the DSM-IV.

12-3.   Which of the following was Freud's major contribution to the understanding of abnormal behavior?
a. his suggestion that the ego demands immediate gratification
b. his suggestion that mental patients should be treated humanely
c. his suggestion that psychological disorders are types of mental illnesses
d. his suggestion that unconscious thoughts or impulses play a role in abnormal behavior

12-4.   Which of the following perspectives suggests that abnormal behavior is best understood through studying processes such as learning, cognition, and perception?
a. the psychological perspective
b. the biological/medical model
c. the psychodynamic perspective
d. the descriptive approach

12-5.   Which of the following statements does not accurately describe the use of the DSM-IV?
a. It provides a useful tool for explaining abnormal behaviors.
b. It provides a useful tool for describing abnormal behaviors.
c. It classifies disorders along five axes.
d. Its use may be subject to bias in making clinical judgments about the severity or presence of psychological disorders.

12-6.   There are two major categories of mood disorders. They are _____ and _____ disorders.
a. bipolar, euphoric
b. euphoric, dysphoric
c. bipolar, unipolar
d. depressive, bipolar

12-7.   The disorder that involves anxieties and repetitive behaviors is called:
a. obsessive-compulsive.
b. phobia.
c. panic.
d. generalized anxiety.

12-8.   Lengthy losses of memory are known as _____ disorders.
a. anxiety
b. personality
c. dissociative
d. emotional

12-9.   People who exhibit physical symptoms that have no underlying physical cause have _____ disorders.
a. anxiety
b. organic
c. dissociative
d. somatoform

12-10.   When a person appears to have two or more distinct personalities, they are said to have which disorder?
    a. dysphoric   c. dissociative memory
    b. bipolar   d. dissociative identity

12-11.   The DSM-IV classifies sexual dysfunctions in terms of:
    a. the object of desire.
    b. conclusions in gender identity.
    c. when in the normal course of sexual activity problems occur.
    d. the capacity of certain stimuli to be sexually arousing.

12-12.   Which of the following has not been found to be a potential cause for depression?
    a. genetic inheritance   c. high levels of neurotransmitters
    b. helplessness   d. faulty cognitive sets

12-13.   Disorders that are associated with collections of long-standing and inflexible traits that cause distress and adjustment problems are:
    a. somatoform disorders.   c. anxiety disorders.
    b. conversion reactions.   d. personality disorders.

12-14.   Which of the following is not discussed as one of the factors related to the occurrence of the anti-social personality syndrome?
    a. poor homes   c. abnormalities in brain EEG
    b. exposure to criminal activity   d. the Oedipal conflict

12-15.   When schizophrenics believe they are manipulated by outside forces they have delusions of:
    a. grandeur.   c. persecution.
    b. control.   d. power.

12-16.   The type of schizophrenia that involves a frozen posture is:
    a. disorganized.   c. catatonic.
    b. paranoid.   d. undifferentiated.

12-17.   An excess of the neurotransmitter _____ seems to be implicated in schizophrenia.
    a. dopamine   c. epinephrine
    b. serotonin   d. norepinephrine

12-18.   When individuals are very fearful of gaining weight and fail to maintain a normal body weight, they have:
    a. paraphilia nervosa.   c. bulimia nervosa.
    b. anorexia nervosa.   d. neologism nervosa.

12-19.   A schizoid personality disorder is characterized by:
    a. physical symptoms that have no underlying cause.
    b. a desire to alter primary and secondary sex characteristics.
    c. social detachment and emotional coldness.
    d. multiple personalities.

12-20.   Suicide attempts are more common among _____, while more _____ actually commit suicide.
    a. women; men   c. children; adults
    b. men; women   d. adults; children

Answers and Feedback for Sample Test Questions:

12-1.   C Fifty percent of all persons have had some type of psychological disorder during their lives. (p. 446)

12-2.   B The Greeks believed that psychological disorders had natural causes. Focusing of attention to natural vs. supernatural causes of abnormal behavior led to the development of the biological/medical model.

12-3.   D Freud's suggestion that unconscious thoughts play a role in abnormal behavior is seen as his major contribution. (p. 448)

12-4.   A In contrast to the other perspectives listed in this question, the psychological approach concentrates on cognitive, learning, and perception processes as a basis for developing abnormal behavior. (p. 449)

12-5.   B The importance of the DSM-IV is that it provides a tool for describing, not explaining, abnormal behavior. (p. 450)

12-6.   D Depression and bipolar disorders are the two forms of mood disorders. (p. 445)

12-7.   A Obsessive-compulsive disorders are characterized by repetitive behaviors and irrational thoughts. (p. 461)

12-8.   C Memory disorders are classified as dissociative disorders. (p. 464)

12-9.   D Somatoform disorders involve physical symptomology, without corresponding physical causes. (p. 463)

12-10.   D A person with dissociative identity appears to have two or more distinct personalities. (pp. 464-465)

12-11.   C Sexual dysfunctions are classified in the DSM-IV in terms of when, in the normal cause of sexual activity, the problem occurs. (p. 466)

12-12.   C High levels of neurotransmitters are not associated with depression. The other characteristics are associated with depression. (p. 456)

12-13.   D Personality disorders are associated with collections of traits (inflexible and long-standing) that cause distress. (p. 468)

12-14.   D The Oedipal conflict is not implicated in the development of anti-social personalities. All the other factors do seem to be present. (pp. 469-470)

12-15.   B Delusions of control are characterized by feelings of being manipulated by outside forces. (p. 472)

12-16.   C Catatonic schizophrenia is characterized by a frozen posture. (p. 474)

12-17.   A Excessive dopamine is implicated as a biological basis for schizophrenia. (p. 476)

12-18.   B Anorexia nervosa is characterized by a fear of gaining weight. (p. 468)

12-19.   C Social detachment and emotional coldness characterize the schizoid personality. (p. 469)

12-20.   A Research suggests that more women attempt suicide, but more men actually commit suicide. (p. 458)

Glossary of difficult words and expressions	Definition
Annoying	bothersome; irritating
Apprehension	fear; dread of something
Atrophy	decrease in size; shrink; the tissue dies
Bearable	tolerable; can deal with or cope with
Binge-purge	eating abnormally large amounts of food and then vomiting it up
Bizarre	strange; completely unexpected and abnormal
Charmed	enchanted, lucky
Clenched	press or clasp firmly together
Clinging	holding tight; grasping something very tightly
Clues	facts that suggests a possible answer to a problem
Continuum	range or spectrum; along some dimension
Cryptic	secret; with a hidden meaning; hard to figure out
Dazzling	sparkling; magnificent and wonderful
Deceitful	misleading; purposely concealing something
Delusion	false opinion or belief; not in contact with reality
Distractible	easily distracted; one's attention is on something else
Dungeons	dark, underground cells used as prisons
Giggling	laughing in a nervous and silly way
Grudges	feeling of resentment; holding something against someone
Harsh	cruel; treating unkindly
Heaves	raises; lifts up; a heavy object
Impassive	not displaying emotion; showing no feeling
Jumbled	mixed or confused
Lingerie	women's underwear
Mumbling	saying something that can be heard; garbled speech
Neologisms	meaningless words
Pierced ears	holes in ears made to wear earrings
Reckless	not thinking or caring about consequences or safety
Shackled	chained or restricted
Shortcomings	failure to reach a standard or to develop properly

Glossary of difficult words and expressions	Definition
Shrieks	scream or yell
Slashing (their wrists)	cutting their wrists
Sprawled	spread out loosely and irregularly
Sprees	occasion of extravagant unusual spending of money
Spurious	false; not reliable or replicable
Subtle	not obvious or noticeable
Swelling	increasing in volume or thickness
Toil	working long/hard hours on something
Thug	criminal; person who performs illegal acts
Unhesitatingly	with a sense of certainty; not holding back
Vanish	disappear or make something go out of sight

CHAPTER 13
THERAPY:
DIMINISHING THE PAIN OF PSYCHOLOGICAL DISORDERS

OUTLINE: Develop a Study Plan

Use this outline to help you grasp the organizational structure of the chapter contents. The learning objectives (LOs) for each section are included. Use them as tools for developing your study plan. Space has been provided for you to write any notes or questions that come to mind as you begin your exploration into this material.

Heading:	Learning Objective:	Your Notes:
I. Psychotherapies: Psychological Approaches To Psychological Disorders	**L.O. 13.1:** Provide an overview of the different types of therapy and know the two crucial features of psychotherapy.	
A. Psychodynamic Therapies: From Repression To Insight	**L.O. 13.2:** Discuss the basis and application of psychoanalysis and evaluate psychoanalysis.	
B. Humanistic Therapies: Emphasizing The Positive	**L.O. 13.3:** Describe person-centered and Gestalt therapy.	
C. Behavior Therapies: Psychological Disorders And Faculty Learning	**L.O. 13.4:** Discuss the application of classical conditioning, operant conditioning, and modeling in behavior therapies.	
D. Cognitive Therapies: Changing Disordered Thought	**L.O. 13.5:** Outline the basic assumptions underlying the cognitive approach to therapy, the characteristics of rational emotive therapy, and Beck's cognitive behavior therapy for treating depression.	
II. Group Therapy: Working With Others To Solve Personal Problems	**L.O. 13.6:** Outline the characteristics of the different types of group therapy and the use of self-help groups.	
A. Psychodynamic Group Therapies		
B. Behavioral Group Therapies		

Heading:	Learning Objective:	Your Notes:
C. Humanistic Group Therapies		
D. Self-Help Groups: Help From Our Peers		
III. Therapies Focused On Interpersonal Relations: Marital And Family Therapy		
A. Marital Therapy: When Spouses Become The Intimate Enemy	**L.O. 13.7:** Discuss the basic assumptions of therapies focusing on interpersonal relations and the characteristics of marital and family therapy.	
B. Family Therapy: Changing Environments That Harm		
IV. Psychotherapy: Some Current Issues		
A. Does Psychotherapy Really Work? An Optimistic Conclusion	**L.O. 13.8:** Discuss the major findings concerning the effectiveness of psychotherapy and whether some forms of therapy are more successful than others.	
B. Are Some Forms Of Therapy More Successful Than Others? Solving A Persistent Puzzle	**L.O. 13.9:** Discuss the importance of including multicultural awareness in psychotherapy.	
V. Biologically Based Therapies		
A. Early Forms Of Biological Therapy	**L.O. 13.10:** Discuss the basic assumption that underlies the biological approach to psychotherapy and survey the early forms of biological therapy.	
B. Electroconvulsive Therapy		
C. Psychosurgery		
D. Drug Therapy: The Pharmacological Revolution	**L.O. 13.11:** List the types of drugs used in therapy and discuss their effectiveness.	

Heading:	Learning Objective:	Your Notes:
VI. The Setting For Therapy: From Institutional Care To The Community	**L.O. 13.12:** Survey the different types of environments that were created as alternatives to psychiatric hospitals.	
A. State Institutions: Custodial Care		
B. Community Mental Health Centers: Bringing Care To Where It's Needed		
C. Prevention: Heading Off Trouble Before It Begins -- Or Becomes Serious	**L.O. 13.13:** Know the goals of the different types of prevention programs and be able to discuss the research concerning their effectiveness.	
VII. Making Psychology a Part of Your Life		
A. How to Choose a Therapist: A Consumer's Guide	**L.O. 13.14:** What are two steps in finding a psychologist?	

SURVEY AND QUESTION

This section presents the major topics and ideas from the chapter. Use it as a tool for seeing how the components of the chapter fit together. At the end of each major topic, we have asked you questions that relate to the major learning objectives. If you can answer these questions, you have taken a major step toward mastering this material.

I.   Psychotherapies: Psychological Approaches to Psychological Disorders

Psychotherapies are procedures in which a trained person establishes a professional relationship with the patient in order to remove or modify existing symptoms, change disturbed behavioral patterns and promote personal growth and development.

Contrary to the image of the Freudian couch, psychotherapy employs a varied range of procedures. These diverse procedures have two crucial features. First, they involve establishing a special relationship between client and therapist in which the client feels free to confide in the therapist. Second, psychotherapy involves attempts to bring about beneficial changes in the client's thoughts, feelings, or behavior.

A.   Psychodynamic Therapies: From Repression to Insight

Psychodynamic therapies are based on the assumption that psychological disorders are caused primarily by the inner workings of personality. Psychoanalysis was developed by Freud and is the most famous psychodynamic therapy. Freud believed that the personality consists of three major parts. The id corresponds to "desire." The ego corresponds to "reason." The superego corresponds to "conscience." Freud suggested that psychological disorders stem from the repression of id impulses. To keep these impulses in check, individuals expend considerable psychic energy and use defense mechanisms to reduce feelings of anxiety. These hidden conflicts between the basic components of personality can, if left unresolved, interfere with normal psychosexual development.

The goal of Freud's psychoanalysis was to overcome repression by having the patient gain insight about hidden feelings. This would be accompanied by a release of emotion or abreaction. The technique involves having the patient report everything that comes to mind or free associations. Dreams are also analyzed for their latent content, the actual motives symbolized in the dream. The therapist asks questions and provides suggestions. This is the process of interpretation. During the early part of the therapy the patient may show resistance. Later, intense feelings for the therapist or transference may develop.

The effectiveness of classical psychoanalysis is limited: it is costly and time-consuming, its scientific base is weak, it is suitable only for people with good verbal skills, and it is not open to criticism. Modern forms of psychoanalysis are briefer than classical psychoanalysis. They also put more emphasis on ego functioning and less on unconscious conflicts; in addition, they also rely on social factors and the client's present life situation.

B.   Humanistic Therapies: Emphasizing the Positive

For humanistic psychologists, psychological disorders arise because the environment interferes with personal growth and fulfillment. Unlike psychoanalysts, in this approach the therapist is primarily a guide or facilitator. The client must take responsibility for success.

According to Rogers, people have psychological problems when they lose contact with their own feelings and form a distorted self-concept. The therapy designed to correct this is person-centered. This involves unconditional acceptance of the individual. A high level of empathy and an interest in the patient that is genuine are also critical components of this therapy. The therapy developed by Perls that focuses on helping individuals become aware of themselves and their true current feelings is Gestalt therapy.

Humanistic therapies share the view that people have the capacity to reflect upon their problems, to control their own behavior, and to make choices that will lead to satisfying lives. All suggest that flaws in our self-concept produce psychological distress. All reject the Freudian idea that psychological disorders stem from repressed urges that must be forced from patients who are unwilling to gain self-insight.

C. Behavior Therapies: Psychological Disorders and Faulty Learning

Therapies that are based on the principles of learning and that focus primarily on individuals' current behavior are behavior therapies. Several are based on the type of learning that occurs when one stimulus comes to serve as a signal for the occurrence of the other (or classical conditioning). Many phobias may be acquired in this manner. To reduce these fears, various techniques, derived, at least in part, from the principles of classical conditioning have been used by behavioral therapists. One technique is flooding. This involves long exposure to the feared stimuli or some representation of it. Because the person is not allowed to avoid these stimuli, extinction of fear can occur. Systematic desensitization is another technique. In this technique, individuals first experience relaxation training. Then, while in a relaxed state, they are exposed to stimuli that elicit anxiety. The technique that involves associating stimuli previously associated with positive feelings with negative ones is aversion therapy. This can be used with inappropriate sexual feelings. Covert desensitization is similar to aversion therapy. However, with covert desensitization, individuals do not experience negative stimuli directly; rather they are merely asked to imagine negative stimuli.

Therapies are also based on operant conditioning. This involves three basic steps: identifying undescribable behaviors, identifying the reinforcers that maintain these behaviors, and, then attempting to change the context so that reinforcement is no longer provided for these behaviors.

Shaping is a technique that involves helping individuals acquire novel and desired responses by offering reinforcement for responses that resemble the desired ones more and more closely. Token economies have been established in hospitals whereby tokens can be exchanged for the performance of adaptive behavior. Another technique that may decrease the probability of an undesirable behavior involves increasing the probability of a response that is incompatible with the undesirable behavior.

The process through which behavior is influenced by exposure to others is modeling. Modeling has been used to change a wide range of behaviors such as sexual dysfunctions. Its most impressive application has involved its use in reducing various phobias. It has also been used to change the behavior of highly aggressive children and adolescents.

D. Cognitive Therapies: Changing Disordered Thought

The basic idea behind cognitive therapy is that psychological disorders come from faulty or distorted modes of thought. The approach by Ellis to change these is called rational emotive therapy. He holds that most problems come from irrational beliefs that are a reaction to frustrations. Ellis feels people should be forced to recognize this irrationality. Because people often are unwilling to give up their irrational beliefs, the therapist first identifies these beliefs and then tries to persuade the client to recognize the irrationality of these beliefs.

Beck's cognitive behavior theory assumes that depression results from illogical thinking about self, the world, and the future. These ideas are often self-defeating and self-fulfilling. Several tendencies foster depression. Seeing oneself as totally worthless because of a few setbacks is an example of overgeneralization. There is also a tendency to interpret positive experiences as exceptions to the general rule of failure and incompetence. The tendency to see the world as a dangerous place is an example of selective perception. There is a tendency to magnify the importance of undesirable events. All-or-more thinking involves the tendency to engage in absolutistic thinking.

Mahoney's constructivist cognitive therapy attempts to change distorted thought patterns as well as associated emotions. Techniques involve asking clients to write stories or letters they won't mail or directing them to observe themselves in a mirror.

Questions:

13-1.   What are the different types of psychotherapy and what are the two crucial features?

_____

_____

_____

13-2.   What is the basis and application of psychoanalysis? _____

_____

_____

_____

13-3.   What are person-centered and gestalt therapy? _____

_____

_____

13-4.   How have classical conditioning and operant conditioning been applied to therapy? _____

_____

_____

_____

13-5.   What are the basic assumptions underlying the cognitive approach to therapy and the characteristics of rational-emotive therapy? _____

_____

_____

_____

13-6. How has Beck's cognitive-behavior therapy been used to treat depression? _____

_____

_____

_____

II. Group Therapy: Working With Others to Solve Personal Problems

A. Psychodynamic Group Therapies

Psychoanalytic procedures have been modified to operate in group settings. This therapy is called psychodynamic group therapy and its goal is to show clients how they actually behave and what hidden inner conflicts lie behind their overt actions. Psychodrama is one form of this therapy in which group members act in front of other group members. Techniques involve role reversal, in which group members switch parts, and mirroring, in which they portray one another.

B. Behavioral Group Therapies

This therapy involves using the basic principles of learning to solve specific behavioral problems in a group setting. For example, individuals practice desired skills in front of and with others.

C. Humanistic Group Therapies

Group therapy originated with humanistic psychologists in the 1940s. The Humanists developed encounter groups and sensitivity-training groups. By having group members talk about their problems, these therapies are designed to promote personal growth, increased understanding of self, and increased openness and honesty with others.

D. Self-Help Groups: Help From Our Peers

Self-help groups, like alcoholics anonymous, bring individuals who share a problem together. They believe that those who share a problem have a unique understanding and can provide a higher level of empathy for one another than those who have not experienced the problem.

Questions:

13-7. What are the characteristics of the different types of group therapy? _____

_____

_____

_____

III. Therapies Focused on Interpersonal Relations: Marital and Family Therapy

The therapies discussed in the previous section all share in common the assumption that psychological disorders stem from processes operating within individuals. In contrast, therapies that focus on interpersonal relations assume that psychological disorders can only be fully understood in terms of the individual's social environment.

A. Marital Therapy: When Spouses Become the Intimate Enemy

Couple or marital therapy focuses on improving the communication skills of partners. This goal is attained through the use of role-playing techniques and through the use of videotapes that depict the couple's interaction. Poorly adjusted couples tend to make unfavorable attributions about the causes of their partner's behavior. Couple therapy attempts to help the partners recognize and change these attributional patterns.

B. Family Therapy: Changing Environments That Harm

Family therapy is based on the recognition that the gains people make through individual therapy often disappear when the person returns home. This relapse pattern suggests that the problems experienced by such persons can be traced, in part, to disturbed patterns of interaction among family members. Once maladaptive patterns have been identified, often through the therapist interacting almost as an insider within the family, he/she uses a wide variety of techniques to alter those patterns. One common pattern involves mother and child subsystems that all but exclude the father. Research that has assessed the effectiveness of family therapy suggests that it is a promising new approach for dealing with psychological disorders.

Questions:

13-8. What are the basic assumptions of therapies focusing on interpersonal relations and the characteristics of marital family therapy? _____

_____

_____

_____

13-9. Why is family therapy beneficial and what are the various kinds of family therapy? _____

_____

_____

_____

IV. Psychotherapy: Some Current Issues

Nearly 10 percent of the population in the U.S. have consulted a therapist. Negative attitudes toward psychotherapy have weakened considerably.

A. Does Psychotherapy Really Work? An Optimistic Conclusion

Contrary to the earlier conclusion of Hans Eysenck, recent research suggests that, although therapy is not equally effective for all persons and all disorders and does not totally eliminate various psychological problems, it is effective. In addition, certain forms of psychotherapy are at least as effective as drug therapy, and in some respects, may be superior to it.

B.   Are Some Forms of Therapy More Successful Than Others?   Solving a Persistent Puzzle

The various forms of therapy seem to produce roughly similar benefits. It is possible that for certain types of disorders (and therapists), certain techniques may be more effective than others. Therapies may be similarly effective because they all provide individuals with positive expectations about their future and a heightened sense of personal control.

Racial and ethnic factors can influence diagnosis and effective communication between therapist and client. Most forms of psychotherapy were originally developed for persons of European decent. Because of these issues, there is an attempt to make psychotherapies more culturally sensitive. First, there is an attempt to make it accessible to the economically disadvantaged. Second, efforts are being made to employ a type of therapy that is consistent with the client's cultural, economic, and educational background. Third, it is believed that therapy should consider the established values and traditions within various cultures. Finally, therapy should consider the unique problems of various groups.

Questions:

13-10. What are the major findings concerning the effectiveness of psychotherapy? _____

_____

_____

_____

13-11. What are the important implications of including a multicultural perspective in psychotherapy?

_____

_____

_____

V.   Biologically Based Therapies

A.   Early Forms of Biological Therapy

Biologically based therapies rest on the belief that everything we think, feel, remember, and do reflects activity in the central nervous system. Early forms of biological therapy were based on primitive notions that drastic procedures freed persons from the evil influences that were thought to cause their psychological disorders.

B.   Electroconvulsive Therapy

The therapy that involves the use of strong electric shock is electroconvulsive therapy. It seems to be effective with severe depression and with a smaller percentage of schizophrenics. It is a therapy that should be used with extreme caution, only when other forms of therapy are ineffective.

C. Psychosurgery

Surgical procedures on the brain to treat mental disorders are forms of psychosurgery.   Prefrontal lobotomy is the technique that involved surgery on the prefrontal lobes and was used to control aggression. A major problem with this technique is unwanted side-effects.   This procedure is not now in use. Evidence for the benefits of psychosurgery is uncertain and its use raises important ethical questions.

D. Drug Therapy: The Pharmacological Revolution

Drug therapy is by far the most common type of biological based therapy. Antipsychotic drugs are highly effective in reducing the symptoms of schizophrenia and other psychoses.   Antidepressants are often effective in reducing depression, while antianxiety drugs are helpful in combating anxiety. All these drugs, however, have potentially dangerous side effects which must be taken into account.

Questions:

13-12. What is the basic assumption that underlies the biological approach to psychotherapy and what are the early forms of biological therapy? _____

_____

_____

_____

13-13. What is drug therapy and how effective is it? _____

_____

_____

_____

VI.   The Setting For Therapy: From Institutional Care to the Community

A.   State Institutions: Custodial Care

Large state-supported institutions provided little in active treatment.   They were largely custodial. Therefore, private institutions were developed and provided active care to patients.   Many were psychodynamic whereas some had ties to humanistic therapies and practiced milieu therapy -- a therapy that provides an environment designed to foster independence and self-respect among patients.

B.   Community Mental Health Centers: Bringing Care to Where It Is Needed

As drug therapy flourished, many patients were discharged from hospitals. Community mental health centers provided these persons with an environment for continued treatment.   These centers provided outpatient services, aftercare treatment, inpatient services, emergency services and consultation services.

C. Prevention: Heading Off Trouble Before It Begins -- Or Becomes Serious

Recently, prevention has become an important approach to mental health. It has three goals. (1) Primary prevention -- preventing disorders from developing. (2) Secondary prevention -- preventing minor disorders from becoming major ones. (3) Tertiary prevention -- minimize the harm done to the individual and society. Results from several research projects indicate that child abuse can be substantially reduced through appropriate preventive programs.

Questions:

13-14. What are the different types of environments that were created as alternatives to state psychiatric institutions? _____

_____

_____

_____

13-15. What are the goals of the different types of prevention programs and what are the research findings concerning their effectiveness? _____

_____

_____

_____

VII. Making Psychology A Part of Your Life: How To Choose a Therapist: A Consumer's Guide

Effective help for psychological disorders is available. To start the process of looking for a therapist, you can contact the psychology department at any university, even if you are not a student there. You could also ask your physician or a member of the clergy for suggestions. Next, you should make sure that the therapist is well qualified and that their specialty matches your needs.

Question:

13-16. Explain how to choose a therapist. _____

_____

_____

_____

MAKING PSYCHOLOGY PART OF YOUR LIFE: Key Terms and Concepts

Knowing the important concepts and key terms contained in this chapter is a very important part of mastering the material. We have presented a sample of these concepts below. Define each concept and check your definition with that presented in the chapter. It will also be beneficial for you to think of an example of each concept. Whenever possible, use your own personal experience to provide an example of each term below.

13-1.   **Behavior Therapies:** _____

        Example: _____

13-2.   **Biologically Based Therapies:** _____

        Example: _____

13-3.   **Client-Centered Therapy:** _____

        Example: _____

13-4.   **Cognitive Behavior Therapy:** _____

        Example: _____

13-5.   **Cognitive Therapy:** _____

        Example: _____

13-6.   **Community Mental Health Centers:** _____

13-7.   **Conditions of Worth:** _____

        Example: _____

13-8.   **Constructivist Cognitive Therapy:** _____

        Example: _____

13-9.   **Drug Therapy:** _____

        Example: _____

13-10.   **Electroconvulsive Therapy:** _____

13-11.   **Encounter Groups:** _____

       Example: _____

13-12.   **Family Therapy:** _____

       Example: _____

13-13.   **Free Association:** _____

       Example: _____

13-14.   **Gestalt Therapy:** _____

       Example: _____

13-15.   **Group Therapies:** _____

       Example: _____

13-16.   **Humanistic Therapies:** _____

       Example: _____

13-17.   **Marital Therapy:** _____

       Example: _____

13-18.   **Primary Prevention:** _____

       Example: _____

13-19.   **Psychotherapies:** _____

       Example: _____

13-20.   **Psychodrama:** _____

       Example: _____

13-21.   **Psychodynamic Therapies:** _____

       Example: _____

13-22.   **Psychosurgery:** _____

      Example: _____

13-23.   **Rational Emotive Therapy:** _____

      Example: _____

13-24.   **Resistance:** _____

      Example: _____

13-25.   **Secondary Prevention:** _____

      Example: _____

13-26.   **Self-Help Groups:** _____

      Example: _____

13-27.   **Sensitivity Training Groups:** _____

      Example: _____

13-28.   **Systematic Desensitization:** _____

      Example: _____

13-29.   **Tardive Dyskinesia:** _____

13-30.   **Tertiary Prevention:** _____

      Example: _____

13-31.   **Therapeutic Alliance:** _____

      Example: _____

13-32.   **Token Economies:** _____

      Example: _____

CHALLENGE: Develop Your Critical Thinking Skills

Summarizing and Evaluating Evidence

Rather than passively accepting the recommendation of experts, the critical thinker is able to evaluate evidence that is related to a problem. This aids the person in assessing the strengths and weaknesses of various courses of action. As an exercise in developing this skill, complete the following analysis of biological intervention treatments:

13-1.   Summarize the main ideas and key issues relating to the use of biological interventions (e.g., drugs) in the treatment of psychological disorders.

13-2.   Identify and evaluate the evidence used to support each of the main ideas.

13-3.   Assess the importance of this research to our society.

CHALLENGE: Making Psychology Part of Your Life

Smoking Cessation Programs

In this chapter, you learned about the various forms of therapy that are available. Although it takes years of education to practice these therapies, the information you have learned should enable you to understand the basic components. Practice applying this knowledge to the following situation.

Situation

Your best friend is a "smoker." She wants to quit, but hasn't been able to do so. Although you have urged your friend to seek help with this problem, she wants to try quitting on her own before seeking professional help. Can you use what you've learned to help her sketch-out a smoking cessation program?

Questions

13-1.   What approach would you take from a humanistic perspective?

13-2.   What procedures would you employ based on the behavioral view?

13-3.   Could you make use of cognitive therapies to help your friend?

13-4.   What are the strengths and weaknesses of each view?

CHALLENGE: Review Your Comprehensive Knowledge

SAMPLE TEST QUESTIONS

Once you have worked through the preceding sections, you should be ready for a comprehensive self-test. You can check, your answers with those at the end of this section. An additional practice test is given in the supplementary section at the end of this study guide.

13-1.   Procedures in which a trained person establishes a special relationship with the patient in order to bring about beneficial changes in the patient's thoughts, feelings, or behavior are:
a. psychotherapies.   c. biologically-based.
b. drug therapies.   d. psychosurgeries.

13-2.   Which of the following is not one of the characteristics of psychoanalysis?
a. empathy   c. transference
b. free association   d. abreaction

13-3.   Freud suggested that psychological disorders stem from the _____ of id impulses.
a. interpretation   c. transference
b. repression   d. abreaction

13-4.   Which of the following is not one of the primary features of person-centered therapy?
a. unconditional acceptance   c. genuine interest in patient
b. interpretation of dreams   d. empathy

13-5.   Therapies based on the principles of learning are:
a. person-centered therapies.   c. Gestalt therapies.
b. psychoanalytic therapies.   d. behavioral therapies.

13-6.   The basic assumption underlying cognitive therapies is that psychological disorders stem from:
a. faulty modes of thought.   c. biological causes.
b. repressed impulses.   d. faulty conditioning.

13-7.   Which of the following is not one of the assumptions of humanistic therapies?
a. People have control over their own behavior.
b. Flaws in self-concept produce psychological distress.
c. People have the ability to make choices.
d. The therapist must force repressed urges from patients.

13-8.   Which therapy is not based on classical conditioning?
a. shaping   c. flooding
b. systematic desensitization   d. aversion therapy

13-9.   In Beck's model of depression, seeing oneself as totally worthless because of one or two failure experiences is an example of:
a. absolutistic thinking.   c. exceptions to the rule.
b. overgeneralization.   d. selective perception.

13-10.   According to the cognitive therapy called rational emotive therapy, most psychological problems come from _____ beliefs that stem from _____.
a. rational, frustrations   c. irrational, frustrations
b. irrational, objective information   d. rational, childhood experiences

13-11.   Encounter groups and sensitivity-training groups are a product of:
    a. behavioral group therapies.   c. psychodynamic group therapies.
    b. humanistic group therapies.   d. behavioral individual therapies.

13-12.   This type of family therapy involves careful analysis of patterns of interactions.
    a. constructivistic family therapy   c. communications approach
    b. psychodynamic family therapy   d. structural family therapy

13-13.   Which of the following is not one of the features held in common by the different therapies?
    a. therapeutic alliance
    b. psychodrama
    c. special kind of setting
    d. suggestion of specific actions in order to cope with problems

13-14.   To reduce the side-effects of antipsychotic drugs, many psychiatrists use:
    a. maintenance dosing.   c. target dosing.
    b. reserpine.   d. reserpine and maintenance dosing.

13-15.   Which of the following is not true about depression?
    a. There appear to be several different types of depression.
    b. The biochemical mechanisms underlying depression are complex.
    c. Antidepressant drugs can have dangerous side-effects.
    d. Psychotherapy is very rarely as effective as drug therapy in the treatment of depression.

13-16.   Electroconvulsive therapy should be used with caution. However, it appears to be effective with severe:
    a. drug addictions.   c. dissociative disorders.
    b. depression.   d. alcohol addictions.

13-17.   Which of the following is true of antipsychotic drugs?
    a. They do seem to relieve the major symptoms of schizophrenia.
    b. They do seem to eliminate the causes that underlie schizophrenia.
    c. They are not often associated with side-effects.
    d. They are sometimes known as minor tranquilizers.

13-18.   The technique that involves helping individuals acquire novel and desired responses by offering reinforcement for responses that resemble the desired ones more and more closely is:
    a. flooding.   c. extinction.
    b. fading.   d. shaping.

13-19.   The basic assumption underlying all interpersonal therapies is that psychological disorders can only be understood in terms of the individual's:
    a. learning history.   c. relationship with his/her mother.
    b. mode of thinking about the world.   d. social environment.

13-20.   Which of the following drugs is helpful in treating bipolar or manic disorders?
    a. barbiturates   c. valium
    b. lithium   d. fluoxetin

Answers and Feedback for Sample Test Questions:

13-1.   A Psychotherapies involve establishing a special relationship with a trained person with the goal of bringing about beneficial changes in the client's thoughts, feelings, and/or behaviors. (p. 484)

13-2.   A Empathy is a characteristic of person-centered therapy, not psychoanalysis. (pp. 485-486)

13-3.   B Repressed id impulses are the basis for psychological disorders, according to Freud. (p. 485)

13-4.   B Dream interpretation is a characteristic of psychoanalysis, not person-centered therapy. (p. 488)

13-5.   D Behavioral therapies are based on learning principles. (p. 490)

13-6.   A Cognitive therapies assume that faulty modes of thinking underlie psychological disorders and, therefore, seek to change these patterns. (p. 493)

13-7.   D Humanistic therapies do not force repressed urges from clients. They do, however, assume the other information given in this question. (p. 489)

13-8.   A Shaping is based on instrumental or operant conditioning, not classical conditioning. (p. 490)

13-9.   B Beck's model assumes that depressed individuals overgeneralize failure experiences. (p. 495)

13-10.   B Rational emotive therapy is based on the assumption that individuals often form irrational beliefs from objective information. (p. 494)

13-11.   B Humanistic group therapies often involve encounter groups and sensitivity-training groups. (p. 497)

13-12.   D Structure family therapy involves careful analysis of interaction patterns. (p. 499)

13-13.   B Psychodramas are used in therapies, but are not held in common by all therapies. (p. 504)

13-14.   C Target dosing is used to reduce aversive side-effects of antipsychotic drugs. (p. 509)

13-15.   D Psychotherapy is often used as an effective treatment for depression. (p. 502)

13-16.   B ECT is an effective treatment for depression. (p. 506)

13-17.   A Antipsychotic drugs do seem to relieve the major symptoms of schizophrenia. The other options in this question are not true. (p. 509)

13-18.   D Shaping involves reinforcing individuals for responses that closely resemble target behaviors. (p. 491)

13-19.   D Interpersonal therapies are based on the assumption that psychological disorders stem from problems in a person's social environment. (p. 498)

13-20.   B Lithium is used in treating bipolar mood disorders. (pp. 510-511)

Glossary of difficult words and expressions	Definition
Acquaint	get to know; become familiar with
Akin	like; similar to something
Array of	variety of; many examples of
Attest	to give proof of, to indicate something is correct
Aversive	negative, unpleasant
Bear	carry, hold-up
Bizarre	strange, bold, unusual
Blurred vision	not clear; hard to see
Brace yourself	get ready; get ready for
Breakthrough	new discovery or finding
Carnage	killing of many people
Chores	everyday tasks usually around the house
Compelling	convincing, overpowering
Conjure up	create in the mind
Craving	strong desire to have something
Desensitization	reduce sensitivity
Dismal	gloomy; miserable
Disowned	no longer wishing to have any connection with
Distressed	do not have peace of mind
Drowsiness	feeling sleepy
Eclectic	selecting or employing individual elements from a variety of sources, systems or styles
Empathetic	an understanding person
Escalate	to increase or expand
Firm grip	strong hold
Forged	created
Gaps	break or opening in a wall, hedge, etc.
Harbor hostility	conceal hostility
Hasty	hurried
Hushed tones	in a silent or quiet way

Glossary of difficult words and expressions	Definition
Inducing	persuade or influence; causing to happen
No matter how trivial	no matter how insignificant or small
Pitfalls	unsuspected snare or danger
Pop (as piece of gum)	put a piece of gum in the mouth
Relapse	fall back again; have another occurrence of something
Render	make; cause something to occur
Roughly	approximately; almost or approximated
Scope	range of action or observation; the extent of coverage
Strain	put pressure on
Strives to	makes an effort to; tries to; works toward
Stuttering	tendency to repeat rapidly the same sound or syllable
Sustain	maintain or keep going
Tantrums	fit of temper or anger
Underlie	form the basis of
Unflattering	not complimentary; insulting
Urges	immediate needs or an impulses that can be resisted
Wanderings	long travels; journeys
Wring	twist; squeeze

CHAPTER 14
SOCIAL THOUGHT AND SOCIAL BEHAVIOR

OUTLINE: Develop a Study Plan

Use this outline to help you grasp the organizational structure of the chapter contents. The learning objectives (LOs) for each section are included. Use them as tools for developing your study plan. Space has been provided for you to write any notes or questions that come to mind as you begin your exploration into this material.

Heading:	Learning Objective:	Your Notes:
I. Social Thought: Thinking About Other People **A.** Attribution: Understanding The Causes of Others' Behavior	**L.O. 14.1:** Be able to define attribution and identify the conditions leading to internal and external causal attributions according to Kelley's model. **L.O. 14.2:** Describe the various attributional biases.	
B. Social Cognition: How We Process Social Information	**L.O. 14.3:** Know the definition of social cognition and sources of error in social thought, including the false concensus effect, automatic vigilance, motivated skepticism, and counterfactual thinking.	
C. Attitudes: Evaluating The Social World	**L.O. 14.4:** Know the general definition of an attitude and the influence of conditioning. **L.O. 14.5:** Describe the general conclusions derived from the early work on persuasion. **L.O. 14.6:** Discuss the role of cognitive dissonance in attitude change and the practical implications of cognitive dissonance theory.	

Heading:	Learning Objective:	Your Notes:
II. Social Behavior: Interacting with Others		
A. Prejudice: Distorted Views of the Social World...and Their Consequences	**L.O. 14.7:** Understand the different views on the origins of prejudice and discrimination and be aware of methods that can be used to reduce prejudice and its impact.	
	L.O. 14.8: Describe the three components of racial identification and the factors that influence its strength.	
B. Social Influence: Changing Others' Behavior	**L.O. 14.9:** Discuss the nature and predominance of conformity as well as the factors that influence it.	
	L.O. 14.10: Define compliance and understand the various techniques for gaining compliance.	
	L.O. 14.11: Define obedience and discuss the factors that increase the extent of obedience to authority.	
C. Prosocial Behavior: When We Help...And When We Don't	**L.O. 14.12:** Define prosocial behavior and the factors that influence it.	
D. Attraction, Love, and Close Relationships	**L.O. 14.13:** Discuss the factors that influence interpersonal attribution.	
	L.O. 14.14: Discuss the nature and varieties of love as well as factors that influence it.	
E. Environmental Psychology: How the Physical Environment Affects Social Behavior -- and Vice Versa	**L.O. 14.15:** Understand how the field of environmental psychology investigates interactions between human behavior and the physical environment.	
	L.O. 14.16: Describe what love scales can tell us about our feelings.	
III. Making Psychology Part of Your Life: Are You in Love? One Way of Telling		

SURVEY AND QUESTION

This section presents the major topics and ideas from the chapter. Use it as a tool for seeing how the components of the chapter fit together. At the end of each major topic, we have asked you a question that relates to the major learning objectives. If you can answer these questions, you have taken a major step toward mastering this material.

I. Social Thought: Thinking about Other People

A. Attribution: Understanding the Causes of Others' Behavior

Our attempts to understand the causes of others' behavior are known as attributions. One of the major concerns is whether the causes stem from internal or external factors. According to Kelley, we make attributions about the causes of others' behaviors by focusing on consistency, distinctiveness, and consensus factors. If a person acts in the same way over time, he/she has high consistency. If the person acts in the same way to other stimuli, he/she has low distinctiveness. If others react the same way as the person, there is high consensus.

We tend to attribute behavior to internal causes if consistency is high, consensus is low, and distinctiveness is low. We tend to attribute behavior to external causes if consistency is high, consensus is high, and distinctiveness is high. We tend to attribute behavior to a combination of these factors when consensus is low, but consistency and distinctiveness are high. This type of attributional process is most likely to occur when we are faced with unexpected events that can't easily be explained -- or when it is important to understand why others acted as they did. Quite often, we do not expend cognitive effort in our attributional processes and do not perform this kind of detailed, rational analysis.

There are some basic sources of bias in the attribution process. The tendency to explain the behavior of others in terms of internal causes and to overlook external ones is the fundamental attribution error. This may occur because people do not pay attention to context or give it less importance. This tendency appears to weaken over time.

The tendency to interpret the causes of our behavior in a positive way is the self-serving bias. For example, we may attribute success to internal causes and failure to external causes. This may be based on a desire to enhance one's self-esteem and a desire to look good to others.

B. Social Cognition: How We Process Social Information

Social cognition is an area of study concerned with understanding the processes through which we notice, interpret, remember, and use social information.

We tend to use various mental short-cuts or heuristics in making judgments. The tendency to believe that others share our views is the false consensus effect. It may occur because of the availability heuristic -- the easier it is to bring information to mind, the more important it is judged to be. Several factors play a role in this effect. The false consensus effect does not occur all of the time. People also desire to perceive themselves as unique when highly desirable attributes are involved.

There appears to be an automatic vigilance (a powerful and automatic tendency) to pay attention to negative information or stimuli. Negative information may alert us to dangers and save us cognitive effort; but it can lead us into errors in our perceptions of others. We appear to possess several kinds of cognitive filters that make it more difficult for some information to be processed and shape our conclusions. Motivated skepticism refers to the tendency to be more skeptical about information that doesn't support our current views.

When we imagine events and outcomes that are different from the ones we actually experienced, we are engaging in counterfactual thinking. This kind of thinking often leads us to have more sympathy for persons who experience negative outcomes that follow their atypical behavior. This is the case, in part, because it is easier to imagine alternatives to unusual than to typical forms of behavior.

The tendencies described above sometimes cause us to make errors. However, they may also allow us to process complex information quickly and efficiently without making serious errors.

C. Attitudes: Evaluating the Social World

Attitudes can be defined as mental representations and evaluations of various aspects of the social world. They may be formed by such processes as operant and classical conditioning, as well as from observational learning.

Efforts at persuasion involve the following basic elements: a source directs a message or communication to some target audience. The traditional approach was concerned primarily with the "when" and "how" of persuasion. Research generated from this approach has found that people who are experts are more persuasive than those who are not. Messages that do not appear to be designed to change our attitudes are more successful than ones that seem intended to manipulate us. The attractiveness and popularity of the source are also important factors in persuasion. Individuals who are low in self-esteem are often easier to persuade than persons high in self-esteem. When an audience holds attitudes contrary to the would-be persuader, it is often more effective to use a two-sided approach (i.e., it is better to present both sides of an issue). A one-sided approach is most effective when the audience holds attitudes that are already consistent with the would-be persuader. People who speak rapidly are generally more effective than those who speak slowly.

The cognitive approach is concerned primarily with the "why" of persuasion -- or what cognitive processes determine when someone is actually persuaded. When we carefully evaluate the arguments and are convinced by their logic, we are experiencing the central route to persuasion. This route is followed when the issues are important or personally relevant to recipients. Persuasion takes the peripheral route when we are not fully attending to the arguments and are influenced by persuasion cues -- information relating to the source's prestige, credibility or likability, or to the style and form of the message. This is likely to occur with issues that are relatively unimportant and not personally relevant to recipients, or when recipients are distracted. These routes are described by the elaboration likelihood model of persuasion.

When inconsistencies arise between attitudes, or between attitudes and behavior, an unpleasant feeling known as cognitive dissonance can occur. This produces a negative motivational state -- people experiencing it want to reduce cognitive dissonance. One way of reducing it is to change your attitudes. In many situations, we are forced to say or do something that is against our true attitudes. This is called forced compliance. The weaker the reasons individuals have for saying or doing things that are inconsistent with their attitudes, the stronger the dissonance generated. Therefore, the greater the pressure for attitude change. This is known as the "less leads to more" effect. This effect is most likely to occur when individuals believe they have free choice and feel personally responsible for their actions.

Questions:

14-1. What are the topics that serve as the major focus of social psychology? _____

_____

_____

_____

14-2. What is the definition of attribution? _____

_____

_____

_____

14-3. What are the conditions leading to internal and external causal attributions from Kelley's model?

_____

_____

_____

14-4. What are the various attributional biases? _____

_____

_____

_____

14-5. What is the definition of social cognition? _____

_____

_____

_____

14-6. What is the research on sources of error in social thought, including the false consensus effect, automatic vigilance, motivated skepticism, and counterfactual thinking? _____

_____

_____

_____

14-7. Are inaccurate judgment and decisions the rule or the exception? Why or why not? _____

_____

_____

_____

14-8. What is the general definition of an attitude and the influence of conditioning on attitudes?

_____

_____

_____

14-9.   What are the general conclusions derived from the early work on persuasion? _____

_____

_____

_____

14-10. What is the elaboration likelihood model? _____

_____

_____

_____

14-11. What is the role of cognitive dissonance in attitude change? _____

_____

_____

_____

II.   Social Behavior: Interacting With Others

A.   Prejudice: Distorted Views of the Social World...and Their Consequences

Prejudice involves negative attitudes toward members of specific groups that are based solely on persons' memberships in these groups. The realistic conflict view suggests that prejudice arises out of economic competition between various groups. The social categorization view suggests that our tendency to divide the social world into distinct categories of "us" versus "them" contributes to the development of prejudice.

The fact that infants do not show prejudice suggests that it emerges through the process of social learning. According to the cognitive perspective of prejudice, prejudice not only involves powerful emotional reactions, but also involves the ways we think about others and process various types of social information. The cognitive perspective emphasizes the role of stereotypes in prejudice, which are widely shared assumptions about the characteristics of social groups. Stereotypes exert strong effects on the ways in which we process social information. For example, information relevant to a particular stereotype is processed more quickly than unrelated information. Stereotypes also determine what we remember about other persons.

Increased contact between groups can sometimes reduce prejudice. This occurs only under the following conditions: (1) the groups are approximately equal in status, (2) the situation involves cooperation and interdependence so that the groups work toward shared goals, (3) contact between groups is informal, (4) existing norms favor group equality, and (5) the persons involved view one another as typical members of their respective groups. Research has found that procedures designed to shift or recategorize the boundaries between "us" and "them" can be a valuable approach to lessening prejudice. In addition, the operation of cognitive dissonance can be a powerful force against prejudice. If we can induce people to act in a non-prejudice way, sometimes attitude change occurs.

B. Social Influence: Changing Others' Behavior

Social influence involves attempts by one or more persons to change the behavior of others. In many contexts, there are social rules or social norms indicating how we should or ought to behave. These rules exert pressure toward conformity -- toward thinking or acting like most other persons. In one classic study on conformity by Asch, accomplices of the experimenter gave their answers on a line judgment task. These accomplices gave the wrong answer on twelve of the eighteen problems. Seventy-six percent of the participants went along with the group's wrong answers at least once; whereas, only five percent of respondents in a control group -- a group not exposed to the accomplices' answers -- made such errors.

The degree of conformity can be influenced by a number of factors. Group size is one factor. As the number of influencing people increases to three or four, conformity increases. Beyond this amount, it tends to increase very little. One reason why compliance may "flatten out" is that we may suspect that these persons are in collusion. Degree of conformity can be greatly reduced by the support of others who also deviate from the norms. Another factor that was once assumed to strongly affect conformity is gender. It is no longer believed to be a factor.

Earlier studies indicated that females were more susceptible to conformity. This difference no longer exists. The greater conformity of females may have been related to the use of materials familiar to men. Another reason involves shifts in gender roles and stereotypes. Persons holding low status are often expected to be easier to influence than those holding higher status. When status differences are eliminated, expectations for greater conformity by females is also eliminated. When females have demonstrated their competence on a task, they are no more likely to yield than males. In fact, in one study, under conditions where females have shown superior knowledge, males yielded more to the judgments of females than vice versa.

Compliance involves one person asking another to do something that the requester wants. There are various techniques for gaining compliance. Ingratiation involves efforts to increase one's appeal to a target person before asking that person to grant a request. This can be done by the use of agreement, emitting positive non-verbal cues, enhancing personal appearance, name dropping, self-deprecating remarks, and flattery.

The strategy of going from a small request to a large one is the foot-in-the-door technique. This technique seems to be effective in increasing compliance. It seems to be related to changes in self-perception. People may see themselves as more helpful after the first request and act consistently with this perception in response to the large request.

The technique of beginning with a large request and switching to a small one after it is rejected is the door-in-the-face technique. The reduction in the size of the request places pressure on the other person to also make a concession. This technique also leads to increased compliance. The that's-not-all approach throws something extra into the situation before the person has made a decision.

Expressions of discontent or dissatisfaction with yourself is called complaining. It has also been found to be a tactic that can increase compliance. There appear to be differences in how males and females react to another's complaints and gender differences in how this technique is used. Women tend to complain about themselves and men tend to complain about others. Women show more supportive reactions to others' complaints than do men.

Social influence by demand is called obedience. In the classic Milgram study, in which people were told to shock another person, about 65 percent of participants showed total obedience. Similar findings have been obtained in studies conducted in Jordan, Germany, and Australia -- and with children as well as adults. An important factor in these results is that the person in authority relieves the subjects of responsibility for the actions. The experimenter possessed clear signs of authority and existing social norm suggest that authority figures are to be obeyed. The fact that increasing obedience is requested in a gradual manner is also important. These effects can be overcome if individuals are held responsible, witness others disobeying, and there is clear evidence that authorities are pursuing selfish goals. You should remember that, in this research, no one was actually shocked.

C. Prosocial Behavior: When We Help...And When We Don't

Prosocial behavior is defined as actions that benefit others without necessarily providing direct benefits to the helpers. Studies have shown that as the number of bystanders to an emergency increase, helping decreases. This seems to be due to the assumption that others will help, known as diffusion of responsibility.

Good moods will increase helping when it results in pleasant consequences. If helping may end the good feelings, tendency to help is reduced. A bad mood can reduce helping if the potential helpers concentrate on their own needs or misfortunes. Sometimes a bad mood can increase helping because it provides negative state relief. This can occur when persons can observe the positive effects of helping and can praise themselves for having helped.

There are large individual differences in tendencies to help. In one study, persons who helped were compared to those that did not. Those that helped had stronger beliefs in a just world -- were higher in internal locus of control, higher in social responsibility and lower in terms of egocentrism.

D. Attraction, Love, and Close Relationships

Friendship or liking is often increased by the close physical distance between people, known as propinquity. This may lead to repeated exposure, which in turn leads to more liking. Similarity often leads to increased liking. One possibility is that similarity provides validation for our views and personal characteristics. In addition, the more others like us, the more we tend to like them. This may be because we enjoy receiving positive evaluations and dislike negative ones. This tendency is so strong that it can occur in situations where we believe that the assessments are inaccurate or represent an attempt at flattery. Physical attractiveness is another factor influencing attraction. It is a factor for men and women, although the effects appear to be stronger for males.

The characteristics that define physical attractiveness vary greatly from culture to culture. In Western societies, faces are perceived as attractive when they don't depart in any pronounced way from the "typical" face in the culture. Most men appear to find two facial "types" attractive in women: youthful, child-like features or bolder, more "mature" features. For body features, many men find medium-size breasts and a slim figure attractive in women, whereas women find men with broad shoulders, small backsides, and a narrow waist attractive. Height is related to attractiveness, especially for women. Females prefer men who are taller than themselves, and men prefer women somewhat shorter than themselves.

According to one approach, three conditions must be met for a person to conclude that they are in romantic or passionate love: a) it requires the experience of strong emotional arousal, b) a suitable object, and c) the concept of romantic love must be present in the culture. Passionate love is dominated by strong physical attraction whereas companionate love emphasizes commitment and concern for the loved-one's well-being. Table 14.1 describes six distinct types of love (see p. 554).

According to a biochemical approach to love, the presence of one's lover triggers the release of amphetamine-like substances within the body. This is associated with romantic love. Over time, the presence of one's lover produces lower levels of these substances. At this point, the "emotional high" is gone and both partners may seek a new relationship. In other cases, the presence of one's lover becomes a stimulus for the production of endorphins that generate feelings of calmness or contentment. These feelings serve as one basis for companionate love. There is not sufficient evidence to evaluate this approach, but it is interesting.

Several factors may contribute to troubled relationships. These include jealousy, the discovery of dissimilarities, boredom, and self-defeating patterns of behavior. These factors contribute to the dissolution of relationships.

E. Environmental Psychology: How the Physical Environment Affects Social Behavior - - and Vice Versa

Environmental psychology investigates how the physical environment influences behavior and how human behavior, in turn, affects the environment. Most research has focused on three influences: temperature, noise, and air quality.

It appears that aggression increases as the air temperature rises. However, at some point, increasing heat may lead to lethargy or heat exhaustion, which would decrease the tendency to aggress unless people take steps to alleviate these states.

We also have an effect on our physical environment. The greenhouse effect, the destruction of rainforests, and the spread of viral diseases are frightening examples of the negative influence of our presence on the planet.

Questions:

14-12. What are the different views on the origins of prejudice and discrimination? _____

_____

_____

_____

14-13. What methods can be used to reduce prejudice and its impact? _____

_____

_____

_____

14-14. What are the three components of racial identification and the factors that influence its strength?

_____

_____

_____

14-15. What are the research findings concerning sex differences in conformity? _____

_____

_____

_____

14-16. What is compliance and the role of ingratiation in this process? _____

_____

_____

_____

14-17. What are the various techniques for gaining compliance? _____

_____

_____

_____

14-18. What is obedience and what are the factors that increase the extent of obedience to authority?

_____

_____

_____

14-19. What is prosocial behavior and what are the factors that influence the bystander intervention effect?

_____

_____

_____

14-20. What are the research findings on mood and prosocial behavior? _____

_____

_____

_____

14-21. What are the personal characteristics that are associated with helpful persons? _____

_____

_____

_____

14-22. What are the factors that influence interpersonal attribution? _____

_____

_____

_____

14-23. What are the approaches to the nature and interpretation of love and what are the factors that influence it? _____

_____

_____

_____

14-24. How does the physical environment affect our behavior and, in turn, how do we affect our environment? _____

_____

_____

_____

III.   Making Psychology Part of Your Life: Are You in Love? One Way of Telling

In this section, Baron provides a questionnaire designed to measure the intense emotional reactions characteristic of love. It is based on systematic research.

Question:

14-25. How do you score on this scale? What can we learn from such questionnaires? _____

_____

_____

_____

MAKING PSYCHOLOGY PART OF YOUR LIFE: Key Terms and Concepts

Knowing the important concepts and key terms contained in this chapter is a very important part of mastering the material. We have presented a sample of these concepts below. Define each concept and check your definition with that presented in the chapter. It will also be beneficial for you to think of an example of each concept. Whenever possible, use your own personal experience to provide an example of each term below, whenever possible.

14-1.   **Attitudes:** _____

Example: _____

14-2.   **Attribution:** _____

Example: _____

14-3.   **Automatic Vigilance:** _____

Example: _____

14-4.   **Bystander Effect:** _____

Example: _____

14-5.   **Central Route:** _____

Example: _____

14-6.   **Cognitive Dissonance:** _____

Example: _____

14-7.   **Cognitive Perspective on Persuasion:** _____

Example: _____

14-8.   **Companionate Love:** _____

Example: _____

14-9.   **Complaining:** _____

Example: _____

14-10.   **Compliance:** _____

Example: _____

14-11.   **Conformity:** _____

Example: _____

14-12.   **Consensus:** _____

Example: _____

14-13.   **Consistency:** _____

Example: _____

14-14.   **Contact Hypothesis**: _____

Example: _____

14-15.   **Counterfactual Thinking**: _____

Example: _____

14-16.   **Diffusion of Responsibility**: _____

Example: _____

14-17.   **Distinctiveness:** _____

Example: _____

14-18.   **Door-in-the-face Technique**: _____

Example: _____

14-19.   **Elaboration Likelihood Model**: _____

14-20.   **Environmental Psychology**: _____

14-21. **Foot-in-the-door Technique**: _____

Example: _____

14-22. **Forced Compliance**: _____

Example: _____

14-23. **Fundamental Attribution Error**: _____

Example: _____

14-24. **Impression Management**: _____

Example: _____

14-25. **Ingratiation**: _____

Example: _____

14-26. **Interpersonal Attraction**: _____

Example: _____

14-27. **Less-Leads-to-More Effect**: _____

Example: _____

14-28. **Love**: _____

Example: _____

14-29. **Motivated Skepticism**: _____

Example: _____

14-30. **Obedience**: _____

Example: _____

14-31. **Peripheral Route**: _____

Example: _____

14-32.   **Persuasion:** _____

Example: _____

14-33.   **Prejudice:** _____

Example: _____

14-34.   **Propinquity:** _____

Example: _____

14-35.   **Prosocial Behavior:** _____

Example: _____

14-36.   **Racial Identification:** _____

Example: _____

14-37.   **Realistic Conflict Theory:** _____

14-38.   **Recategorization:** _____

Example: _____

14-39.   **Repeated Exposure Effect:** _____

Example: _____

14-40.   **Romantic Love:** _____

Example: _____

14-41.   **Self-Serving Bias:** _____

Example: _____

14-42.   **Social Categorization:** _____

Example: _____

14-43.   **Social Cognition**: _____

Example: _____

14-44.   **Social Influence**: _____

Example: _____

14-45.   **Social Norms**: _____

Example: _____

14-46.   **Social Psychology**: _____

14-47.   **Stereotypes**: _____

Example: _____

14-48.   **That's Not All Approach**: _____

Example: _____

CHALLENGE: Develop Your Critical Thinking Skills

Introspection: Prejudice and Discrimination

Unfortunately, prejudice and discrimination are common in our social world. Rather than denying this fact, it is useful to recognize the instances in which we have been both victims and instigators of prejudice and discrimination. A critical thinker is able to recognize instances in which he/she has been affected by these social forces. Recognizing these instances is the first step toward reducing these negative forms of social behavior. As an exercise in developing these skills, look within yourself and your past experiences (i.e., introspect) for instances in which prejudice and discrimination have affected your thought and behavior.

14-1.   List the social labels that can be applied to you (e.g., male, female). _____

_____

_____

_____

14-2.   When has prejudice touched your life? Have you ever felt "put-down," excluded or discriminated against because you were in any of the social groups you listed above? Describe an occasion. _____

_____

_____

_____

_____

14-3.   Describe your feelings about the occasion described above. _____

_____

_____

_____

14-4.   Have you ever felt that anyone responded to you based on assumptions that they made concerning your social group (what you are) vs. your individual characteristics (who you are)? If so, describe an occasion.

_____

_____

_____

14-5.   If you answered "yes" to question 4, describe the feelings you experienced in this occasion. _____

_____

_____

_____

14-6.   Have you ever felt that you responded to another person based upon his/her social group membership? If so, please describe an occasion. _____

_____

_____

_____

14-7.   Do you ever feel as if you are prejudiced? For example, have you ever had immediate prejudice reactions -- regardless of how you then acted? If so, describe an occasion. _____

_____

_____

_____

14-8.   If you answered "yes" to either question 6 or 7, speculate on why you had these reactions. Does the material you've learned in this chapter give you insight into the reason? _____

_____

_____

_____

14-9.   Have you ever felt that others responded to you as if you were prejudiced? If so, describe an occasion.

_____

_____

_____

14-10. If you answered "yes" to question 9, how did this make you feel? _____

_____

_____

_____

14-11. After completing questions 1-10, you may want to ask your friends and/or classmates these questions. You may be surprised to find that so many people feel they have been both victims and instigators of prejudice. How might you use the information you've learned to reduce prejudice in your social world? _____

_____

_____

_____

_____

_____

CHALLENGE: Making Psychology Part of Your Life

<u>Attribution</u>

As an exercise in seeing how the research on attribution discussed in your text applies to you, complete the following questionnaires:

Questionnaire I

14-1. From the following, circle the trait that is most applicable to the President of the United States.

1.	a. trustworthy	b. untrustworthy	c. depends on the situation
2.	a. friendly	b. unfriendly	c. depends on the situation
3.	a. intelligent	b. not intelligent	c. depends on the situation
4.	a. insincere	b. sincere	c. depends on the situation
5.	a. humorous	b. serious	c. depends on the situation
6.	a. anxious	b. calm	c. depends on the situation
7.	a. easy going	b. stubborn	c. depends on the situation
8.	a. conscientious	b. unconscientious	c. depends on the situation
9.	a. agreeable	b. disagreeable	c. depends on the situation
10.	a. unattractive	b. attractive	c. depends on the situation

14-2. From the following list, circle the trait that is most applicable to you.

1.	a. trustworthy	b. untrustworthy	c. depends on the situation
2.	a. friendly	b. unfriendly	c. depends on the situation
3.	a. intelligent	b. not intelligent	c. depends on the situation
4.	a. insincere	b. sincere	c. depends on the situation
5.	a. humorous	b. serious	c. depends on the situation
6.	a. anxious	b. calm	c. depends on the situation
7.	a. easy going	b. stubborn	c. depends on the situation
8.	a. conscientious	b. unconscientious	c. depends on the situation
9.	a. agreeable	b. disagreeable	c. depends on the situation
10.	a. unattractive	b. attractive	c. depends on the situation

14-3. Count the number of times you circled "depends on the situation" when you made judgments about the President vs. yourself. Record the tally below:

<u>The President</u>   <u>You</u>

<u>Analysis</u>: Did you circle "depends on the situation" more often when describing your characteristics vs. those of the President? If so, you demonstrated the **fundamental attribution error** -- our tendency to explain others' actions in terms of dispositional (internal) factors vs. seeing the situation factors that may influence others' behavior. See page 523 in your text for further discussion.

Source: Suggested by R. E. Nisbett Attribution Scale.

Questionnaire II

14-1. Imagine the following situation: You have just received an A+ on your psychology exam. To what extent do you think your grade was affected by:

a. the amount you studied for the exam. (Mark the scale point that corresponds with your feeling.)

Not at all   1   2   3   4   5   6   7   a great deal

b. the difficulty of the exam.

Not at all   1   2   3   4   5   6   7   a great deal

c. your talent for psychology.

Not at all   1   2   3   4   5   6   7   a great deal

d. the instructor's grading standards.

Not at all   1   2   3   4   5   6   7   a great deal

14-2. Imagine the following scenario: You have just received a failing grade on your psychology exam. To what extent do you think that your grade was affected by the following:

a. the amount you studied for the exam. (Mark the scale point that corresponds with your feeling.)

Not at all   1   2   3   4   5   6   7   a great deal

b. the difficulty of the exam.

Not at all   1   2   3   4   5   6   7   a great deal

c. your talent for psychology.

Not at all   1   2   3   4   5   6   7   a great deal

d. the instructor's grading standards.

Not at all   1   2   3   4   5   6   7   a great deal

<u>Analysis:</u>

1. Tally the numbers you placed on the scales for items A and C and items B and D in scenario 1 and 2.

    A & C = _____   2. A & C = _____

    B & D = _____   B & D = _____

    What pattern do you see? Did you tend to place higher numbers for options A and C in scenario 1 vs. scenario 2? And did you give higher numbers to B & D in scenario 2 vs. 1? _____

    _____

2. Options A and C represent internal causal dimensions and options B and D represent external causal dimensions.   If you made more internal vs. external causal attributions for scenario 1 vs. 2, you demonstrated what's known as "the self-serving bias" -- our tendency to take credit for positive behavior or outcomes by attributing them to internal causes, but to blame negative ones on external causes. See page 524 in your text for further discussion.

    Source: Suggested by B. Weiner attribution scale.

CHALLENGE: Review Your Comprehensive Knowledge

SAMPLE TEST QUESTIONS

Once you have worked through the preceding sections, you should be ready for a comprehensive self-test. You can check your answers with those presented at the end of this section. An additional practice test is given in the supplementary section at the end of this study guide.

14-1.   According to Kelley, if a person reacts the same way to a given stimulus or situation on different occasions (i.e., across time), he/she exhibits:
a.   low distinctiveness.
b.   high consistency.
c.   high consensus.
d.   low covariation.

14-2.   According to Kelley, we tend to attribute behavior to external causes if consistency is _____, distinctiveness is _____, and consensus is _____.
a.   high, low, low
b.   high, high, high
c.   low, low, low
d.   low, high, high

14-3.   The fundamental attribution error is the tendency to explain the behavior of others in terms of _____ causes.
a.   internal
b.   external
c.   stable
d.   unstable

14-4.   The tendency to interpret the causes of our behavior in a positive way is the:
a.   fundamental attribution error.
b.   basis of most gender differences.
c.   illusory correlation.
d.   self-serving bias.

14-5.   The tendency to overestimate the extent to which we are similar to others is the _____ effect.
a.   false consensus
b.   priming
c.   illusory correlation
d.   false uniqueness

14-6.   Advertisements that are designed to sell by having a "star" endorse the products use the:
a.   peripheral route to persuasion.
b.   central route to persuasion.
c.   counterfactual thinking route to persuasion.
d.   foot-in-the-door technique.

14-7.   The central route to persuasion refers to:
a.   the careful processing of arguments.
b.   the impact of persuasion cues on attitude change.
c.   attitude change that occurs because an individual recognizes inconsistencies between their attitudes and behavior.
d.   persuasion induced by fear.

14-8.   When we imagine events and outcomes that are different from the ones we actually experienced, we are engaging in:
a.   counterfactual thinking.
b.   internal attributions.
c.   high distinctiveness thinking.
d.   illusory correlation.

14-9.   The view of prejudice that suggests that prejudice stems from competition between social groups over valued commodities or opportunities is the:
a.   realistic conflict theory.
b.   cognitive dissonance theory.
c.   social learning theory.
d.   social categorization perspective.

14-10. This view suggests that prejudice results from our tendency to divide the social world into "us" versus "them."
    a. conflict
    b. social categorization
    c. social learning
    d. cognitive dissonance

14-11. This view of prejudice emphasizes the role of stereotypes.
    a. realistic conflict
    b. peripheral cue
    c. learning
    d. cognitive

14-12. According to dissonance theory, the _____ the obvious pressure for attitude change, the _____ the pressure to change one's own view.
    a. more stable, more stable
    b. greater, weaker
    c. greater, greater
    d. less stable, less stable

14-13. Early research on gender differences indicated that females were more susceptible to conformity. Evidence for this effect:
    a. is getting stronger.
    b. occurs only on intellectual tasks.
    c. no longer exists.
    d. occurs only in western societies.

14-14. The foot-in-the-door technique seems to be effective because it produces changes in:
    a. self-image.
    b. attitudes.
    c. motivation.
    d. self-confidence.

14-15. In the door-in-the-face technique, the first request is a _____ one and the second request is a _____ one.
    a. large, small
    b. small, large
    c. large, large
    d. small, moderate

14-16. Bystanders may not help in emergencies because they presume others will help. This is known as:
    a. pluralistic ignorance.
    b. nonempathy.
    c. diffusion of responsibility.
    d. division of impact.

14-17. An important factor in getting participants to obey in the obedience studies is that the person in authority relieves the participant of:
    a. responsibility.
    b. emotion.
    c. awareness.
    d. none of the above

14-18. Increased contact between groups can sometimes reduce prejudice, especially if several conditions are met. Which of the following is not one of the conditions?
    a. the groups are approximately equal in status
    b. existing norms favor equality
    c. the persons involved view one another as atypical members of their respective groups
    d. the groups work toward shared goals

14-19. This type of love emphasizes commitment and concern for the loved-one's well-being.
    a. passionate love
    b. companionate love
    c. responsible love
    d. motivated love

14-20. In one study, the characteristics of persons who helped were compared to those who did not. Which of the following characteristics did helpers not have?
    a. a stronger belief in a just world
    b. lower in internal locus of control
    c. lower in terms of egocentrism
    d. higher in social responsibility

Answers and Feedback for Sample Test Questions:

14-1.   B   If a person acts in the same way to a stimulus over time, he/she has high consistency. (p. 521)

14-2.   B   We tend to attribute behavior to external causes if consistency is high, consensus is high, and distinctiveness is high. (p. 521)

14-3.   A   The tendency to explain the behavior of others in terms of internal causes and to overlook external ones is the fundamental attribution error. (p. 523)

14-4.   D   The tendency to interpret the causes of our behavior in a positive way is the self-serving bias. (p. 524)

14-5.   A   The false consensus effect refers to the tendency to overestimate the extent to which we are similar to others. (p. 525)

14-6.   A   Persuasion is taking the peripheral route when we are not fully attending to the arguments and are influenced by information related to such things as the source's prestige. A "star" has prestige for most persons. (p. 529)

14-7.   A   The central route involves careful processing of information. (p. 530)

14-8.   A   Counterfactual thinking occurs when we imagine events and outcomes that are different from the one we actually experienced. (p. 527)

14-9.   A   The realistic conflict theory contends that prejudice stems from competition over valued resources. (p. 535)

14-10. B   The social categorization view suggests that an "us" versus "them" distinction contributes to prejudice. (p. 535)

14-11. D   The cognitive perspective emphasizes the role of stereotypes. (pp. 535-536)

14-12. B   According to cognitive dissonance theory, the greater the obvious pressure for attitude change, the weaker the pressure to change one's own attitude or view. This follows from the less-leads-to-more effect and research on forced compliance. (p. 532)

14-13. C   Current research suggests that females are no more susceptible to conformity than males. (p. 541)

14-14. A   The foot-in-the-door technique seems to be effective because of changes in self-perception in that people may see themselves as more helpful after complying to the first request. (p. 543)

14-15. A   The door-in-the-face technique begins with a large request and switches to a small one after the large request is rejected. (p. 544)

14-16. C   Bystanders may not help in emergencies because the presence of other individuals leads to a diffusion of responsibility. (p. 549)

14-17. A   An important factor in the obedience studies is that the authority figure relieves the participant of responsibility. (p. 545)

14-18. C   The persons involved should view one another as typical (not atypical) members of their respective groups. (pp. 536-537)

14-19. B   Companionate love emphasizes commitment and concern for the loved-one's well-being. (p. 553)

14-20. B   Helpers were higher (not lower) in internal locus of control. (p. 550)

Glossary of difficult words and expressions	Definition
Bigots	people who are strongly partial to their own religion, race or group; people who are prejudiced
Clerk	a person who works in an office performing such tasks as keeping records
Clumsy	lacking physical coordination, skill or grace
Compelled	forced
Coped	managed; attempted to overcome problems and difficulties
Curtailed	to cut short
Drought	state that occurs due to lack of water
Flattery	excessive praise
Fled	left in a hurry
Frown	drawing the eyebrows together forming lines on the forehead; an expression of displeasure
Inept	awkward, incompetent; lacking sense or reason
Jargon-studded paper	paper filled with words that are common to a particular field
Law-abiding citizens	citizens who respect the law
Marshaled	to arrange, place or set
Murky	dark; gloomy
Negligence	carelessness; inattention to one's responsibilities
Onslaught	overwhelming
Pleas for aid	desperate calls for help
Plight	unfortunate situation
Prevail	to win or overcome difficulties
Reluctant	hesitant
Resiliency	marked by the ability to recover; toughness
Shudder	to shake from fear
Slick	smooth, slippery
Sorting	to arrange
Succumb	to give in
Tilt	incline; on its side
Unsettling	uneasy

SUPPLEMENTAL PRACTICE TESTS

This section provides you with additional practice quizzes for each chapter. Review these after you have finished studying for your exam. If you find you cannot correctly answer eight or more questions, you should review the material in the chapter. But be sure and go back to the material in the chapter that discusses any of the questions you missed. The page number in the text where this material can be found is indicated at the end of each question. The answers for each quiz can be found at the end of this section. Good luck!

CHAPTER 1
PSYCHOLOGY: IT'S NATURE AND SCOPE

PRACTICE QUIZ 2

1- 1.   Psychologists who believed that psychologists should study the ways in which consciousness helps us to survive and adapt were called: (p. 5)
a. functionalists.
b. structuralists.
c. behaviorists.
d. experimentalists.

1- 2.   A structuralist who founded the first psychological laboratory was: (p. 5)
a. Wundt.
b. James.
c. Watson.
d. Freud.

1- 3.   One of the major changes in psychology in recent years has been the increased interest in: (p. 13)
a. parapsychology.
b. animal behavior.
c. multi-cultural issues.
d. perception.

1- 4.   The characteristics that define a field as scientific are: (p. 15)
a. systematic observation and direct experimentation.
b. the topics under investigation.
c. the use of particular scientific procedures and equipment.
d. the use of naturalistic observation.

1- 5.   A detailed study of a few individuals is the _____ method. (p. 20)
a. natural observation
b. case
c. survey
d. common sense

1- 6.   One problem with the survey method is that it may be: (p. 21)
a. time consuming.
b. non-representative of larger groups to whom the findings are generalized.
c. too manipulative.
d. difficult to use.

1- 7.   The view that people can choose how to behave (i.e., have free will) is most consistent with the _____ perspective. (p. 9)
a. psychodynamic
b. behaviorist
c. humanistic
d. biopsychological

1- 8.   If one wants to determine why a relationship exists one needs to use: (p. 23)
a. observation.
b. correlation.
c. experimentation.
d. surveys.

1- 9.   In an experiment, the factor that is measured is called the _____ variable. (p. 24)
a. independent
b. dependent
c. control
d. stimulus

1-10.   Theories involve all but one of the following: (p. 30)
a. nontestable predictions.
b. basic concepts.
c. statements about concepts.
d. hypotheses.

CHAPTER 2
BIOLOGICAL BASES OF BEHAVIOR:
A LOOK BENEATH THE SURFACE

PRACTICE QUIZ 2

2- 1. Information is carried to the cell body by: (p. 45)
    a. dendrites.
    b. axons.
    c. glial cells.
    d. dopamine.

2- 2. A change in electric charge is called: (p. 46)
    a. dynamic state.
    b. steady-state stage.
    c. action potential.
    d. resting potential.

2- 3. When the neuron is stimulated it lets _____ charged _____ enter. (p. 46)
    a. positively, ions
    b. negatively, ions
    c. positively, proteins
    d. negatively, proteins

2- 4. Interference with this transmitter is related to paralysis. (p. 50)
    a. norepinephrine
    b. acetylcholine
    c. dopamine
    d. serotonin

2- 5. Opiate-like substances produced by the brain during times of pain or vigorous exercise are: (p. 51)
    a. analgesics.
    b. endorphins.
    c. glutamic acid.
    d. aspartic acid.

2- 6. The part of the autonomic nervous system that readies the body for use of energy is the _____ division. (p. 53)
    a. central
    b. sympathetic
    c. parasympathetic
    d. somatic

2- 7. The part of the brain involved in eating and drinking is the: (p. 58)
    a. midbrain.
    b. hypothalamus.
    c. cerebellum.
    d. medulla.

2- 8. Damage to the right hemisphere of the occipital lobe results in an inability to: (p. 60)
    a. point to objects.
    b. to name objects.
    c. to see objects in the left visual field.
    d. identify features in the right visual field.

2- 9. The two areas of the brain related to speech are: (p. 61)
    a. Wernicke's, Fugua's.
    b. Long's, Fuqua's.
    c. Long's, Broca's.
    d. Wernicke's, Broca's.

2-10. Which of the following is done more accurately by the left side of the brain? (p. 63)
    a. judgment of emotion
    b. judgment of hearing.
    c. word perception.
    d. tilt perception.

CHAPTER 3
SENSATION AND PERCEPTION:
MAKING CONTACT WITH THE WORLD AROUND US

PRACTICE QUIZ 2

3- 1.   Your ability to recognize and interpret odors is referred to as: (p. 80)
    a. perception.   c. neurology.
    b. sensation.   d. transduction.

3- 2.   The fact that rewards and costs affect our ability to detect stimulation is part of the _____ theory. (p. 82)
    a. discrimination.   c. signal detection.
    b. threshold analysis.   d. utility.

3- 3.   The threshold that refers to how much change is required for a physical stimulus to be perceived as noticeably different is called a _____ threshold. (p. 82)
    a. sensitivity   c. detection
    b. variation   d. difference

3- 4.   The receptors in the eye that are involved in color vision are the: (p. 86)
    a. ganglion cells.   c. rods.
    b. blind spot.   d. cones.

3- 5.   Cells in the visual system that respond to length, width, and shape are: (p. 90)
    a. simple.   c. hypercomplex.
    b. complex.   d. geometric.

3- 6.   Which of the following best explains why we first feel cold when we dive into a swimming pool but then feel it is just right a few minutes later? (p. 84)
    a. sensory adaptation   c. sensory deprivation
    b. sensory threshold   d. signal detection theory

3- 7.   The theory that holds that sounds of different pitch cause different rates of neural firing is: (p. 93)
    a. place.   c. neuronal.
    b. frequency.   d. pitch differential.

3- 8.   When we take distance into account in determining size, we are using the _____ principle. (p. 106)
    a. size constancy.   c. size-distance invariance.
    b. relative size.   d. distance-size perspective.

3- 9.   Theories that propose that pattern recognition is based on simple perceptual abilities are called: (p. 111)
    a. prototype.   c. bottom-up.
    b. top-down.   d. feature.

3-10.   The fact that perceived size of an object remains the same when the distance is varied, even when the size of the image it casts on the retina changes greatly is called: (p. 106)
    a. the law of closure.   c. shape constancy.
    b. size constancy.   d. law of similarity.

CHAPTER 4
CONSCIOUSNESS:
AWARENESS OF OURSELVES AND THE EXTERNAL WORLD

PRACTICE QUIZ 2

4- 1. Which of the following is **not** one of the characteristics of REM sleep? (p. 133)
    a. occurs only in humans   c. muscular relaxation occurs
    b. accompanied by rapid eye movements   d. individuals dream during REM sleep

4- 2. Fluctuations in our bodily rhythms that occur throughout the day are called: (p. 123)
    a. circadian rhythms.   c. ultradian rhythms.
    b. nocturnal myoclonus rhythms.   d. REM rhythms.

4- 3. The drugs that reduce the release of excitatory transmitter substances at the synapse are: (p. 147)
    a. opiates.   c. hallucinogens.
    b. amphetamines.   d. barbiturates.

4- 4. The type of processing that does not take much attentional capacity is called: (p. 127)
    a. capacity.   c. automatic.
    b. subconscious.   d. controlled.

4- 5. Daydreams appear to aid in all but one of the following: (p. 129)
    a. psychological escape.   c. self-regulation.
    b. finding solutions to problems.   d. apnea.

4- 6. Which of the following is the sleep disorder in which individuals are overcome by uncontrollable periods of sleep during waking hours? (p. 136)
    a. insomnia   c. narcolepsy
    b. somnambulism   d. apnea

4- 7. As we fall to sleep there is an increase in: (p. 132)
    a. beta waves.   c. delta waves.
    b. alpha waves.   d. macro waves.

4- 8. According to the psychodynamic perspective, the reported content of dreams is: (p. 138)
    a. latent content.   c. unconscious content.
    b. manifest content.   d. delta content.

4- 9. Which of the following is not one of the characteristics of individuals who are very susceptible to hypnosis. (p. 141)
    a. They are prone to fantasies.
    b. They become deeply involved in sensory experiences.
    c. They are dependent on others.
    d. They do not seek direction.

4-10. The procedure that is designed to produce an altered state of consciousness in which awareness and contact with the external world is reduced is called: (p. 151)
    a. hypnosis.   c. delta states.
    b. apnea.   d. meditation.

CHAPTER 5
LEARNING: HOW WE'RE CHANGED BY EXPERIENCE

PRACTICE QUIZ 2

5- 1.   The type of learning that involves pairing unconditioned and conditioned stimulus is: (p. 159)
   a. vicarious.   c. classical.
   b. operant.   d. emotional.

5- 2.   The tendency of stimuli similar to the conditioned stimulus to produce conditioned reactions is called: (p. 164)
   a. stimulus generalization.   c. spontaneous recovery.
   b. response generalization.   d. extinction.

5- 3.   Which of the following statements about conditioned taste aversion is false? (p. 166)
   a. It is a type of conditioning.
   b. The UCS must occur within a few minutes of the CS.
   c. It can occur in a single trial.
   d. The UCS is usually an internal cue.

5- 4.   Stimuli that reward and strengthen the responses that precede them are called: (p. 171)
   a. negative reinforcers.   c. primary reinforcers.
   b. positive reinforcers.   d. secondary reinforcers.

5- 5.   The situation in which people learn to refrain from responses which lead to unpleasant events is called: (p. 172)
   a. escape.   c. extinction.
   b. avoidance.   d. punishment.

5- 6.   The process through which a conditioned stimulus gradually loses the ability to evoke conditioned responses when it is no longer followed by the unconditioned stimulus is called: (p. 164)
   a. extinction.   c. instinctual drift.
   b. spontaneous recovery.   d. natural resemblance.

5- 7.   The reinforcement schedule in which some period of time which varies around an average value must elapse before reward is presented is called: (p. 177)
   a. fixed interval.   c. fixed-ratio.
   b. variable-interval.   d. variable-ratio.

5- 8.   The reinforcement schedule which leads to brief pauses after the delivery of the reward is called: (p. 177)
   a. fixed-interval.   c. variable-interval.
   b. fixed-ratio.   d. variable-ratio.

5- 9.   Learned helplessness may play a role in the disorder of: (p. 180)
   a. schizophrenia.   c. autism.
   b. depression.   d. paranoia.

5-10.   A child learning to share his/her toys by exposure to adult sharing behavior (e.g., giving to the Salvation Army) is an example of: (p. 185)
   a. positive reinforcement.   c. instrumental conditioning.
   b. classical conditioning.   d. observational learning.

CHAPTER 6
MEMORY: OF THINGS REMEMBERED...AND FORGOTTEN

PRACTICE QUIZ 2

6- 1. The earliest systematic study of memory was done by: (p. 194)
a. Pavlov.
b. Freud.
c. Watson.
d. Ebbinghaus.

6- 2. The modal model of memory proposed by Atkinson and Shiffrin suggests that memory consists of _____ different systems. (p. 195)
a. two
b. three
c. four
d. six

6- 3. Information moves from one memory system to another by means of _____ processes. (p. 195)
a. anchoring
b. systemic
c. retrieval
d. control

6- 4. Our general abstract knowledge about the world is known as: (p. 197)
a. semantic memory.
b. long-term memory.
c. episodic memory.
d. procedural memory.

6- 5. The memory system that holds information that is being used in consciousness is known as: (p. 199)
a. short-term memory.
b. long-term memory.
c. sensory memory.
d. parallel memory.

6- 6. Each item in short-term memory can represent several other pieces of information. This is called: (p. 201)
a. grouping.
b. encoding.
c. retrieval.
d. chunking.

6- 7. STM is thought to store _____ chunks of information. (p. 201)
a. 10 to 20
b. 2 to 3
c. 5 to 9
d. unlimited

6- 8. Information enters LTM from STM by means of: (p. 203)
a. elaborative rehearsal.
b. shallow encoding.
c. retrieval.
d. cues.

6- 9. Loss of memory for events that occur after an accident is called: (p. 220)
a. retrograde amnesia.
b. phobic amnesia.
c. Korsakoff's syndrome.
d. anterograde amnesia.

6-10. The memory disorder that develops from prolonged alcohol abuse is: (p. 222)
a. Alzheimer's disease.
b. Korsakoff's disease.
c. Ebbinghaus syndrome.
d. infantile amnesia.

CHAPTER 7
COGNITION AND INTELLIGENCE

PRACTICE QUIZ 2

7- 1. Mental frameworks for categorizing diverse items as belonging together are called: (p. 231)
    a. categories.
    b. frameworks.
    c. concepts.
    d. schemas.

7- 2. Concepts that can be clearly defined by a set of rules are _____ concepts. (p. 231)
    a. artificial
    b. natural
    c. intuitive
    d. semantic

7- 3. A source of error in reasoning that leads us to assume we are better at predicting events than we really are is the: (p. 234)
    a. hindsight effect.
    b. availability heuristic.
    c. perseverance effect.
    d. confirmation bias.

7- 4. Overestimation of chances of being a victim of a violent crime can be understood as an example of the _____ heuristic. (p. 237)
    a. informational
    b. availability
    c. representativeness
    d. perseverance

7- 5. According to the research described in your text, escalation of commitment increases when: (p. 241)
    a. subjects make decisions in groups.
    b. subjects make decisions as individuals.
    c. subjects feel they are not responsible for decisions.
    d. subjects feel they are responsible for decisions.

7- 6. According to Chomsky, speech is based on: (p. 249)
    a. social learning.
    b. cognitive development.
    c. sociobiology.
    d. a built-in neural system.

7- 7. Problem solving strategies suggested by experiences are: (p. 237)
    a. trial-and-error.
    b. heuristics.
    c. algorithms.
    d. inducers.

7- 8. For symbols to be a language, they must meet all but one of the following criteria. Which one is not a criterion? (p. 248)
    a. transmission of meaning
    b. combination into an infinite number of sentences
    c. be logically interrelated
    d. meaning of sentences must be independent of context

7- 9. If one divides a test in half to determine whether scores in both halves are similar, one is assessing: (p. 264)
    a. split-half reliability.
    b. test-retest reliability.
    c. split-half validity.
    d. test-retest validity.

7-10. Cattell proposed that ingellience consisted of two types of intelligence. These are: (p. 254)
    a. primary and secondary.
    b. mental and spatial.
    c. fluid and crystallized.
    d. general and specific.

CHAPTER 8
HUMAN DEVELOPMENT: FROM CHILD TO ADULT

PRACTICE QUIZ 2

8- 1. Development begins when the sperm fertilizes the: (p. 282)
    a. embryo.   c. uterus.
    b. ovum.   d. fetus.

8- 2. Differences between persons of different ages stemming from the contrasting social or cultural conditions in which they grew up are called: (p. 287)
    a. cross-sectional differences.   c. teratogens.
    b. cohort effects.   d. personality effects.

8- 3. Susan is doing developmental research in which she is studying a single group of subjects when they are two years old, then 4 years old and finally six years old to determine whether they change. Which method is Susan using? (p. 287)
    a. the cross-sectional method   c. the age-transfer method
    b. the case-study method   d. the longitudinal method

8- 4. The stage at which children are egocentric and have difficulty with the principle of conservation is: (p. 289)
    a. formal operations.   c. preoperational.
    b. concrete operations.   d. sensorimotor.

8- 5. The judgment of actions in terms of self-chosen moral principles occurs at the _____ level of morality. (p. 296)
    a. preconventional   c. postconventional
    b. conventional   d. abstract

8- 6. Harlow's research on attachment with monkeys led to the conclusion that the important factor was: (p. 302)
    a. contact comfort.   c. instrumental conditioning.
    b. classical conditioning.   d. need reduction.

8- 7. According to Erikson, the last crisis of adult life centers around the issue of: (p. 313)
    a. intimacy vs. isolation.   c. identity vs. role confusion.
    b. integrity vs. despair.   d. generativity vs. self-absorption.

8- 8. Physical or biological changes related to disease, injury, or abuse of the body are called: (p. 316)
    a. secondary aging.   c. the biological clock.
    b. primary aging.   d. lifestyle aging.

8- 9. The genetically-determined upper limit to a lifespan is set by: (p. 324)
    a. a biological clock.   c. disease.
    b. a social clock.   d. physical.

8-10. In Kübler-Ross's views, feelings of depression are often replaced by _____ in the dying process. (p. 324)
    a. anger   c. acceptance
    b. denial   d. bargaining

CHAPTER 9
MOTIVATION AND EMOTION

PRACTICE QUIZ 2

9- 1.   Identify the theory of motivation that stresses physiological needs. (p. 335)
a. instinct theory
b. drive theory
c. expectancy theory
d. behavior theory

9- 2.   Expectancy theory holds that behaviors are motivated by expectations of: (p. 337)
a. control.
b. stimulation.
c. positive incentives.
d. grooming.

9- 3.   Which of the following describes the typical sequence of phases of female sexual behavior described by Masters and Johnson? (p. 344)
a. resolution, orgasmic, excitement, plateau
b. excitement, plateau, orgasmic, resolution
c. excitement, resolution, plateau, orgasmic
d. resolution, excitement, plateau, orgasmic

9- 4.   In Maslow's theory, a person who is motivated to move out of a dangerous neighborhood would be influenced by: (p. 338)
a. growth needs.
b. deficiency needs.
c. self-actualization needs.
d. incentive needs.

9- 5.   Which of the following is **not** thought to be a consequence of exposure to x-rated films? (p. 345)
a. a tendency to overestimate the frequency of unusual sexual practices.
b. a tendency to view some societally disapproved sexual behaviors as less inappropriate
c. a tendency to feel increased satisfaction in one's own sex life
d. a tendency to respond with physiological arousal

9- 6.   The desire to harm a person who has prevented you from obtaining what you want is most consistent with the _____ view of aggression. (p. 348)
a. biological
b. frustration-aggression
c. social-learning
d. depression-aggression

9- 7.   According to your text, emotions involve all but one of the following: (p. 353)
a. subjective cognitive states.
b. instincts.
c. physiological changes.
d. expressive behaviors.

10- 8.   External rewards do not necessarily decrease motivation if such rewards are: (p. 353)
a. seen as a bribe.
b. seen as contingent on performance.
c. seen as signs of recognition.
d. seen as desirable.

9- 9.   Identify the theory that holds that changes within our bodies are the basis for our emotions. (p. 354)
a. James-Lange
b. Cannon-Bard
c. Schachter-Singer
d. Watson-Levin

9-10.   Which of the following is not one of the assumptions of the Schachter-Singer theory? (p. 355)
a. Emotional events produce arousal.
b. We look for environmental cues for bases arousal.
c. We focus on our instincts as a basis for emotion.
d. We label the arousal.

CHAPTER 10
INDIVIDUAL DIFFERENCES:
PERSONALITY CONSISTENCY IN THE BEHAVIOR OF INDIVIDUALS

PRACTICE QUIZ 2

10- 1.   In Freud's theory, the stage at which male children supposedly fantasize about sexual relations with their parents is the _____ stage. (p. 376)
  a. phallic
  b. genital
  c. oral
  d. latency

10- 2.   The part of our personality concerned with morality is the: (p. 374)
  a. id.
  b. ego.
  c. superego.
  d. preconscious.

10- 3.   According to Maslow, our highest need is for: (p. 385)
  a. acceptance.
  b. safety.
  c. self-actualization.
  d. esteem.

10- 4.   Which of the following is a characteristic of low sensation-seekers? (pp. 398-399)
  a. They show stronger orienting responses to stimuli.
  b. They have better abilities to ignore irrelevant stimuli.
  c. They have higher levels of endorphins than high sensation-seekers.
  d. They make fewer errors in shadowing tasks than low sensation-seekers.

10- 5.   For Freud, a defense mechanism whereby a person behaves in a way that is directly counter to a threatening impulse is: (p. 374)
  a. projection.
  b. regression.
  c. reaction formation.
  d. sublimation.

10- 6.   Which of the following ideas is not usually considered a contribution of Freudian theory? (pp. 378-379)
  a. behavior is affected by unconscious thought
  b. anxiety plays a role in many psychological disorders
  c. early childhood development influences adult behavior
  d. during the phallic stage, females experience penis envy

10- 7.   According to Jung, inherited images that shape our perception of the external world are called: (p. 381)
  a. archetypes.
  b. the collective unconscious.
  c. animus.
  d. defense mechanisms.

10- 8.   Which theorists would most likely agree with this statement: "All human beings possess the capacity to become fully-functioning persons. Problems arise when distortions in our self-concepts interfere with our personal growth." (p.3846)
  a. Freud
  b. Adler
  c. Rogers
  d. Jung

10- 9.   Recent findings suggest that there may be _____ key dimensions of personality. (p. 389)
  a. 2
  b. 5
  c. 7
  d. 10

10-10.   Bandura's social learning theory suggests that there are three important forms of learning. They are: (p. 392)
  a. classical, operant, and observational.
  b. classical, operant, and instrumental.
  c. operant, internal, and external.
  d. classical, operant, and internal.

CHAPTER 11
HEALTH, STRESS, AND COPING

PRACTICE QUIZ 2

11- 1.   The sequence of responses to stress noted by Selye were called the general _____ syndrome. (p. 409)
a. stressor
b. alarm
c. adaptation
d. coping

11- 2.   The second stage of stress reactions in Seyle's GAS model is: (pp. 409-410)
a. resistance.
b. alarm.
c. exhaustion.
d. none of the above

11- 3.   Being the target of conflicting demands at work is called: (p. 416)
a. overload.
b. underload.
c. role conflict.
d. demand conflict.

11- 4.   If you are experiencing burnout, which of the following is not likely to be one of your symptoms? (p. 420)
a. emotional exhaustion
b. feelings of low personal accomplishment
c. feelings of underload
d. physical exhaustion

11- 5.   A study of the communication of doctors with their patients found that most of the communication dealt with _____ aspects of the patient's illness. (p. 426)
a. social
b. emotional
c. mental
d. physical

11- 6.   The largest preventable cause of illness and death in the U.S. is: (p. 428)
a. poor diet.
b. lack of exercise.
c. smoking.
d. stress.

11- 7.   Type A individuals are most likely to suffer an increased risk of heart disease if they also exhibit: (p. 432)
a. depression.
b. introversion.
c. cynical hostility.
d. burnout.

11- 8.   Studies on the effect of the media on health promotion have found that: (p. 436)
a. it is very effective.
b. it is totally ineffective.
c. it can be effective when combined with other programs.
d. it is most effective for those who do not believe they are susceptible to a disease.

11- 9.   Time management is an example of: (p. 440)
a. a physiological coping technique.
b. a cognitive coping technique.
c. a belief coping technique.
d. a behavioral coping technique.

11-10.   The personality type that is characterized by high levels of commitment and a sense of control over events is called: (p. 422)
a. optimism.
b. hardiness.
c. pessimism.
d. Type B.

CHAPTER 12
PSYCHOLOGICAL DISORDERS: THE NATURE AND CAUSES

PRACTICE QUIZ 2

12- 1.   The view that mental disorders are caused by physical factors is the basis for: (p. 448)
   a. clinical psychology.   c. social work.
   b. psychiatry.   d. criminology.

12- 2.   Susan washes her hands an average of 100 times a day. She says she cannot control this activity and can't stop
   even though her skin is sore as a result of this activity. Susan may have (p. 461)
   a. a somatoform disorder.   c. an obsessive-compulsive disorder.
   b. a dissociative disorder.   d. a psychogenic disorder.

12- 3.   Your book suggests that phobias may be acquired through: (p. 460)
   a. instrumental conditioning.   c. genetic conditioning.
   b. classical conditioning.   d. conflicts with parents.

12- 4.   When people have losses of memory beyond ordinary forgetfulness, they are said to experience: (p. 464)
   a. a somatoform disorder.   c. an obsessive-compulsive disorder.
   b. a dissociative disorder.   d. a psychogenic disorder.

12- 5.   Jay has no feeling in his leg although multiple tests reveal no physical cause that would produce this symptom.
   Interestingly, he shows little concern over his paralysis. Jay may be experiencing: (p. 463)
   a. fugue.   c. a conversion disorder.
   b. hypochondriasis.   d. reaction formation.

12- 6.   The criteria for the existence of depression include all but one of the following: (p. 455)
   a. intense sadness.   c. physical symptoms.
   b. forgetfulness.   d. negative self-image.

12- 7.   In order for depression to occur in response to lack of control over bad events one must attribute the events to
   _____ causes. (p. 456)
   a. unstable and external   c. general and personal
   b. stable and internal   d. specific and impersonal

12- 8.   People with the antisocial personality disorder have all but one of the following characteristics. (p. 469)
   a. lack of conscience   c. close relationships
   b. impulsive   d. good social skills

12- 9.   The person who shows exaggerated displays of emotion may have the _____ personality disorder. (p. 470)
   a. antisocial   c. dependent
   b. prosocial   d. histrionic

12-10.   The type of schizophrenia that involves delusions of persecution and grandeur is: (p. 473)
   a. disorganized.   c. paranoid.
   b. catatonic.   d. undifferentiated.

CHAPTER 13
THERAPY:
DIMINISHING THE PAIN OF PSYCHOLOGICAL DISORDERS

PRACTICE QUIZ 2

13- 1. Which of the following is not one of the problems of classical psychoanalysis? (p. 487)
a. weak scientific base
b. not suitable for sophisticated patients with good verbal skills
c. time-consuming
d. costly

13- 2. Which of the following assumptions is not shared by all humanistic approaches to therapy? (p. 488)
a. the view that people can reflect on their problems
b. the view that people are unwilling to reflect on their problems
c. the view that people can control their behavior
d. the view that flaws in self-understanding cause problems

13- 3. The therapy developed by Perls that focuses on awareness and understanding of one's own feelings: (p. 489)
a. person-centered.   c. ego analysis.
b. existential.   d. Gestalt.

13- 4. Which of the following is **not** an important factor in Ellis' rational-emotive therapy? (p. 494)
a. dealing with irrational beliefs   c. identifying self-defeating cycles of maladaptive behavior
b. overcoming "awfulizing" tendencies   d. unconditional positive regard

13- 5. In Beck's model of depression, the tendency to see the world as a threatening place would be an example of: (p. 495)
a. overgeneralization.   c. selective perception.
b. absolutistic thinking.   d. an "awfulizing" irrational belief.

13- 6. The treatment that is based on the principle that we cannot have two opposite emotions at once to the same stimulus is: (p. 490)
a. attribution.   c. aversive conditioning.
b. systematic desensitization.   d. activation.

13- 7. The system used in some hospitals which is based on the use of reinforcements is: (p. 491)
a. aversive conditioning.   c. token economy.
b. desensitization.   d. counterconditioning.

13- 8. A form of therapy in which individuals are exposed to others behaving in an adaptive manner: (p. 492)
a. structured family therapy   c. attributional therapy
b. modeling therapy   d. psychotherapy

13- 9. The benzodiazepines seem to have their effects by depressing activity in the _____ system. (p. 510)
a. circulatory   c. immune
b. hormonal   d. central nervous

13-10. A basic assumption underlying various behavior therapies is that a psychological disorder is the result of: (p. 490)
a. unresolved unconscious conflict.   c. failure to achieve self-actualization.
b. low self-esteem.   d. faulty learning.

CHAPTER 14
SOCIAL THOUGHT AND SOCIAL BEHAVIOR

PRACTICE QUIZ 2

14- 1. We tend to attribute behavior to internal causes if consistency is _____, distinctiveness is _____, and consensus is _____. (p. 521)
   a. low, high, high
   b. high, low, low
   c. high, high, high
   d. low, low, low

14- 2. Overestimating the role of dispositional causes in our attributions is the: (p. 523)
   a. fundamental attribution error.
   b. self-serving bias.
   c. availability heuristic.
   d. false consensus effect.

14- 3. Which of the following is not a factor that was identified by research in the traditional approach to persuasion? (p. 529)
   a. expertise of the communicator
   b. attractiveness of the communicator
   c. how distracted the audience is
   d. the self-esteem level of the audience

14- 4. For the person on the peripheral route, persuasion will often occur if: (p. 530)
   a. strong, convincing arguments are used.
   b. careful attention is given to the arguments.
   c. cognitive dissonance is aroused.
   d. the person is distracted to prevent focusing on the content of the arguments.

14- 5. When individuals notice that attitudes they hold and their behavior are inconsistent, they often experience a negative emotional state known as: (p. 532)
   a. commitment.
   b. cognitive dissonance.
   c. false consensus.
   d. forced compliance.

14- 6. The fact that infants do not show prejudice supports the idea that prejudice is due to: (p. 535)
   a. realistic conflict.
   b. social learning.
   c. mutual interdependence.
   d. social categorization.

14- 7. What percentages of subjects obeyed completely in Milgram's obedience study in which they were asked to shock another person? (p. 546)
   a. 25
   b. 40
   c. 65
   d. 80

14- 8. Which of the following does not seem to be related to increased attraction? (p. 551)
   a. high degree of physical distance
   b. similarity
   c. propinquity
   d. physical attractiveness

14- 9. If you are in a bad mood, you should be more likely to help when you think helping is likely to: (p. 549)
   a. be observed by others.
   b. be costly.
   c. unpleasant.
   d. relieve the negative mood.

14-10. Research in environmental psychology suggests that: (p. 557)
   a. heat always decreases aggression.
   b. heat always increases aggression.
   c. heat is unrelated to aggression.
   d. heat can contribute to increased aggression.

Answers For Practice Quizzes

Chapter 1:
Answers: 1a; 2a; 3c; 4a; 5b; 6b; 7c; 8c; 9b; 10a

Chapter 2:
Answers: 1a; 2c; 3a; 4b; 5b; 6b; 7b; 8c; 9d; 10c

Chapter 3:
Answers: 1a; 2c; 3d; 4d; 5c; 6a; 7b; 8c; 9c; 10b

Chapter 4:
Answers: 1a; 2a; 3d; 4c; 5d; 6c; 7c; 8b; 9d; 10d

Chapter 5:
Answers: 1c; 2a; 3b; 4b; 5b; 6a; 7d; 8b; 9b; 10d

Chapter 6:
Answers: 1d; 2b; 3d; 4a; 5a; 6d; 7c; 8a; 9d; 10b

Chapter 7:
Answers: 1c; 2a; 3a; 4b; 5d; 6d; 7b; 8c; 9a; 10c

Chapter 8:
Answers: 1b; 2b; 3d; 4c; 5c; 6a; 7b; 8a; 9a; 10c

Chapter 9:
Answers: 1b; 2c; 3b; 4b; 5c; 6b; 7b; 8c; 9a; 10c

Chapter 10:
Answers: 1a; 2c; 3c; 4c; 5c; 6d; 7a; 8c; 9b; 10a

Chapter 11:
Answers: 1c; 2a; 3c; 4c; 5d; 6c; 7c; 8c; 9d; 10b

Chapter 12:
Answers: 1b; 2c; 3b; 4b; 5c; 6b; 7b; 8c; 9d; 10c

Chapter 13:
Answers: 1b; 2b; 3d; 4d; 5c; 6b; 7c; 8b; 9d; 10d

Chapter 14:
Answers: 1b; 2a; 3c; 4d; 5b; 6b; 7c; 8a; 9d; 10d